Contents

Macmillan Education
4 Crinan Street
London N1 9XW
A division of Macmillan Education Limited

Companies and representatives throughout the world

Ferris Wheel Level 2 Teacher's Book 978-1-380-02670-5
Ferris Wheel Level 2 Teacher's Book with Navio App 978-1-380-02669-9

First published 2019

Teacher's Book credits:
Designed by emc design ltd
All character artwork and main illustrations by Jose Ignacio Gómez (Nacho Gómez); others by Animation Group Sp. z o.o. pp208, 210, 212, 214, 216, 218, 220, 222, 224, 226, 228, 230, 232–241.
Cover design by emc design ltd
Cover illustration by Jose Ignacio Gómez (Nacho Gómez)
Picture research by Lorraine Beck

Author's acknowledgements
I would like to thank everyone at Macmillan Education in the UK, Spain and Mexico who has contributed to the development and production of these materials. I would also like to thank all the teachers who have taken time to read and pilot the materials, and given invaluable feedback at every stage of writing the course. Special thanks as ever go to my husband, Alan, for his encouragement and support, and to our son and daughter, Jamie and Hannah, from whose early childhood days I learnt so much.

Student's Book credits:

Original design by Clare Webber
Page make-up by emc design ltd
Illustrated by Jose Ignacio Gómez (Nacho Gómez) pp3–84(all character artwork and main illustrations);
Animation Group Sp. z o.o. pp85–96.
Cover design by emc design ltd
Cover illustration by Jose Ignacio Gómez (Nacho Gómez)
Picture research by Lorraine Beck

The publishers would like to thank Alex Tamulis, São Paulo, Brazil; Ayşegül Sezer, İNO Schools, Turkey; Daniela Araujo Pielli, Alt Idiomas, São Bernardo Do Campo, Brazil; Daniela Pugliese, Milton's College, Buenos Aires, Argentina; Esra Ezici, Turkey; Fernanda Domeniconi Nery Amorim, São Paulo, Brazil; Gabriela Iocolari, English Schoolhouse, Buenos Aires, Argentina; Gulbin Cin, Bahcesehir College, Turkey; Mariana Pastorino, Em Pi Instituto de Inglês, Santa Fe, Argentina; Marinê Ortiz, Warrington, Buenos Aires, Argentina; Paola Daniela Tuninetti, Academia Argüello, Córdoba, Argentina; Silvana Paola Accardo, Escuela Cooperativa Mundo Nuevo Instituto Casa de Jesús, Buenos Aires, Argentina.

Printed and bound in Brazil

2025
24

The author and publishers would like to thank the following for permission to reproduce their photographs:

Alamy Stock Photo/lee avison p24(pasta), Alamy Stock Photo/Blend Images p11(bmr), Alamy Stock Photo/EyeEm pp75, 76, 83(star), Alamy Stock Photo/Granger Historical Picture Archive pp75, 76, 83(planet), Alamy Stock Photo/Ivan Kmit pp31, 33(trees), Alamy Stock Photo/Fritz Liedtke pp35, 43(living room), Alamy Stock Photo/Radius Images pp75, 76, 83(sun), Alamy Stock Photo/Zoonar GmbH pp25, 33(dress), 65, 69, 73(car); **Getty Images/**3DSculptor p76(rocket), Getty Images/AlexStar p54(l), Getty Images/Alexthq pp25, 32, 33(pants), Getty Images/aluxum pp51, 53(garden), Getty Images/Antagain pp55, 56, 63(hen),Getty Images/ArcaidImages/Diane Auckland pp35, 43(dining room), Getty Images/artpartner-images pp65, 66, 73(plane), Getty Images/Artpilot pp15, 23(legs), Getty Images/baona pp15, 23(tummy), Getty Images/Carolyn Barber pp35, 43(bathroom), Getty Images/CHUYN p71(bmr), Getty Images/David Clapp pp81(r), 83(night sky), Getty Images/cosmonaut p11(bml), Getty Images/Creative Crop pp45, 46, 53(cereal), Getty Images/Dorling Kindersley p32 (shoes), Getty Images/Michael Duva pp55, 56, 63(duck), Getty Images/eurobanks pp5, 6, 13(bag), Getty Images/Fuse pp55, 56, 63(goat), p59(goat insert r), Getty Images/Lenora Gim p41(bl), Getty Images/GlobalP pp55, 56, 61, 63(sheep, cow, dog), pp56, 61(horse), p59(dog, goat insert l), p61(puppy, calf, foal), pp61, 63(lamb), p75(dog, goat insert), p59 Getty Images/Glow Decor pp35, 43(bedroom), Getty Images/Peter Gridley pp75, 83(sky), Getty Images/hadynyah pp71(br), 73(br sky), Getty Images/Hemera Technologies pp6, 74 (paper), Getty Images/hillwoman2 p41(br), Getty Images/hudiemm p51(tomatoes), Getty Images/iStockphoto/DGLimages p11(bl), Getty Images/iStockphoto/sharpshutter pp21, 23(field), Getty Images/iStockphoto/Thinkstock Images/Anson_iStock pp75, 76, 83(moon), Getty Images/j-wildman pp59, 63(farm), Getty Images/Jamakosy pp51, 53(potatoes), Getty Images/Jamesmcq24 pp45, 46, 51, 53(bread), Getty Images/JBryson p11(tmr), Getty Images/JohnnyGreig pp15, 23(arms), Getty Images/kamski pp65, 66, 73(boat), Getty Images/keni1 p11(br), Getty Images/Dave King pp25, 32, 33(coat), 13(br), Getty Images/krungchingpixs pp15, 23(feet), Getty Images/lucielang pp5, 13, 24, 44, 64, 74(crayons), Getty Images/mawielobob pp25, 33(skirt), Getty Images/milanfoto pp46, 51(bananas), Getty Images/moodboard pp15, 23(head), Getty Images/narvikk p56(rooster), Getty Images/Nerthuz pp65, 66, 69, 73(bus), 66(truck), Getty Images/nuiiko pp15, 23(hands), Getty Images/NYS444 pp25, 33(sweater), Getty Images/parinyabinsuk p34(pegs), Getty Images/PeopleImages p11(tr), Getty Images/Per Magnus Persson pp41, 43(toybox), Getty Images/PetrMalyshev pp5, 6, 13(pencil case), Getty Images/PhotoAlto/Laurence Mouton p51(pears), Getty Images/Photodisc p76(astronaut), Getty Images/piovesempre p41(bml), Getty Images/Andrea Pistolesi pp81(l), 83(sky with rainbow), Getty Images/Rawpixel p66(motorcycle), Getty Images/Aigars Reinholds pp25, 32, 33(shirt), Getty Images/Andrea Rugg pp35, 43(kitchen), Getty Images/scanrail pp65, 66, 73(train), Getty Images/Science Photo Library pp46, 51, 53(carrots), Getty Images/Serg_Velusceac pp6, 14, 34, 84(paints), Getty Images/Sergiy1975 pp65, 69, 73(bike), Getty Images/Richard Sharrocks pp5, 6, 13(scissors), Getty Images/SheraleeS p71(bml), Getty Images/Spaces Images p21(climbing frame), Getty Images/STOCK4B/Silas pp35, 43(house), Getty Images/stockcam pp45, 46, 51, 53(eggs), Getty Images/Stocktrek Images pp75, 83(earth), Getty Images/Kutay Tanir p44 (milk carton), Getty Images/Chris Tobin p71(bl), Getty Images/trigga pp45, 46, 51, 53(milk), Getty Images/Tsuji pp45, 46, 51, 53(apples), Getty Images/Udomsook pp5, 13, 14(pencil); **iStockphoto/**alex_kz pp5, 6, 13, 14, 24, 44, 64, 74, 84(glue); **Shutterstock/**Robyn Mackenzie pp51, 53(peas), Shutterstock/M. Unal Ozmen pp45, 46, 53(ice cream); **www.imagesource.com** p34(string).

Commissioned photographs by Helen Marsden/Spectrecom pp7(c), 9, 13(Sam, Anna), 14(c), 15(Anna and Sam), 16(1–3, paper), 19, 21, 25, 27(Anna and Sam), 28(1–3), 31, 33, 37(Anna, Sam), 39(Anna and Sam), 40(1–3), 43, 45, 49(Sam, Anna), 52(1–3), 55(c), 57, 61(c), 63(Anna and Sam), 64(1–3), 67(br), 69, 73(tr), 76(1–3, tissue paper), 79(c), 81, 85(tr), 88(1–3), 91(tr), 93, 97(tr), 100(1–3, tissue paper, stickers); Spectrecom Education Ltd pp11, 14(tr), 23, 26, 35, 38(tl, tc, tr), 47, 50, 51(Anna, Sam and Uncle Dan), 59, 62, 71(Anna and Sam, Uncle Dan), 74, 83(tl), 86, 87(Uncle Dan), 95, 98, 99(Anna, Sam and Uncle Dan).

A letter from the author

Dear Teacher,

I'm delighted to welcome you to *Ferris Wheel*. Get ready to hop on with your children for what I hope will be a truly enjoyable and successful learning journey!

Before we start, I'd like to introduce you to the imaginary world of the meerkats. The delightful Mimi and her family accompany us through the course and provide a rich source of engaging, and often humorous, stories that young children will want to hear again and again.

Mimi is curious about the world, full of fun, at times mischievous, but also sensible, helpful, loving and kind.

Mimi's younger brother, Dylan, is funny, adorable and sometimes a little silly. Together they make an appealing and loveable pair.

Mimi and Dylan's mommy and daddy work at the Ferris Wheel next to the meerkats' house. Mommy and Daddy share roles such as shopping and cooking, and love sports and dancing, too.

In contrast to the fantasy world of the meerkats, *Ferris Wheel 2* also features two real-life children, Sam and Anna, whose favorite animated stories are about the meerkat family. Together with Uncle Dan, Sam and Anna extend the natural contexts in which children are exposed to English. We meet them in lively videos where they interact in everyday situations, or act out traditional rhymes and songs. These provide a realistic and motivating model that supports children as they learn to communicate in English.

The Ferris Wheel, with its brightly colored pods, represents the course's innovative Hop on & Hop off approach to learning. Instead of working through the units in a linear way, you can teach them in the order that best suits your educational context and the children's curriculum, interests and needs. This gives you flexibility and allows your English program to be in sync with children's learning in other areas of the curriculum.

Before writing *Ferris Wheel*, I carried out extensive research to find out what teachers really need and want from a pre-school English language course. My findings led me to adopt a methodological approach for *Ferris Wheel* that takes into account the priorities and everyday concerns of classroom practitioners, as well as applying what we know from academic research about young children's overall development and language learning. It also incorporates many practical techniques from my own experience of teaching young children.

This is reflected in the methodology of *Ferris Wheel* in the following ways:

- Units with a clear, logical structure that build children's linguistic competence and self-confidence.
- Lesson procedures and activities that are easy to implement and manage, even with large classes.
- A wealth of content to foster children's motivation and develop language skills, including stories, songs, culture, values, real-world content and projects.
- A focus on the development of the whole child, including metacognitive, cognitive, psychological and physical development, social and emotional learning (SEL), life skills and values education.
- A balance between fantasy, which builds on children's natural capacity for creativity and play, and reality, which develops children's curiosity in learning about the real world.
- A wide range of resources to ensure lessons are engaging and dynamic, including the Mimi puppet, the *Ferris Wheel* mat, animated stories, videos, songs, Teacher's and Student's Apps, flashcards, story cards and posters.

Ferris Wheel is dedicated to every pre-school teacher who shares a passion for early language learning and believes in the unique learning potential of every child. I hope you and your children enjoy using *Ferris Wheel* as much as I enjoyed writing it!

All the best,
Carol

Ferris Wheel 2 Syllabus

Unit	Main vocabulary	Key language	Values	Content-based learning	Culture	Project
Hello 	Mommy, Daddy, Mimi, Dylan, Ferris Wheel blue, green, orange, pink, red, yellow numbers 1–6 ball, car, doll, teddy, train, scooter	Hello, I'm (Mimi). Where's the (ball)? Here's the (ball)! It's (blue).				
Classroom 	backpack, crayons, glue, paints, paper, pencil, pencil case, scissors	Do you have your/a (pencil)? Yes, I do / No, I don't. I have (red) (paint). I don't have (scissors). I'm good at (home). Go to the (playground). Point to the (ceiling).	**Good behavior:** home, school	**Places at school and what we do there:** cafeteria, classroom, library, playground	***Wind the bobbin up:*** ceiling, clap, door, floor, hands, knee, window	Our Ferris Wheel
My body 	arms, feet, fingers, hands, head, legs, toes, tummy	I can/can't move my (head). Can you? Can you move your (head)? Yes, I can. / No, I can't. What can you do? I can/can't (dance). Move your (head). I can/can't (put on my shoes/cut with scissors).	**Making an effort:** coat, scissors, shoes	**Things we can do with our bodies:** climb, hop, jump, run	***One finger, one thumb, keep moving:*** thumb, stand up, sit down, turn round, keep moving	Dancing pasta pictures
Clothes 	coat, dress, pants, shirt, shoes, skirt, socks, sweater	This is my (skirt). These are my (shoes). What are you wearing? I'm wearing (a white) (hat). I (play) with my (friends). It's (cold). This is the way I put on my (socks).	**Cooperating:** learn, play, share; family, friends	**Clothes for hot and cold weather:** gloves, sandals, scarf; cold, hot	***This is the way I put on my shirt***	Clothes lines with clothes for hot and cold weather
Home 	bathroom, bedroom, dining room, garage, house, kitchen, living room, yard	Is (Sam) in the (garden)? Yes, he/she is. / No, he/she isn't. Where's (Dylan)? In the (dining room). He's/She's in the (house). He/She isn't in the (garage). My family is (small). I have (one brother). I put (paper) in the (recycling bin).	**Families are different:** baby; big, small	**Putting things away where they belong:** box, closet, recycling bin, shelf	***Round and round the garden:*** garden	A model of a street

Unit	Main vocabulary	Key language	Values	Content-based learning	Culture	Project
Food 	apples, bananas, bread, carrots, cereal, eggs, ice cream, milk	I like (carrots). I don't like (cereal). How about you? Do you like (bananas)? Yes, I do. / No, I don't. Put the (eggs) in the cart. I help my (mommy).	**Helping others:** teacher	**Food that grows in the garden:** pears, peas, potatoes, tomatoes	***Peas pudding hot:*** peas, plate, pudding	Food made from modeling clay
Farm animals 	cow, dog, duck, goat, hen, horse, rooster, sheep	There's a (horse). There are (cows). How many (hens)? (Four). The (sheep) goes (baa). I'm kind to animals. The baby is a (calf).	**Being kind to animals:** clean, food, home, kind, water	**Animals and their babies:** calf, foal, lamb, puppy	***Five little ducks:*** little, pond, quack, swimming	Our favorite farm animals poster
Transportation 	bike, boat, bus, car, motorcycle, plane, train, truck	Let's go by (bus)! Yes. / No. I want to go by (car). Do you want to go by (bus)? Yes, I do. / No, I don't. I think of my (daddy). I say (please/sorry/thank you). A (bus) goes (on the road). Row, row, row your boat.	**Thinking of others:** friend, teacher	**Different forms of transportation and where they go:** air, road, track, water	***Row, row, row your boat:*** dream, row, stream	Transportation poster
Space 	astronaut, Earth, moon, planet, rocket, sky, star, sun	What's this? It's (the sun). Can you see (the moon)? Yes, I can. / No, I can't. What can you see? How many (stars) can you see? Sometimes I'm (sleepy). (In the day), I can see (clouds). My favorite character is the (dish).	**Feelings:** angry, calm, happy, sad, scared, sleepy	**What we can see in the sky at night and in the day:** day, night; clouds, rainbow	***Hey diddle, diddle:*** dish, spoon	Model space rockets

Unit	Main vocabulary	Key language
Endmatter	black, blue, brown, green, orange, pink, purple, red, white, yellow numbers 1–20 circle, diamond, oval, rectangle, square, star, triangle hot, cold, noisy, quiet, clean, messy	
Festivals	animals, bird, children, fly, happy, peace, world Carnival, clown, crown, king, pirate, queen; happy children; hug, play, run, talk	I'm a (pirate). I love to (play).

Ferris Wheel 1 Syllabus

Unit	Main vocabulary	Key language	Content-based learning
Hello	Mimi, Dylan, Mommy, Daddy, boy, girl; red; Ferris Wheel	Hello, I'm (Mimi).	
Family	mommy, daddy, grandma, grandpa, brother, sister; blue, green, orange, pink, red, yellow	Where's your (grandma)? Here. This is my (mommy). Here we go. Round and round.	**Wheels go round and round:** round, wheel
Classroom	book, chair, crayon, eraser, pencil, table	Sit down. Stand up. Look! It's a (chair). I don't know. I'm (happy). What color is your (book)? It's (red).	**Putting classroom objects where they belong:** shelf, tray
My face	ear, eye, hair, mouth, nose, teeth	I have (a nose). I have (two) (eyes). It's (a boy) in the water.	**What we do with our ears and eyes:** hear, see
Clothes	boots, coat, hat, shoes, shorts, T-shirt	Put on your (hat). Take off your (shoes). Where are your (boots)? Here.	**Clothes for sunny and rainy weather:** rainy, sunny
Toys	ball, car, doll, scooter, teddy, train	What's this? It's a (train). Let's play with the (ball). What's your favorite toy? It's my (teddy).	**Where we play and where we work:** classroom, playground; play, work
Food	apple, banana, cookie, juice, sandwich, water	I like (bananas). I'm hungry. Can I have (a sandwich), please? Here's (a sandwich) for you. / Here you are. Thank you. Are you hungry?	**Things we drink and things we eat:** drink, eat
Pets	bird, cat, dog, fish, mouse, rabbit	I have a (mouse). Is this your (mommy)? Yes, it is. / No, it isn't. My (fish) is (orange).	**Animals that fly and animals that swim:** fly, swim
Beach	bucket, crab, ocean, sand, shell, shovel	I can see (a crab). Me too. How many (little crabs)? (Five). What color are the (shells)? They're (pink).	**Where animals live:** land, water
Endmatter	blue, brown, green, orange, pink, purple, red, yellow; numbers 1–10; circle, rectangle, square, triangle; happy, sad, big, small, up, down		
Festivals	Carnival, mask, parade; dance, sing happy, family; mommy, daddy, grandma, grandpa, brother, sister eyes, feet, fur; teddy bear		

Ferris Wheel 3 Syllabus

Unit	Main vocabulary	Key language	Content-based learning
Hello	Mommy, Daddy, Mimi, Dylan; Ferris Wheel; blue, green, orange, pink, red, yellow; numbers 1–6	Hello. How are you? I'm fine, thank you. Where's number (one)? It's on (red). I'm (sleepy). Hurry up. Here's your (hat). Goodbye.	
School	color, count, dance, draw, jump, paint, play, run, sing, think	What do you do at school? I (draw) at school. Do you want to (color)? Yes, I do. / No, I don't. I want to (jump). I don't want to (draw).	**Doing exercise:** play soccer, ride my bike, swim, walk (to school)
The park	bench, flowers, grass, merry-go-round, path, pond, seesaw, slide, swing, trees	There's (a path). There are (trees). It's (windy). Is there (a slide)? Are there (swings)? Where's (Mommy)? Under the (tree). On the (bench).	**The life cycle of a plant:** leaves, plant, roots, seed, sun, water
Wild animals	crocodile, elephant, giraffe, hippo, lion, monkey, parrot, snake, tiger, zebra	What's that? It's a (snake). What are those? They're (monkeys). It's (black and white). It has (big teeth). I'm a (crocodile).	**Animal body parts:** claws, fur, tail, whiskers
Daily routines	brush my hair/teeth, get dressed, get up, have breakfast/lunch/dinner, take a shower, wash my face/hands	What do you do every day? I (get up). Do you (wash your hands) (at school)? Yes, I do. / No, I don't. It's time to (get dressed). What do you do at (home)? I (have breakfast) at (home). I don't (have dinner) at (school).	**How and when to wash your hands:** faucet, soap, towel, water; clean
Meals	chicken, fish, pancake, pizza, rice, salad, soup, spaghetti, toast, yogurt	What do you have for (dinner)? I have (soup). Do you want (pancakes)? Yes, please. / No, thank you. I want/don't want (toast).	**Healthy and unhealthy food:** fruit, vegetables; candy, carrots, chips, cupcakes, ice cream, oranges, peas, plums, tomatoes
Town	bookstore, mall, movie theater, museum, park, restaurant, supermarket, swimming pool, toy store, zoo	Do you want to (go to the zoo)? Yes, I do. / No, I don't. Where do you want to go? I want to (go to the museum). Let's (go to the mall).	**Crossing the street safely:** crosswalk, sidewalk, stoplights, street; stop, look, listen
Music	drum, guitar, maracas, piano, recorder, tambourine; clap, dance, listen, sing	What are you doing? I'm (playing the piano). Do you like (playing the maracas)? Yes, I do. / No, I don't. I like (playing the drum).	**Different rhythms:** fast, slow, loud, quiet
Bugs	ant, bee, butterfly, ladybug, snail, worm; legs, spots, stripes, wings	Does (a snail) have (spots)? Yes, it does. / No, it doesn't. Ask the (ladybug), please. It doesn't have (stripes).	**The life cycle of a butterfly:** caterpillar, chrysalis, egg, leaf
Endmatter	black, blue, brown, gray, green, orange, pink, purple, red, white, yellow; numbers 1–100; circle, diamond, oval, rectangle, square, star, triangle; hungry, thirsty, clean, dirty, old, young	It's (red). It's a (star). I can see (three) (diamonds). I'm (hungry). He's/She's/It's (old).	
Festivals	animals, people, pictures, stories, words, world; elephant, gorilla, panda, polar bear, rhino, tiger; beach, countryside, forest, mountains	I like books about (people). I like books with (pictures). Save the (panda). I go to the (countryside). Let's protect the (beach).	

What's in *Ferris Wheel*?

Student's Book

The *Ferris Wheel* Student's Book has a flexible, Hop on & Hop off approach that allows you to adapt to the unique needs and requirements of your class, and align children's English learning with the content and sequence of the wider curriculum. Hop on and off the Ferris Wheel wherever you wish or follow the unit sequence given in the book – it's up to you! Each unit has ten lessons that follow a logical structure in order to develop children's language skills and understanding of the chosen topic.

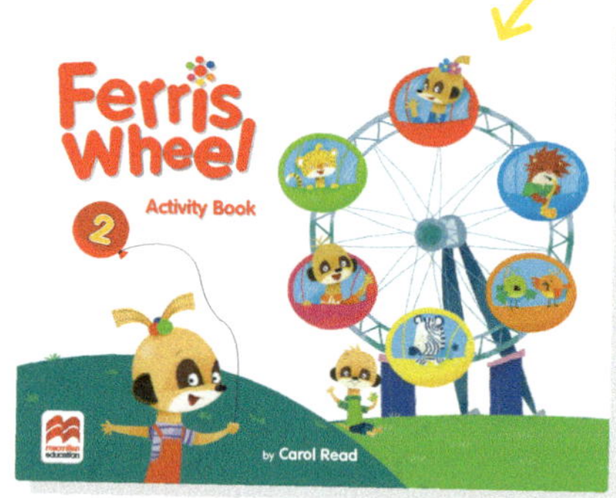

Activity Book

The full-color Activity Book mirrors the Student's Book structure and provides additional practice of key language and content. Activities such as visual discrimination, matching, pre-literacy and numeracy support and develop children's cognitive and fine motor skills.

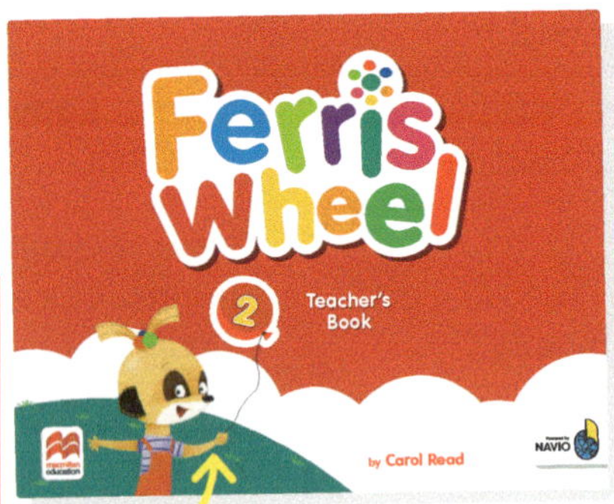

Teacher's Book

Detailed lesson plans, interleaved with the Student's Book pages, allow you to navigate the course with ease. Learning objectives, materials, teacher's tips and audioscripts are all at your fingertips.

***Ferris Wheel* mat**

The *Ferris Wheel* mat is a flexible teaching resource. Place it on the floor during Circle time, or hang it on the wall or board, and put flashcards or real objects in the pockets to play motivating language games. Practical ideas for using the mat can be found on p20.

Mimi puppet

Mimi the meerkat is an engaging puppet who will bring your classes to life. The use of a puppet has a positive impact on children's motivation and participation. Practical ideas for using the puppet can be found on p21.

Teacher's App on Navio

The Teacher's App on Navio offers one-stop access to the digital resources, including Tap & Teach Lessons with integrated audio and video, the Rewards tool to award points for good behavior or success, and a Progress Tracker. You'll also find additional resources in the Resource Bank, including posters, story cards, word cards, worksheets, evaluation materials, extra flashcards, alternative festivals, and letters to parents.

Student's App on Navio

The Student's App allows students to explore Navio's immersive worlds. They complete game-based activities designed to practice and review language and content. The App also includes all the songs, videos and animated stories from the course. The access code can be found on the inside front cover of the Student's Book.

Class CDs

All the audio material, including stories, songs, rhymes, chants, games and dialogues, can be found on the Class CDs.

Flashcards

Photographic flashcards are provided for every key vocabulary item. See page 19 for ideas for using the flashcards.

Ferris Wheel's Hop on & Hop off approach

Ferris Wheel's **unique and innovative Hop on & Hop off approach** offers teachers the flexibility to teach the eight core units in any order. Topics can be aligned with the wider curriculum, or sequenced according to your and your class's preferences.

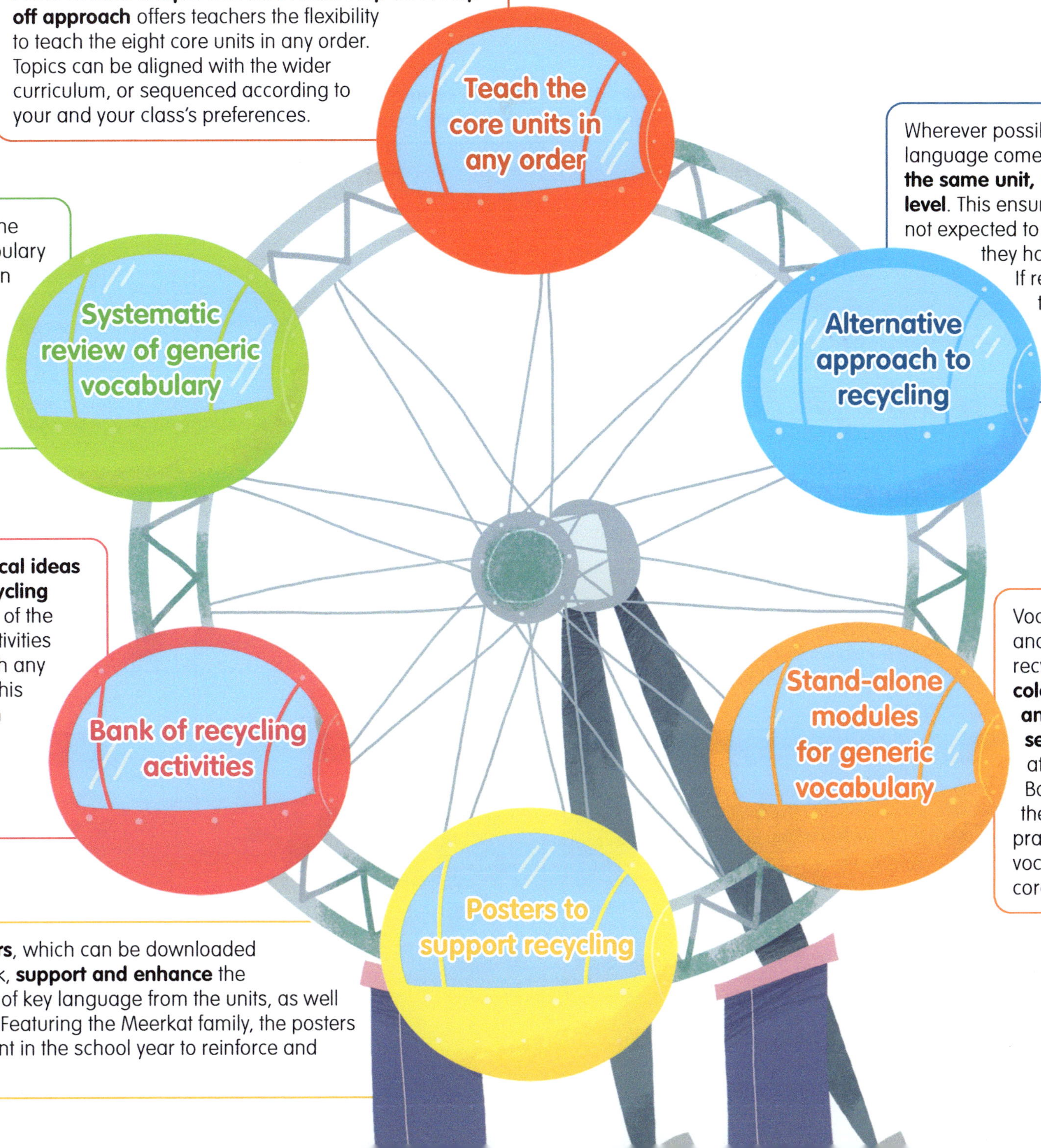

Wherever possible, recycled language comes either from **within the same unit, or from the previous level**. This ensures that children are not expected to use language that they haven't yet covered. If recycled language is taken from other units in the same level, it is for receptive understanding only.

Vocabulary that is generic and can be applied and recycled in any unit, such as **colors**, **numbers**, **shapes and concepts**, appear in **separate short modules** at the back of the Student's Book. This gives teachers the flexibility to present, practice and review this vocabulary outside of the core units.

The *Ferris Wheel* **posters**, which can be downloaded from the Resource Bank, **support and enhance** the teaching and recycling of key language from the units, as well as generic vocabulary. Featuring the Meerkat family, the posters can be used at any point in the school year to reinforce and recycle key language.

There is a **bank of practical ideas and suggestions for recycling known language** on p19 of the Teacher's Book. These activities are designed to work with any vocabulary set or topic. This means you can use them to recycle vocabulary and language from any unit that you have previously covered.

This overall approach to the teaching of generic vocabulary and the recycling of known language allows for **regular and systematic review**, while removing the need to work through the units in chronological order.

About the Student's Book and Activity Book

The *Ferris Wheel* Student's Book and Activity Book have eight core units, plus a *Hello* unit. The course's Hop on & Hop off approach allows you to teach the core units in the order you prefer. Each unit features ten varied lessons to consistently develop a range of skills, as well as motivating children and promoting the use of English in their daily classroom interactions.

Student's Book

Lesson 1, Vocabulary

Six new topic-based vocabulary items are introduced by Mimi and Dylan. Children practice the new words through a rhythmic chant, play a memory game, and stick the vocabulary stickers on the Ferris Wheel.

Lesson 2, Language

The **target language structure and two additional vocabulary items** are introduced through an appealing and memorable song.

Lesson 3, Story

Children listen to the story using the printable story cards, or watch a **delightful animated version.** They then do a comprehension activity, stick the story sticker and share their opinion about the story.

Lesson 4, Story Song

Children listen to, sing and act out the story song using the audio or an animated version. This **reinforces and reviews the concepts and key language in the story**. They then do a comprehension activity related to the song.

Lesson 5, Speaking

Children watch a **video** showing Sam, Anna and Uncle Dan using the **unit language in a realistic context.** Children are then encouraged to use some of the key language in a speaking activity that also practices **life skills.**

Lesson 6, Values

Children sing a song that develops their awareness of a specific value related to the story. They also practice **social and emotional (SEL) skills**.

Lesson 7, Content

Children are introduced to new vocabulary items and learn about **content from the wider world** related to the unit topic.

Lesson 8, Culture

Children are introduced to culture from the English-speaking world through listening to or watching the video of Sam and Anna singing and acting out a **traditional song**.

Review
With the help of Mimi and Dylan, children **review their learning**, including key language and the main activities they did. They then complete a **self-evaluation** activity.

Project
The unit culminates in a creative and **cooperative project** related to the topic, providing a natural context in which to practice and review known language.

Endmatter
Colors, numbers, shapes and **key concepts** are covered in short modules at the back of the Student's Book. This allows frequently-used vocabulary to be introduced, practiced and reviewed at any stage of the course. This supports *Ferris Wheel*'s Hop on & Hop off approach and facilitates regular recycling. There are also three **Festivals** pages and pull-out **Stickers** pages.

Activity Book

Lessons 1–8, Review and Project
The Activity Book **mirrors the Student's Book unit structure** exactly. The activities are designed to **consolidate children's understanding** of the new language and content presented in the Student's Book, whilst **simultaneously developing skills** such as visual discrimination, pre-literacy, matching, coloring, sequencing, and numeracy.

Endmatter
The Activity Book endmatter provides **further practice of the frequently-used vocabulary** presented in short modules at the back of the Student's Book: **colors, numbers, shapes** and **key concepts**. There are also three Festivals pages with activities to extend and develop this content.

Teacher's and Student's Apps on Navio

The Navio app that accompanies this course offers one-stop access to the wide range of resources that come with *Ferris Wheel*. Tap & Teach Lessons enable you to move seamlessly between the book and digital components. You can track your students' progress using the Progress Tracker and find additional resources in the Resource Bank.

Accessing the app

To access Navio, go to www.macmillaneducationeverywhere.com to create a Macmillan Education account, or log in with your existing account. Then you can enter your access code and download the app for your device (see system requirements at www.macmillaneducationeverywhere.com/system-requirements).

Setting up a class

You can use Navio's Learning Management System to set up a class and register your students with their names and the email address of their parents or guardians. You can then provide login details to parents so that they can log in to the Student's App and enter the code from the inside front cover of the Student's Book to access the 3D worlds and practice activities. Alternatively, parents can register their children directly at www.macmillaneducationeverywhere.com and students can then join your class using a class code.

Managing your downloads

Navio makes it easy to manage the storage space on your device, as you can control how much material you download at one time. Navio makes it clear how much storage space your chosen content will need. You can download the complete Teacher's and Student's Apps at once or, if your device has limited storage capacity, you can choose to download only one or two units. When you complete a unit, you can safely delete the content from your device. You won't lose your students' data, as this information is stored online.

Using the Progress Tracker

All the work your students complete in the app is recorded in the Progress Tracker. You can monitor the progress of a whole class or any individual student. Every activity in the app is mapped against the course learning objectives and skills, so you can easily identify where your students need extra support.

Teaching a lesson

Navio makes it easy to plan and teach your lessons with fully interactive **Tap & Teach Lessons**. Find the lesson you want to teach and click to open it. A thumbnail view of all activities in the lesson is available via the toolbar at the bottom of the page. The toolbar also contains the Tap & Teach tools you need to teach heads-up, whole-class activities, including a timer, pen tool, and mask tool. Lessons include all the audio and video you need for the lesson, as well as some extra tools such as digital flashcards.

Using the Rewards tool

Navio's Rewards tool is a great way to keep your students engaged in class. Much more than just a record of attendance, you can also use it to award points for good behavior or success in activities. You can even organize your class into teams, and you can award points to individuals, groups or the whole class at any time. When students earn points, they appear in the Student's App the next time they log in, so parents can see their performance.

Student's App

As a teacher you can also access a version of the Student's App from the main menu of the Teacher's App. This has all the same content that your students can access at home, but your version is set in teacher mode. This means that all the activities and worlds are already unlocked, and the app does not record any scores to the Progress Tracker. We recommend using teacher mode when students share devices to avoid mixing up students' grades and progress. However, if students have individual devices or are using the app at home, they should always log in with their own username and password. In this way they can earn points and badges, set up and customize their avatar and build a record of their progress in the Progress Tracker.

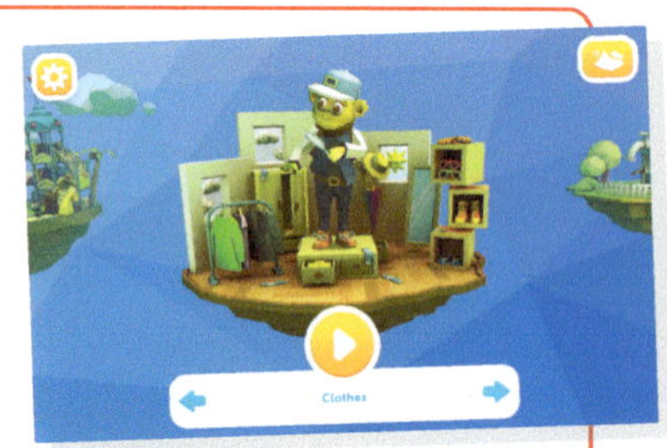

Features of the Teacher's Book

The *Ferris Wheel* Teacher's Book lesson plans are interleaved with the Student's Book pages. Each lesson plan follows the same structure: **Circle time**, **Table time** and **Closing time**.

Each unit begins with an overview of the **vocabulary, language** and **objectives** for the unit.

The audioscripts for the **unit story** and **songs** are also provided at the start of the unit for easy reference.

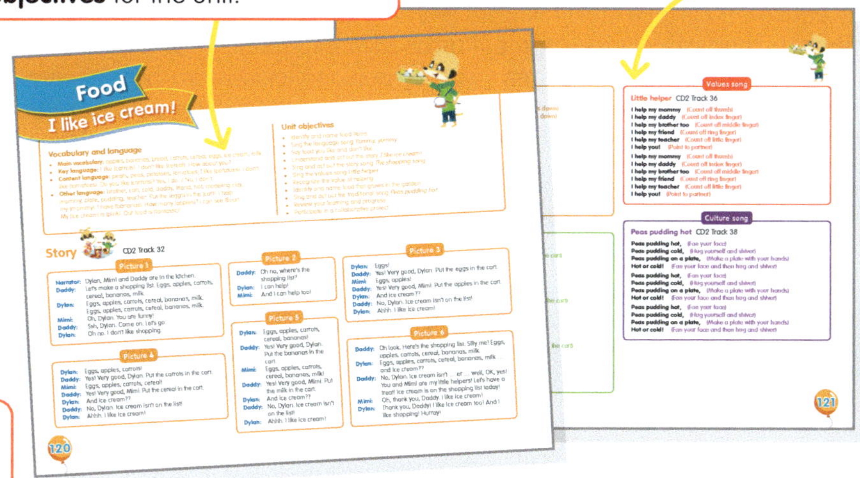

The detailed lesson plans are **interleaved** with full-size reproductions of the Student's Book pages.

Each lesson plan has an overview of the lesson's **learning objectives** and **language aims**, along with the **materials** you need.

A **facsimile and instructions for the Activity Book** are also provided.

Teacher's tips provide helpful advice and suggestions to enrich the teaching experience.

Each lesson begins with **Circle time**. Children come together for the opening learning routines (see p16). They are also introduced to the lesson aims and then engage in a variety of games and activities using the Mimi puppet and the *Ferris Wheel* mat. Circle time focuses children's attention and is an opportunity for key input and new learning.

During **Table time**, children do a range of language and skills activities in the Student's Book. Step-by-step instructions, as well as audioscripts for the listening activities and chants, allow you to guide children through these activities smoothly and effectively.

Closing time ends the lesson with a learning review (see p18) and closing routines (see p16). Children then sing the *Bye bye song* as they wave goodbye to the Mimi puppet.

Additional resources

Activities Banks with ideas on how to use the Mimi puppet and *Ferris Wheel* mat in class, as well as recycling activities, and ways to specifically promote social and emotional learning, life skills and learning enrichment, can be found on pp19–25. There are also guidelines for how to incorporate **learning reviews** and **learning routines** into your lessons, along with audioscripts for the *Ferris Wheel* routine songs, on pp16–18.

Photocopiable templates specifically designed for the **Project** lessons can be found at the back of the Teacher's Book.

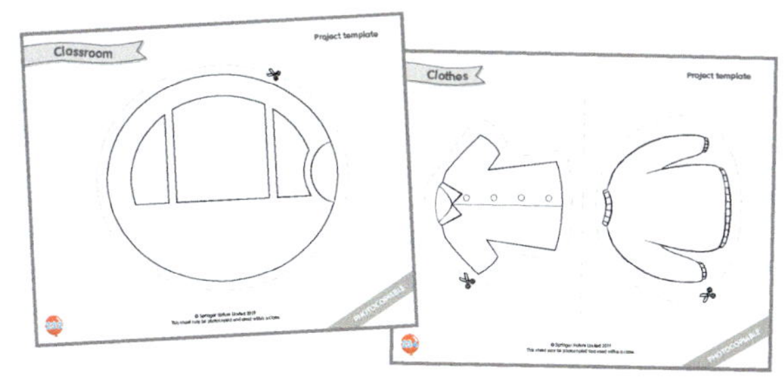

Whole child development

What is whole child development?

Many educators believe that children's learning success, both now and in the future, depends as much on their overall development as on their academic achievements. Developing the whole child means that we not only rely on traditional classroom-based learning, but give children the space and the opportunity to develop their creativity, physical, social and emotional expression, empathy, and understanding of the world around them.

A child's emotional, social, physical, creative and cognitive capacities are all intertwined and of equal importance. As language teachers, we also need to give all aspects of a child's development equal attention in order to achieve well-being, and create the optimal conditions for learning and growth. The development of a child's sense of self-worth and self-determination during the pre-school years is likely to be much more influential on positive long-term outcomes than a focus on standard academic achievements alone.

Ferris Wheel and whole child development

Ferris Wheel aims to integrate whole child development in a holistic way, including natural exposure to meaningful language, with the systematic development of age-appropriate language, thinking and social skills. This ensures that children are given the opportunities they need to develop all aspects of themselves, while simultaneously working towards the language and academic objectives in each unit.

Each level of *Ferris Wheel* was written to reflect the ages and stages of social, emotional, psychological, physical and cognitive development of pre-schoolers. Key child development goals, such as the development of creative thinking, personal autonomy, social and emotional learning, life skills, values, cognitive and metacognitive skills, and deliberate memory, are integrated and addressed throughout the course. On-the-page activities include ordering, matching, sequencing, tracing and visual discrimination to encourage effort, persistence, concentration and the development of early cognitive skills. Many of the songs in *Ferris Wheel* have accompanying actions to develop gross motor skills and coordination. There is a focus on creativity and personal expression, e.g. in the Story and in the Project lessons, and on emotional intelligence, self-esteem and autonomy, e.g. in the Values lessons. Metacognitive skills are developed through regular learning reviews, reflection and self-assessment.

Life skills

Life skills are the strategies needed to deal effectively with the challenges of everyday life. Life skills enable children to effectively problem-solve, adapt, take responsibility for their actions, cooperate and collaborate with others, make decisions, and interact with their peers.

Life skills are integrated across all levels of *Ferris Wheel*. In the Speaking lessons, children watch videos demonstrating how the real-life characters respond and behave in a variety of typical, everyday scenarios that are relevant to young children. On page 23 of the Teacher's Book, you will also find a bank of practical activities to help children develop and practice age-appropriate life skills.

Social and emotional learning (SEL)

Social and emotional learning (SEL) is essential for success at school and in life. Children who develop social and emotional awareness and skills find it easier to manage themselves, relate to others and resolve conflict. This creates positive self-esteem and provides a healthy foundation for children's learning and well-being.

Pre-schoolers are naturally egocentric and are still in the process of learning how to understand and interpret other people's emotions and intentions. This ability to "de-center" or move away from their own limited viewpoint to integrate other people's perspective is a skill that requires practice. SEL is an integrated part of the methodology of *Ferris Wheel* and is also reflected in the learning routines (see p16), unit stories and Values lessons, in which children rehearse strategies for handling their emotions, having empathy for others and making good choices about behavior. On p22, you can also find a bank of activity ideas for the development of social and emotional skills, including self-awareness, self-management, social awareness, relationship skills, responsible decision-making and autonomy.

Values education

The Values education lessons in every unit of *Ferris Wheel* encourage children to think about a range of age-appropriate values in relation to themselves, other people and their immediate environment. The Values lessons link back to a theme or issue that arose in the unit story. Children sing and act out a values-related song and are given options and choices that encourage them to reflect on specific values and apply them to their own lives.

About the projects

Each unit of *Ferris Wheel* culminates with an enjoyable and motivating project, which acts as a final outcome to children's learning in the unit. The projects are simple and achievable, and require only basic materials. The *Ferris Wheel 2* projects include painting and making a Ferris Wheel, creating a pasta picture, making a model of a street, modeling food from clay, and using paper shapes to create a transportation poster. Photocopiable templates for the projects can be found in the back of the Teacher's Book.

Cooperative learning, or working together to accomplish **shared goals**, can be beneficial for both the group and the individual. By encouraging children to work with others, we nurture their ability to be **considerate, patient, kind and collaborative**. By following the simple steps in each Project lesson, children work individually, and then in small groups or with the class, to contribute towards a shared outcome. This brings **a sense of satisfaction and boosts self-esteem**.

Three numbered photographs clearly demonstrate **the steps children must follow** to achieve the final outcome, developing **logic and sequencing skills**, and giving them the confidence to attempt the project with **minimal teacher intervention**.

Activities such as painting, gluing and decorating promote the development of **fine motor skills**.

By showing **images of the materials**, rather than a written list, children are empowered to identify and collect the materials they need independently. This promotes **organizational skills and autonomy**.

In the Activity Book, children complete a motivating **art and craft activity** that practices **the key language** from the unit.

There are **photocopiable templates** provided at the back of the Teacher's Book so only **minimal forward planning** is needed.

The project creates a natural context for **production of the unit language**, and any other known language. This opportunity is fully exploited through a group discussion in which children express their personal opinions and give each other positive feedback.

The Teacher's Book provides **step-by-step guidance** on how to prepare children before they embark on their project, as well as **classroom management techniques** to ensure your project lessons run smoothly.

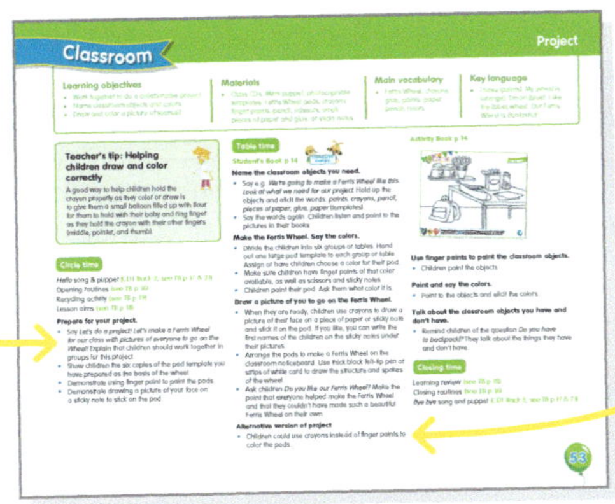

Simpler alternatives are suggested for most projects.

Learning routines

Learning routines are established procedures and patterns of behavior that you teach children and then use to signal and punctuate everyday classroom activities. Learning routines impact positively on children's behavior, participation, and social and emotional well-being, as well as on your ability to manage your classes and hold children's attention. Audioscripts for *Ferris Wheel*'s learning routine songs and chants can be found on p17.

Some typical learning routines include:

- **Opening routines** at the start of lessons, such as greeting the puppet, singing the *Hello song* (see p17), taking the register, identifying the day of the week, or talking about the weather.
- **Activity routines** to create the appropriate atmosphere for specific activities, such as Circle time and Story time.
- **Transition routines** to help children make the transition from one stage of the lesson to another in an orderly way.
- **Classroom routines** for specific tasks, such as giving out and collecting materials.
- **Energy-building routines** to use when children are losing concentration and need a short, physical break.
- **Settling routines** to use when children need to calm down and refocus their attention, e.g. after doing a lively, physical activity.
- **Thinking and feeling routines** to foster certain skills and attitudes, such as explicit thinking, cooperation, mindfulness, and social and emotional learning (SEL).
- **Closing routines** at the end of lessons, such as learning reviews (see p18), cleaning up and singing the *Bye bye song* (see p17).

For **children**, learning routines:

- give security and confidence about what they are expected to do;
- help them manage and regulate their behavior;
- provide frequent, repeated exposure to the same language in a meaningful context;
- provide opportunities for guided interaction and turn-taking in a familiar context;
- develop a sense of responsibility and autonomy in carrying out everyday classroom tasks;
- foster active participation in a safe environment;
- create a sense of community and positively develop social and emotional skills.

For **the teacher**, learning routines:

- allow you to create a safe and caring learning environment;
- allow you to manage your class positively and effectively;
- enable you to carry out essential routine classroom tasks more quickly and efficiently;
- provide for smoother transitions between activities;
- provide opportunities for you to communicate naturally with children;
- cut down on lesson preparation time;
- help you create a positive socio-affective atmosphere in your lessons and develop relationships with all children based on care, respect and trust.

The following guidelines will help you make the most of learning routines in your lessons:

- Decide on the learning routines that you are going to introduce in your lessons and the exact procedure and language you will use to carry out each one. For example, as part of your opening routines, you could:
  i) Hold up a feely bag with the puppet inside. Ask children *Who's here?*
  ii) Encourage children to answer *Mimi* and call to the puppet to come out of the bag.
  iii) Use the puppet to say *Hello, children!* and get children to respond *Hello, Mimi!*
  iv) Get the puppet to greet individual children, e.g. *Hello, Lucía. How are you today?*, and encourage children to respond *Hello, Mimi. I'm fine.*
- Repeat the learning routines in every lesson. To begin with, use exactly the same procedure and language pattern each time. Explicitly model language and be ready to support children in either non-verbal or verbal responses until they become familiar with the routine.
- Once children are responding confidently to a learning routine, you can start to gradually adjust the procedure and extend the language.
- Use opening and closing routines to provide a clear framework and structure to lessons. However, be careful not to spend too long on these stages of the lesson.
- Be aware that although learning routines may feel repetitive for you, children will love to do them over and over again!
- If you have an English Language Area (ELA) (see p25) in your classroom, it is a good idea to resource it with materials you use for learning routines, such as the *Ferris Wheel* mat, flashcards and Mimi puppet, so children can use the learning routines as a starting point for improvisation and free play.

Ferris Wheel 2 learning routine audioscripts

Hello song CD1 Track 2

Ferris Wheel, Ferris Wheel, (Draw a circle in the air with finger)
Hello, hello, hello. (Wave to the Mimi puppet)
Ferris Wheel, Ferris Wheel, (Draw a circle in the air with finger)
Hop on! Hop on! Let's go! (Beckon with hand)
[Repeat]

Bye bye song CD1 Track 3

Ferris Wheel, Ferris Wheel, (Draw a circle in the air with finger)
Bye bye, bye bye, bye bye. (Wave to the Mimi puppet)
Ferris Wheel, Ferris Wheel, (Draw a circle in the air with finger)
Hop off! Hop off! Bye bye! (Wave to the Mimi puppet)
[Repeat]

Story rhyme CD1 Track 4

It's time for a story. (Open palms of hands as if opening a book)
One, two, three. (Hold up three fingers one by one)
Are you ready? (Hold out hand to the class)
Listen to me! (Hold hand to your ear)

Circle time chant CD1 Track 5

Sit down,
Cross your legs,
Hands together,
Just like me!
Ready to learn,
Ready to play,
Let's start our lesson,
One, two, three!
[Repeat]

Table time train chant CD1 Track 6

It's table time, it's table time! (Form a train and lead children to their tables)
Ch-ch-ch-ch, ch-ch-ch-ch
Off we go, off we go!
Ch-ch-ch-ch, ch-ch-ch-ch
[Repeat]

Mimi's action rhyme CD1 Track 7

Follow, follow, follow me. (Signal for children to copy you)
Walk, walk, walk. (Walk purposefully around the classroom)
One, two, three!

Follow, follow, follow me. (Signal for children to copy you)
Run, run, run. (Run slowly around the classroom)
One, two, three!

Follow, follow, follow me. (Signal for children to copy you)
Jump, jump, jump. (Jump around the classroom)
One, two, three!

Follow, follow, follow me. (Signal for children to copy you)
Sit down, shhh … (Sit down and put your finger to your mouth)
One, two, three!

Weather chant CD1 Track 8

Sunny? Cloudy? Rainy? Windy? (Point to pictures of the weather)
What's the weather like today? (Point to the window)
Sunny? Cloudy? Rainy? Windy? (Point to pictures of the weather)
What's the weather? Can you say?

Is it hot? Is it cold? (Mime being hot and cold)
What's the weather like today? (Point to the window)
Is it hot? Is it cold? (Mime being hot and cold)
What's the weather? Can you say?

Clean up song CD1 Track 9

Let's clean up, clean up,
And put our things away.
Let's clean up, clean up,
It's time to stop today!
[Repeat]

Days of the week chant CD1 Track 10

Monday, Tuesday,
Wednesday, Thursday
Friday, Saturday, Sunday!
[Repeat]
And today is …! (Children say the correct day)

Mimi's recycling chant CD1 Track 11

Remember, remember,
One, two, three.
Look and say
The words with me! (Hold up six flashcards in turn for children to say the words.)

Very good! Very good!
Great! Hurray!
For all the words
That we can say!

Mimi's recycling song CD1 Track 12

Ask a question, Ask a question.
Say the answer.
"Yes" or "No!"
Take turns
With your partner.
Here we go! Here we go!

Feelings song CD1 Track 13

Be kind to your friends
When they're happy, happy, happy. (Draw a smile on your face with a finger and smile)
Be kind to your friends
When they're sad, sad, sad. (Draw a sad mouth on your face with a finger and frown)

Be kind to your friends
As they're kind to you.
Remember your friends
Have feelings too.

Cooperation song CD1 Track 14

Let's work together! (Have the class join hands in a circle)
Let's cooperate!
I help you,
You help me.
It's great! It's great!

Let's work together!
Let's cooperate!
I share with you,
You share with me.
It's great! It's great!

Learning reviews

Much of children's learning during the pre-school years takes place in an implicit, natural way when children are engaged in meaningful and enjoyable activities. However, as teachers, we also need to encourage children to reflect on their learning in child-friendly ways. This helps develop metacognitive skills – children's ability to think about, plan, monitor, reflect on and evaluate their learning. It also allows you to introduce a range of learning strategies that, over time, will inform and support children's learning. As well as providing immediate benefits, such as giving children agency and choice in their learning, this also lays the foundations for becoming responsible and motivated learners in the future.

The learning reviews in *Ferris Wheel* offer children an opportunity to think about both what they are learning (the product) and how they are learning (the process). It is recommended that a short learning review is carried out as a regular part of the Closing time routines at the end of every lesson. At the end of each unit, the Review lesson also offers an opportunity for children to evaluate their learning during the whole unit.

Learning reviews are most effective when they form part of a three-stage learning cycle:

- **Before:** understand the aim and purpose of the lesson;
- **During:** participate in the lesson;
- **After:** think about the outcomes of the lesson and how they were achieved.

Establishing lesson aims

At the start of lessons, briefly explain the lesson aims in simple, child-friendly language. You may like to use the Mimi puppet to do this. Examples of generic lesson aims are as follows:

- **Lesson 1 (Vocabulary):** *Today we're going to learn words for … . We're also going to do some activities to help us learn to say and remember the words.*
- **Lesson 3 (Story):** *Today we're going to listen to, and watch, a story about Mimi and Dylan. We're also going to do activities to check that we understand the story.*

Conducting a learning review

At the end of the lesson, conduct a learning review either in English or in the children's shared language, or using a mixture of the two. Initially, you may wish to use English to name activities and the learning content, and the children's shared language to express ideas about the learning process. You can either do all or select only some of the steps described below:

i) Refer back to the lesson aims communicated to children at the start of the lesson.
ii) Ask children *What did we do first/next/then?* Elicit their ideas. Be ready to use prompts and reminders as necessary.
iii) Ask further questions about each activity, e.g. *What did you learn when we played the* Ferris Wheel *mat game?* Encourage personal responses and make sure it's clear that there are no correct answers.
iv) Extend children's thinking by asking further questions about each activity, e.g. *How did the* Ferris Wheel *mat game help you learn?* Be prepared for children to find questions about the learning process challenging, especially at first. Model possible responses to clarify what you mean, e.g. *The* Ferris Wheel *mat game helped me see pictures of the words in my head.*
v) Ask children for their personal views of the activities they have done, e.g. *Did you like the* Ferris Wheel *mat game? Why? / Why not?* Again make it clear that there are no correct answers.
vi) Refer back to the lesson aims and ask, e.g. *How well did you learn to say and remember the words?* Encourage children to evaluate their work in the lesson positively with a focus on what they have achieved.
vii) Ask children to talk about their progress in the lesson when they go home. Brief parents and carers to show interest, ask further questions and respond positively. When children do the Review lesson, add your own comment, stamp and/or signature to endorse the children's self-evaluation, and make sure that this is shared with parents.

Activities Bank: Recycling

1. Slow reveal
Hide some flashcards from previous units behind a book. Slowly reveal a flashcard so it is just visible over the top of the book. Children say the word as soon as they recognize it.

2. Quick flash
Hold flashcards from previous units facing you. Quickly, show children the top flashcard, then turn it back to you again. Children name the item they saw. If they can't name it, quickly show the same flashcard a second time.

3. Odd one out
Choose three flashcards from two different units, e.g. *eggs, milk, sweater.* Display the flashcards and encourage children to point and say the odd one out.

4. Point to the …
Display some flashcards from previous units around the classroom. Choose one of the words at random and say *Point to the (dress).* Children point to the correct flashcard.

5. What's in the bag?
Use the flashcards to review vocabulary from a previous unit. Then choose four of the flashcards (or real objects) and place them in a bag without the children seeing. Children talk to a partner and guess which four items are in the bag. Ask different pairs to share their guesses. When children guess correctly, remove the flashcard or object from the bag and show it to the class.

6. Can you remember?
Display six flashcards from different units and allow children to observe them for about 30 seconds. Remove the flashcards and place them face down. Ask children to name the items they remember. Each time a child remembers a word, show the corresponding flashcard to the class.

7. Secret word
Use the flashcards to review vocabulary from a previous unit. Put the flashcards away. If you have space, sit all the children in a circle. If not, have children play this game at their desks in small teams. Choose one of the words you reviewed and whisper it to the child on your left or to one child in each team. That child then whispers the same word to the child on their left. Continue around the circle or team until the word reaches the final child. Ask him/her to say the word aloud. If it is the correct word, show the corresponding flashcard. If not, ask the other children to say the word. (You could also try the game with full sentences, e.g. *I'm wearing a dress.*)

8. Order the flashcards
Choose flashcards from previous units and place them on the floor or board. Slowly say three of the words at random. Ask a volunteer to pick up the three corresponding flashcards and put them in the correct order.

9. Stand up!
Give all or some of the children a flashcard from any previous unit and tell them to sit down. Name one of the flashcards. The child holding that flashcard stands up and says the word. If necessary, the rest of the class can help by saying *Stand up, (Jack)!* Ask the class to repeat the word.

10. Which side?
Use the flashcards to review the words from two previous units. Place one flashcard from each set on opposite sides of the room and ask children to stand in the middle of the room. Shuffle the remaining flashcards and place them face down. Take a flashcard from the pile and show it to the class. Children run, jump or walk to the side of the room that has a flashcard from the same unit.

11. I spy
Choose flashcards from previous units that show different-colored objects. Display them around the classroom. Choose a color and say *I spy something (blue).* Children name the item of that color. Allow a child who answers correctly to take your role and play again.

12. Question chain
Choose flashcards from previous units and sit in a circle with the children if you have space. If not, have children play this game in small teams. Take a flashcard and make a question using that word, e.g. *Do you have your (backpack)? Can you move your (feet)? I like (carrots) – how about you?* Pass the flashcard to the child on your left, or the first child in each team, and encourage them to answer the question. They then turn to the child on their left, ask the same question, and pass the flashcard. Children continue asking and answering questions as they pass the flashcards around the circle or team.

13. 20-second time bomb
Use the flashcards to review the vocabulary from several previous units. Put the flashcards away. Set a timer to 20 seconds and name a unit topic, e.g. *Food/Clothes/Space.* Children must say as many words as they can from that unit before the timer goes off. As children name the words, show the corresponding flashcards.

14. Which one's missing?
Choose five flashcards from previous units and display them on the board. Ask children to close or cover their eyes. Remove one of the flashcards. Ask children to open their eyes and name the missing flashcard.

15. Relay race
Display flashcards from previous units on the board at the children's height. Divide the class into two teams. Ask a child from each team to stand next to each other a few meters away from the board. Name one of the flashcards. The two children race to touch the correct flashcard. The first child to touch the named flashcard wins a point for their team.

16. What do I have?
Place flashcards from previous units face down on the floor or board. Ask a volunteer to pick one up and show it to the class without you seeing it. Ask questions to help you identify the flashcard, e.g. *Is it big? Is it blue? Is it an animal?* When you are ready to guess, ask *Do you have a (ball)?*

17. Twister
Choose flashcards from previous units and stick them face up on the floor so they are secure. Name a flashcard and ask a volunteer to put one hand or foot on that flashcard. Repeat until both the child's hands and feet are touching flashcards, and he/she is in a position that is difficult to maintain. Count to ten with the class and tell the child to try to stay in the same position until you reach number 10. Repeat with different volunteers.

18. No!
Use the flashcards to review vocabulary from different units. Put the flashcards away. Start to name items from the same topic, e.g. *cow, goat, duck, horse.* Then say an item from a different topic, e.g. *planet.* When you say an item from a different topic, the children shout *No!*

19. Yes or no?
Choose flashcards from previous units. Hold up each flashcard in turn and either say the correct name or an incorrect name. If you say the correct name, the children say *Yes* and wave their arms in the air. If you say the incorrect name, they say *No* and fold their arms.

20. Karaoke
Place one flashcard from each previous unit on the board. Ask a child to touch the flashcard from their favorite unit. Play the songs from that unit. Encourage children to sing along and do the actions.

Activities Bank: The *Ferris Wheel* mat

Note: For larger classes, create a *Ferris Wheel* mat learning station (see p25) and do these activities with small groups. When demonstrating a new mat activity, ensure the other learning stations are familiar activities so the rest of the class can work independently.

1. Where's the …?
Hide six flashcards or objects in different pockets of the mat. Ask *Where's the (teddy)?* Children take turns guessing, e.g. *It's in the (blue) pocket!* or *Is it in the (green) pocket?* When a child guesses correctly, remove the object and show it to the class. Alternatively, ask children *What's in the (blue) pocket?* and encourage them to guess, e.g. *It's the teddy.*

2. Listen and do!
Display some objects or flashcards. Put children in pairs and give each pair an instruction, e.g. *Put the pencil in the pink pocket!* If they follow the instruction correctly, encourage the class to clap and say *Fantastic!* You can also instruct each pair to remove an object, e.g. *Give me the pencil, please.*

3. Remember, remember!
Put six flashcards or objects in different pockets of the mat. Talk to the children as you do this, e.g. *Let's put the ball in the yellow pocket.* Then ask *Can you remember where the (ball) is?* Ask children to raise their hands if they remember. Choose a child and encourage them to say *It's in the (yellow) pocket.* Ask the child to remove the object and show it to the class.

4. My favorite color
Write each child's name on a small piece of white construction paper. Ask children to color their card using their favorite color from the Ferris Wheel. Children take turns naming the color and putting their card inside the corresponding pocket. At the end, count the cards in each pocket. Ask children which pocket has the most cards and say *(Red) is our favorite color!*

5. Hide and seek
Ask children to turn around as you place the Meerkat family flashcards in different pockets of the mat. Leave a small part of each character's body visible. Have children turn around. Ask *Where's (Dylan)?* Ask a volunteer to point and say *(Dylan) is in the (blue) pocket!*

6. Mimi's magic
Hold up the mat. Ask individual children to check the pockets are empty, e.g. *Please look in the green pocket. Nothing there? Thank you!* Turn the mat around so the pockets are facing you and hide a flashcard or object in one of them. Show the mat to the class and have the Mimi puppet wave a "wand" (a ruler or pencil) as you say *Abracadabra! Listen to me. Look in the (red) pocket. What can you see?* Invite a child to remove and name the object.

7. *Ferris Wheel* ride
You will need small passport-sized photos of the children with reusable sticky tac on the back for this activity. Children choose the pod they want to ride in and stick their photo on it. Encourage them to say *I'm in (red)!* Then ask them to make big circles with their arms as they say the following rhyme: *Round and round and round we go! Oh, Ferris Wheel, we love you so!* Alternatively, ask children to bring in a favorite doll or teddy from home. Invite children to place their toys inside the pockets and say *My (teddy) is in (green)!*

8. Color swat!
You will need two plastic fly swatters for this activity. Hang the mat on the wall. Ask two children to stand either side of the mat and give each child a fly swatter. Name a color. The children should swat the correct color on the mat. Alternatively, place the mat on the floor and ask two or three children to walk around the mat. When you name a color, children must quickly touch the correct color.

9. Action game
Hang the mat on the wall. Over several lessons, teach children an action for each color, e.g. *When I say red, jump!* Introduce no more than two actions per lesson, and review the previous colors and actions each time. Once children are familiar with the colors and associated actions, point to a pocket on the mat and say *(Red)!* Children respond by doing the action and saying the word, e.g. *Jump!*

10. Odd one out
Arrange flashcards in six groups of four – three of the items in each group should be from the same lexical set and one should be from a different set. Put each group of flashcards inside a pocket on the mat. Invite a child to choose a color and remove the flashcards from that pocket. The child names each flashcard and then identifies the odd one out.

11. Sorting shapes
Ahead of time, cut out a selection of shapes from construction paper in the colors from the Ferris Wheel. Put children in small groups and give each group a variety of shapes. Ask them to organize them by color. Have a volunteer from each group place the shapes in the same-colored pocket as they say *A (green) (circle).*

12. Musical mat
Place six flashcards in different pockets and lay the mat on the floor. Ask six children to stand around the mat, one next to each pocket. Play music and ask children to dance around the mat. Pause the music and have children stand still. Say a color and ask the child next to that pocket to take out the flashcard and name the item. Ask the class to shout *Yes* and wave their arms if the child is correct and shout *No* and fold their arms if the child is incorrect.

13. Number game
You will need a big dice for this activity (you can make this out of construction paper). Hide a flashcard in each pocket of the mat. Write the numbers 1–6 on pieces of paper and place these clockwise on the pockets of the mat. Ask children to take turns throwing the dice and counting and saying the number. The child then removes the flashcard from the pocket with that number and names the item.

14. Mood mat
You will need pictures of emojis, e.g. happy, sad, scared, surprised, angry, calm, for this activity. Show each emoji and ask children to act out the emotion using facial expression and body language. Ask a child to choose an emoji and place it in the pocket with the color they associate with that emotion. Encourage them to name the emotion and the color. Make sure children understand that there are no correct answers.

15. *Ferris Wheel* role-play
If you like, prepare simple "tickets" for the role-play. Hang the mat on the wall and ask a small group of children to make a line in front of the mat. Use the Mimi puppet to act out a simple role-play with each child. For example: Mimi: *Hello, (David).* / Child: *Hello, Mimi.* / M: *Welcome to the Ferris Wheel! Choose a color.* / C: *(Orange), please.* [the child touches the correct pocket] / M: *Here's your ticket!* / C: *Thank you.*

Activities Bank: The Mimi puppet

The use of a puppet helps create a positive and warm environment for learning and playing in English. Children will develop a familiarity and fondness for Mimi, making the course materials even more engaging and appealing. Using the Mimi puppet as an integral part of your daily activities and routines brings fantasy, magic and humor into the classroom and creates opportunities for children to use English as part of their real-life interactions. Children will feel more secure and confident speaking English to Mimi and are more likely to actively participate, especially as they know she doesn't understand their first language!

1. Daily routines

Use the puppet to greet and say goodbye to children in every lesson. You can also use her for other classroom routines, such as the weather, the day of the week and taking attendance.

2. Social and emotional learning

Use the puppet to show affection towards the children and encourage the children to show affection back. Establish that the puppet has feelings and moods, e.g. happy, sad, tired. Encourage them to empathize with and respect these feelings, as well as telling Mimi how they feel.

3. Boosting confidence and self-esteem

Use the puppet to encourage and praise children. Ask children to show Mimi their work and get her to show interest and give positive feedback. If the class does a task well, use the puppet to praise and reward them with stickers or similar.

4. Demonstrating and modeling activities

Demonstrate and model activities with the puppet, e.g. act out a conversation or role-play. Do a cooperative activity using the puppet as your partner so children can see what to do. You can also use Mimi to drill vocabulary or short sentences. Children repeat what Mimi said in exactly the same way.

5. Linking fantasy and reality

Use the puppet as a bridge between the imaginative world of the Meerkat family and the real world. For example, use the puppet to show how language introduced in the stories is also applicable and relevant to the context of the classroom.

6. Introducing humor

Use the puppet to introduce an element of humor to lessons, e.g. when you want to surprise children or need to get their attention. For example, the puppet can be naughty, moody, make mistakes, answer questions incorrectly, or refuse to follow your instructions.

7. Learning reviews

Use the Mimi puppet when conducting learning reviews and have her take on the role of teacher. Alternatively, pretend she forgot what the children learned and ask them to remind her, or have Mimi answer your questions incorrectly and encourage children to correct her.

8. Managing your class positively

Use the puppet to help you manage your class, e.g. tell children that Mimi's sleeping or has a headache so they need to be quiet, or have Mimi give them instructions to form a line or a circle, e.g. *Come here, please, (Alex).* Similarly, when conflicts arise, have Mimi ask children to say sorry and be friends again. When selecting children to participate in activities, use Mimi to point to children and say a little rhyme, e.g. *Red, yellow, blue. I love YOU!*

9. Role-play and drama

You can use the puppet to act out simple role-plays or short versions of the unit stories, with the puppet taking on Mimi's role and children acting out the other parts.

10. Games and play

Have Mimi take your role in games to engage children's interest. If you have learning stations or an English Language Area (ELA) in your classroom (see p25), put the puppet there along with other resources, such as flashcards, for use during child-led play.

11. Hello, Mimi!

Ask children to sit in a circle. Play music as children pass the puppet around the circle. Whenever you pause the music, the child who has the puppet holds it up and says *Hello, Mimi!* If you wish, encourage the child to tell the puppet something about themselves, e.g. *I'm Maria. I have a ball.* You could also ask children to bring a stuffed animal from home and have their toys greet Mimi.

12. Do what Mimi says

Use the puppet to give instructions for children to follow, e.g. *Stand up. Sit down. Jump. Run. Stop.* Alternatively, display some flashcards and use the puppet to say, e.g. *Touch the (apple).*

13. Guess what Mimi's thinking

Display 3–6 flashcards on the floor or board. Hold up Mimi and put her in a thinking pose. Encourage children to guess which flashcard Mimi is thinking about. Have Mimi nod or shake her head and say *Yes/No.* When a child guesses correctly, Mimi gives them a high five.

14. Guess what's in Mimi's bag

Put several different objects or flashcards in a non-transparent bag. Make the puppet hold up the bag and ask *What's in my bag?* Children take turns guessing. If a child guesses correctly, Mimi removes the object or flashcard from the bag and shows it to the children.

15. Hide and seek

Choose two children and ask them to cover their eyes. Hide the puppet somewhere in the classroom so it is still partially visible. Ask the two children to open their eyes. Ask *Where's Mimi?* As the two children search, encourage the class to say *no, no, no* softly when they are far from the puppet, and *YES, YES, YES!* loudly when they get close to the puppet.

16. Mimi's song choice

When children learn a new song, draw a picture to illustrate it on a piece of construction paper. Keep the cards in a box. Use the puppet to take a card, show it to the class and say *Please sing this song.* Use Mimi as a conductor while children sing by having her hold a pencil or ruler. Hold her high for children to sing more loudly and low for children to sing quietly.

17. Taking Mimi home

Allow children to take turns taking the puppet home. When children bring the puppet back, encourage them to tell the class about the visit, e.g. where Mimi slept and where she went. If you wish, you could ask parents/carers to take photos of the visit and add them to a shared photo album, *Mimi's Travel Diary.*

Activities Bank: Social and emotional learning (SEL)

By integrating the development of social and emotional learning (SEL) skills into your teaching, you will enable children to deal confidently with the psychological, social and academic demands of pre-school, and lay the foundations for their future educational and life success.

1. Social development

Show that you value the way children relate to each other. Encourage children to think through any social difficulties that arise by asking questions such as *How do you feel when someone …?* This will help children see situations from other people's point of view.

2. Emotional development

Observe children's body language, eye contact, behavior and participation in class. Acknowledge children's emotions, while also making it clear that certain behavior is not acceptable. Provide a positive role model in the way that you express and manage your own emotions. Make discussing your feelings (happy, sad, angry, calm, sleepy, etc.) part of your daily class routine. Sharing your feelings will facilitate an emotional connection with children and give them the confidence to talk about how they feel.

3. Curiosity and confidence

Create a warm and supportive environment in which children feel secure about taking risks, asking questions, sharing ideas or making mistakes. Ask questions to scaffold children's understanding and promote further learning. Give praise and feedback that honestly acknowledges children's achievements and efforts. Make it clear that making mistakes is an important part of learning. Establish regular routines in class so that children feel secure about what is expected of them.

4. Resilience

Resilience is the ability to bounce back and keep going after a difficult or stressful experience. Two significant ways to help children develop resilience are i) to foster positive self-esteem and ii) to reinforce and promote self-belief. A safe and caring learning environment allows children to try to achieve their goals independently while always feeling that they are supported by the adults around them.

5. Responsible decision-making

Children need to practice making positive choices about both their personal and social behavior, and their academic work. Start with simple choices and decisions that are age-appropriate, e.g. the order in which to do activities or which materials to use. Model thinking through the options, making it clear that there are no correct answers. Avoid making decisions for children as, although this may often be quicker and easier, it denies children the opportunity to consider the different options and select the most appropriate action.

6. Self-management

Giving children strategies to control and manage their behavior will contribute to a positive atmosphere in the classroom. After a lively activity, introduce a calming technique to regain children's attention. Ask the children to sit down very slowly while you count down from six. By the time you reach number one, the children should be seated and calm enough to move on to the next activity. Teach children to use language, e.g. *I don't like it when …*, rather than physical actions to express displeasure. Provide them with strategies to calm down, such as relaxing and breathing deeply or deliberately moving away from the upsetting situation. If possible, create a "peace corner" where children can go when they feel angry or upset. Provide cushions, books and stuffed animals to help children relax and process their emotions.

7. Cooperation and empathy

Pair and group work gives children the opportunity to interact positively and show empathy towards their peers. It is also helpful in developing cooperation skills. Encourage children to listen to and show an interest in others and see things from their point of view. When a child shares something about themselves, encourage them to ask a classmate to do the same by asking *How about you?* Be inclusive at all times and encourage children to behave respectfully towards their classmates by using language such as *please*, *thank you* and *sorry*.

8. Supportiveness and self-esteem

Encourage children to support and help their classmates. Pairing shy children with a more confident classmate can be beneficial for the self-esteem of both children. Encourage children to help and guide each other throughout the day, not only with academic tasks, but also with daily routines, such as putting on coats and shoes, etc. When playing games or doing other activities, remind children to use positive language. If the answer is incorrect, encourage them to say, e.g. *Try again.* If the answer is correct, encourage them to offer praise, e.g. *Great job! Very good!*

9. Autonomy

Little by little, encourage children to become more independent and responsible for their learning and behavior in class. Provide them with simple age-appropriate strategies for everyday tasks, such as putting on their coats, and allow them to make their own choices wherever possible. As part of developing autonomy and metacognitive skills, encourage children to regularly reflect on their learning (see p18). Use the Review lessons in each unit to foster self-awareness and an ability to self-evaluate.

10. Making an effort

Encourage children to believe in their ability to master different skills through effort and persistence. Praise achievement while, at the same time, focusing on the underlying effort. If children find an activity challenging, encourage them not to give up by singing the song: *I can do it if I try* (CD1 Track 41). Monitor children's response to their learning in each unit using the self-evaluation in the Review lesson and emphasize that increased effort will lead to more progress.

11. Free play

Child-led play is one of the key ways in which children naturally develop SEL skills, such as relating to friends, managing emotions, solving problems, resolving conflict, developing autonomy and making decisions. An English Language Area (ELA) (see p25) can be a great way to provide opportunities for free play.

Activities Bank: Life skills

Life skills

Pre-school may be children's first experience of extended separation from their family. By teaching basic life skills, you help children adapt to the new social context of life at school. Teaching life skills also enriches children's exposure to English and allows them to acquire new language in a natural and meaningful way.

1. Put on your coat
Show children how to put on their coats by placing the coat on the floor with the hood or collar at their feet. The child inserts their arms in the armholes, and then lifts the coat up and over their head and into position.

2. Find your coat hook or shelf
In addition to labelling coat hooks or shelves with children's first names, add a picture so children can recognize it easily. Provide a selection of pictures showing English vocabulary children already know or will soon learn. Allow children to choose their picture.

3. Look after your clothes
Teach children to put their jacket, hat and gloves into the pockets of their coat before they put it on their coat hook. This way, they will always know where to find them.

4. Clean up
Allow time for children to clean up materials. Ensure everyone knows where each kind of material belongs and have children work together in teams to get the classroom clean and neat. Use the *Clean up song* (see p17) to signal when it's time to clean up.

5. Little helpers
Nominate helpers to give out or collect classroom materials. Rotate the helpers on a daily or weekly basis so everyone gets a turn. This will make children feel valued and help them see the importance of their contribution.

6. Put it in the trash can
Encourage children to use the trash can when clearing up waste paper and snack wrappers. You could also show them how to sharpen their own pencils over the trash can.

7. Make a line or circle
To make a line, use gesture to show that children should stand one behind the other and place their hands on the shoulders or waist of the child in front of them. To make a circle, stand at the front of the line and ask everyone to hold hands. Lead children around to form a circle.

8. Put belongings in your backpack
Encourage children to take responsibility for their own possessions. Give time for children to take out and put away belongings in their backpacks. Praise children who do this independently.

9. Share materials
Encourage children to take turns and share materials. Show that you value a willingness to share materials and cooperate as much as completing the activity.

10. Say "please" and "thank you"
Teach these words early on. Consistently remind children to say *please* and *thank you* both to you and to each other. Make it clear that children are more likely to get a positive response when they use these words.

11. Motor skills and projects
Project work provides an opportunity for the integrated development of both language and fine motor skills, such as rolling modeling clay, tearing tissue paper and using finger paints. Demonstrate these skills before asking children to use them. Praise and value children's efforts.

12. Wash and dry your hands
Teach the procedure for washing hands (see Level 3 Student's Book, p41). Establish when and why it is important for children to wash their hands, e.g. before and after meals, after going to the playground and bathroom, and encourage them to do this independently.

13. Be active
Teach children the importance of moving their bodies every day. Incorporate physical activity into your classroom routines by using action songs and games. This will help develop coordination and gross motor skills. Show children how to place a hand on their heart after physical activity to show that it's beating faster and explain why this is good for them.

14. Wait your turn
Gently insist that children wait their turn to speak, and listen to others without calling out or interrupting. Explain or elicit why this is important. During Circle time, it may help to have an object, e.g. a soft ball, to show whose turn it is to speak. Similarly, when playing classroom games, explain that everyone has equal right to participate and praise children who wait their turn.

15. Cover a cough or sneeze
Explain basic hygiene about spreading germs from coughs and colds. Train children to hold up their arms to cover their mouths when they cough or sneeze. This is preferable to using hands, which they may then use to touch classmates or shared materials.

16. Care with scissors
If children use scissors, make sure that they are holding the scissors correctly. When they get up to put any scraps of paper in the trash can, make sure they leave the scissors on the table.

17. Safe in the sun
Explain to children why it is important to wear a sunhat and sunscreen to protect them from the sun. Ask children to put on their hats before going outside and not to take them off until they come back inside.

18. Bathroom visits
Build in opportunities for children to go to the bathroom either before or after lessons and at recess. Make it clear, however, that if children need to go to the bathroom at any other time, they are free to do so. If the bathrooms are not in the classroom, children could wear a card around their necks to show that they have been authorized to leave the classroom.

19. Drink water
Explain to children why it is important to keep hydrated and drink water throughout the day. Make sure children know that they can ask for water if they feel thirsty.

20. Pleasure in participating
It is important not to force children to participate unless they are willing to do so. At the same time, it is crucial to create an environment in which children take pleasure in participating and learning with their peers. This will help children to develop other life and SEL skills, such as cooperation, tolerance, empathy and respect.

Activities Bank: Learning enrichment

Ferris Wheel provides everything you need to teach children English in an enjoyable and effective way. However, if you also have the time and opportunity to incorporate additional materials, resources and activities, this will enrich children's learning experience and ensure maximum appeal and motivation.

1. Picturebooks

Picturebooks are a great way to expose children to new language in a natural, motivating context. It is a good idea to focus on picturebooks that relate to the topic of the current unit, e.g. Clothes, Food, Farm animals, and that contain simple and repetitive language. However, keep in mind that children don't need to understand every word to enjoy the story, and you can make use of the illustrations, intonation, facial expression, questions and repetition to support understanding. Once children become familiar with a picturebook, encourage them to join in with repeated phrases and, if appropriate, to act out the story.

You may also like to encourage children to bring English picturebooks from home to share with the class. Put children in small groups to look at their picturebooks together. Encourage them to talk about what they like and can see on each page.

2. Dressing up

Provide a selection of dress-up clothes. Encourage children to practice fine motor skills by putting on and removing the clothes independently, asking for help from their classmates if needed. Encourage children to give each other instructions as they get dressed, e.g. *Put on your shirt.* Allow them to play freely and imaginatively with the clothes, e.g. organizing a costume party or drawing pictures of themselves and each other wearing their costumes.

3. Posters and visual images

As well as using the *Ferris Wheel* posters (see Resource Bank) to decorate the classroom walls and reinforce key language, topics and concepts, collect and display other visuals that relate to the topic of the current unit. Make use of the posters to recycle language and play games, e.g. by asking children to run and touch something on the poster. You may also like to use children's artwork for recycling activities. This gives a specific purpose to the work children produce and raises self-esteem.

4. Toys and realia

Wherever the unit topic allows, try to provide real-life objects or toys that children can touch and interact with. This will help create a direct connection in children's minds between their language learning and the real world. It will also make children's learning feel less abstract and more meaningful. Use the toys and objects in place of, or as well as, flashcards when you present and practice vocabulary. You can also use them as props for role-plays, drama and "feely bag" games.

5. Mime and drama

Mime allows children to produce a non-verbal response to language and helps boost confidence and self-esteem. Children can mime what happens as you tell a familiar story about Mimi and Dylan, for example, or they can mime in response to a set of instructions you give. Drama enables you to create a realistic context for children to practice using English they know. For example: you can create simple role-plays using dress-up clothes and props; get children to act out a simplified version of the Mimi and Dylan stories; pretend to be the Meerkat family or the real children; or allow them to take on the role of teacher, as Mimi does in the Review lessons. Use the Mimi puppet to help you transition from the real world to fantasy, and vice versa.

6. Music, movement and dance

Music, movement and dance develop gross motor skills and rhythm, and provide an engaging context in which to respond to simple instructional language. You may like to use the karaoke version of a favorite song from the course as the basis for teaching children a simple dance. It is also beneficial to teach children simple movement sequences, in which you start with one or two instructions, e.g. *Put your arms in the air. Jump three times.*, and build additional actions cumulatively. You can then use these sequences at moments when you feel children's energy levels are getting low and they need to get up and move around.

7. Movies, TV and video clips

In addition to the *Ferris Wheel* animated stories, songs and real-life videos, you may like to select other short movies and video clips from online sources that relate to the current unit topic. You could also occasionally allow children to watch their favorite TV show in the original English language version. This will expose them to natural English being spoken in a familiar context by well-loved characters. You may also like to suggest that parents or carers show children the English version of their favorite TV shows at home.

8. Children's multilingual identities

The children in your class may have diverse cultural backgrounds and speak another language at home, in addition to the shared language of the classroom and English. It is important to show that you respect and value each child's culture and language. Encouraging children to talk about their culture in class will help reinforce a positive sense of identity and create an atmosphere of tolerance and mutual respect. For example, when learning a new word in English, you could ask children to tell you the word in the language they speak at home. Alternatively, you could ask *How many different words do we know for "lion?"* Show your own enthusiasm for learning words in different languages and ask *Do any of the words sound similar?* Similarly, you can ask questions that get children to compare aspects of their culture with North-American culture, e.g. *Do you have toast for breakfast? What do you have?*

9. Home-school link

Working in partnership with parents and carers can be a hugely beneficial way to enrich children's learning. Regular letters to parents (see Resource Bank) with information about your approach, content and expectations, along with specific guidance on how parents and carers can support their children's learning, will facilitate communication. It is also a good idea to hold regular meetings with parents and carers, and to ensure they know you are available whenever they have questions or concerns. Given that parents and carers are likely to have had a different experience of learning a foreign language, it may help them to understand your approach if they can informally observe a lesson. Alternatively, you could share video clips of your lessons during an explanatory talk. If parents have a good level of English, invite them to visit the class as a volunteer, either to assist children with individual work, read a story or give a short talk related to the current unit topic.

10. Out and about

Whenever appropriate and possible, it is beneficial to take children on trips outside the classroom in order to make the connection between their learning and the real world. This may involve visiting different places within the school, e.g. the playground or music room, or finding a window overlooking a street where children can identify different forms of transportation. If there is a school garden, children could visit the vegetable patch and identify food that is growing there. If possible, plant some seeds, water them regularly and monitor how they grow. Trips further afield might include a visit to a local park, farm, zoo or museum.

11. Learning stations

Learning stations provide meaningful, self-directed language practice and develop skills such as autonomy, responsible decision-making and cooperation. When organized during lesson time, learning stations also provide you with an opportunity to give extra support to small groups of children. Start off with two or three learning stations, and add new stations gradually through the year. Ensure you use activities that children have already practiced with you before they use the station independently. Organize children in pairs or small groups and have them take turns visiting each station. Some ideas for learning stations include:

- **Feely bag:** Children take turns feeling and guessing the objects in a non-transparent bag.
- ***Ferris Wheel* mat games:** see p20.
- **Drawing station:** Children draw their favorite animal, toy, family member, etc.
- **Matching pairs:** Provide two copies of a selection of five to six flashcards, mix them up and place them face down. Children take turns turning over two cards. If they are a matching pair, they keep the cards. If not, they turn them back over in the same place and continue the game.
- **Watch and learn:** Play videos or animations from the current unit or previous units for children to watch and enjoy. For the songs, encourage them to sing along and join in with the actions.
- **Classification station:** Children work together to classify objects or flashcards using different criteria, e.g. colors, shapes, size, etc.

12. English Language Area (ELA)

In some educational contexts, it is usual practice to divide the pre-school classroom into different learning areas or activity centers. These provide opportunities for children to play and experiment with a range of resources and to interact with their peers in an autonomous, child-led way. Typical learning areas or activity centers include: a reading area (with soft cushions, books, audio devices and headphones); a communication and drama area (with props, e.g. store items or kitchen utensils, and dress-up clothes); a science area (with small slides, weights, balances, sand and water); and a modeling and construction area (with building blocks and modeling materials).
You can also create an English Language Area (ELA) using course materials, such as the *Ferris Wheel* mat, the Mimi puppet, a selection of flashcards and story cards, and a computer or tablet with headphones and access to the digital materials. Ensure that the activities and materials are familiar to the children so they can repeat, imitate, and create activities and games closely based on teacher-led activities using known language. For example, children may pretend to take on the role of teacher and use the *Ferris Wheel* mat and flashcards to play a well-known game, or use the Mimi puppet to test a friend on vocabulary, as Mimi does with Dylan in the Review lessons.
As the idea is for the teacher to monitor and observe, but not directly intervene, it is essential for each learning area to have clear rules, e.g. the reading area is strictly for quiet reading and only English can be spoken in the ELA. Observing children as they play in the ELA will also provide you with invaluable feedback on their learning and progress to date.

Hello I'm Mimi!

Vocabulary and Language

- **Main vocabulary:** Mommy, Daddy, Mimi, Dylan, Ferris Wheel; blue, green, orange, pink, red, yellow; numbers; ball, car, doll, scooter, teddy, train
- **Key language:** Hello, I'm (Mimi). Where's the (ball)? Here's the (ball). It's (blue).

Unit objectives

- Say *Hello, I'm …*
- Identify and name colors
- Count to six
- Sing *Hello, I'm Mimi.*
- Identify and name the course characters
- Identify and name toys
- Sing *Where's the ball?*
- Ask and say where things are
- Say what color things are

Songs

Language song

Hello, I'm Mimi CD1 Track 16

Hello, I'm Mimi (Wave to Mimi puppet)
I'm happy today. (Dance around)
Hello, I'm Mimi (Wave to Mimi puppet)
Come and play. (Beckoning gesture)
Here's the Ferris Wheel (Make big circle with arms)
Hurray! Hurray! (Wave arms in air)

Hello, I'm Dylan (Wave to Dylan flashcard)
I'm happy today. (Dance around)
Hello, I'm Dylan (Wave to Dylan flashcard)
Come and play. (Beckoning gesture)
Here's the Ferris Wheel. (Make big circle with arms)
Hurray! Hurray! (Wave arms in air)
Here's the Ferris Wheel. (Make big circle with arms)
Hurray! Hurray! (Wave arms in air)

Language song

Where's the ball? CD1 Track 18

Where's the ball, ball, ball? (Shrug shoulders and mime bouncing a ball)
Where's the ball? (Shrug shoulders and mime bouncing a ball)
Here's the ball. (Point to the ball flashcard)
It's blue, blue, blue! (Throw arms up in air)

Where's the car, car, car? (Shrug shoulders and mime turning a wheel)
Where's the car? (Shrug shoulders and mime turning a wheel)
Here's the car. (Point to the car flashcard)
It's red, red, red! (Throw arms up in air)

Where's the teddy, teddy, teddy? (Shrug shoulders and mime hugging a teddy)
Where's the teddy? (Shrug shoulders and mime hugging a teddy)
Here's the teddy. (Point to the teddy flashcard)
It's yellow, yellow, yellow! (Throw arms up in air)

Where's the train, train, train? (Shrug shoulders and mime a train chugging)
Where's the train? (Shrug shoulders and mime a train chugging)
Here's the train. (Point to the train flashcard)
It's green, green, green! (Throw arms up in air)

Hello I'm Mimi!

Vocabulary Lesson 1

Listen, point and repeat. Sing *Hello, I'm Mimi.* Stick the color stickers. Color the flag your favorite color. Language: Mommy, Daddy, Mimi, Dylan; Ferris Wheel; blue, green, orange, pink, red, yellow; numbers; Hello, I'm (Mimi).

3

Learning objectives

- Say *Hello, I'm …*
- Identify and name colors
- Count to six
- Sing *Hello, I'm Mimi*
- Identify and name the course characters

Materials

- Class CDs, flashcards, *Ferris Wheel* mat, Mimi puppet

Main vocabulary

- Mommy, Daddy, Mimi, Dylan; Ferris Wheel; blue, green, orange, pink, red, yellow; numbers 1–6

Key language

- Hello, I'm (Mimi).

Teacher's tip: Circle time and Table time

Circle time is a great way to gather children together at the start of the class. If there isn't space for children to sit on the floor, children can sit at their desks. For the *Circle time chant* (see p 17), when it says "hands together", have them hold hands with the children at their table to show they are a team.

Table time is when children work with their books. When it's time to do so, ask them to stand up and form a train with the children at their table. All the trains then link up to make a whole-class train. Say the *Table time train chant* (see p 17) as you move around the room, dropping each team off at their table. When each team sits, they give each other a high five!

Circle time

Hello song & puppet (CD1 Track 2; see TB p 17 & 21)
Opening routines (see TB p 16)
Lesson aims (see TB p 18)

Introduce the Meerkat family.

- Use the flashcards and puppet to introduce the characters.
- Say *Hello, I'm …* and name the characters *(Mommy, Daddy, Mimi, Dylan)*. Children wave and say *Hello*.
- Use the puppet to say *Hello, I'm Mimi* and encourage children to respond *Hello, I'm (Sara)*.

Introduce the Ferris Wheel.

- Put the *Ferris Wheel* mat on the floor or the board. Explain that the Meerkat family live near the Ferris Wheel.
- Use the puppet to point and elicit or name the colors. Children repeat.
- Use the puppet to count the pods on the Wheel.

Sing *Hello, I'm Mimi.*

CD1 Track 16

- Say *Let's sing "Hello, I'm Mimi."*
- Play the song. Hold up Mimi (puppet) and Dylan (flashcard) in turn and point to the Ferris Wheel when it's mentioned in the song.
- Teach actions for the song (*hello*: wave; *happy*: dance around; *come and play*: beckoning gesture; *Ferris Wheel*: make big circle with arms; *hurray*: wave arms in the air.) Children sing and act out the song (see TB p 27).

Game: *Find the meerkats!*

- Put the character flashcards face down on different pods of the *Ferris Wheel* mat without the children seeing. Name a color and the children guess the character. Repeat. Then reverse the procedure. Name a character and the children guess the color.

Table time

Student's Book p 3

Listen, point and repeat.

- Hold up your book. Point to the Meerkat family and colors on the Ferris Wheel as Mimi speaks.
- Play the audio again. Children join in, pointing to the picture in their books and saying the names of the characters and colors.

CD1 Track 15

Mimi: I'm Mimi. This is my brother, Dylan. This is my mommy and daddy. We live near the Ferris Wheel. The Ferris Wheel is red, blue, orange, yellow, pink and green.

Sing *Hello, I'm Mimi.*

CD1 Track 16

- Children sing and act out the song, waving to the characters in the book.

Stick the color stickers. Color the flag your favorite color.

- Children stick the color stickers in the correct places and name the colors.
- Children choose their favorite color and color the flag.
- Explain that children will "meet" the other characters on the Ferris Wheel in stories later in the book.

Activity Book p 3

Point and say the names.

- Point to each course character and have children say the name.

Trace and color the Ferris Wheel. Say the colors

- Children trace and color the Ferris Wheel. Point to each pod and have them name the color.

Closing time

Learning review (see TB p 18)
Closing routines (see TB p 16)
Bye bye song and puppet (CD1 Track 3; see TB p 17 & 21)

Use the **Navio App** to play the vocabulary game, and encourage children to do the same at home.

Lesson 2 Language

Listen, find and point. Sing *Where's the ball?* Circle the toys. Draw your favorite toy. Ask and say. Language: ball, car, doll, scooter, teddy, train; blue, green, orange, pink, red, yellow; Where's the (ball)? Here's the (ball)! It's (blue).

4

Learning objectives

- Identify and name toys
- Sing *Where's the ball?*
- Ask and say where things are
- Say what color things are

Materials

- Class CDs, flashcards, *Ferris Wheel* mat, Mimi puppet

Main vocabulary

- ball, car, doll, scooter, teddy, train; blue, green, orange, pink, red, yellow

Key language

- Where's the (ball)? Here's the (ball)! It's (blue).

Teacher's tip: Forming a bond with the puppet

Allow the children to come close and stroke Mimi's head or hold her hand as they greet her. Initially, some children may feel shy, so invite confident children to come first. At the end of the lesson, ask them again. You may find more children feel confident enough to stroke Mimi or hold her hand and begin to form a bond with her.

Circle time

Hello song & puppet (CD1 Track 2; see TB p 17 & 21)
Opening routines (see TB p 16)
Lesson aims (see TB p 18)

Introduce toys.

- Use the puppet to introduce the new vocabulary by pointing to the toy flashcards. Say the words and encourage children to repeat them with you. Repeat for all the words.
- Put the *Ferris Wheel* mat on the board or the floor with the toy flashcards face down (one on each color). Use the puppet to turn the flashcards over and name them. The children repeat the words.

Game: *Play with your scooter!*

- Point to the flashcards in turn. Use the puppet to give instructions. Children mime playing with each toy.

Game: *Say the color!*

- Name the toys on the Ferris Wheel and children name the color. Then do it in reverse.

Game: *Guess the toys!*

- Turn the flashcards face down and mix them up so that they are on different colors of the wheel.
- Point to one flashcard. Children guess what it is. Then say *Let's find out!* Turn the flashcard over and children say the word. Repeat with all the flashcards.

Table time

Student's Book p 4

Listen, find and point. Sing *Where's the ball?*

CD1 Track 18

- Play the song. The children listen and point to each toy as they hear it in the song.
- Play the song again. Children sing the song and do the actions (see TB p 27)

Circle the toys.

- Children find and circle the toys.

Draw your favorite toy.

- Demonstrate that children should draw their favorite toy in the white space.

Ask and say.

- Encourage children to show their pictures and say, e.g. *Here's the (scooter). It's (red).*

Activity Book p 4

Find and color the toys.

- Children find and color the six toys in the picture.

Point and say. Ask and say.

- Point to each toy in turn and have children say the name. Then ask *Where's the (ball)?* and encourage children to answer *Here's the (ball)! It's (blue).*

Closing time

Learning review (see TB p 18)
Closing routines (see TB p 16)
Bye bye song and puppet (CD1 Track 3; see TB p 17 & 21)

Use the **Navio App** to listen to the song, and encourage children to do the same at home.

Classroom

Fun with paint!

Vocabulary and language

- **Main vocabulary**: backpack, crayons, glue, paints, paper, pencil, pencil case, scissors
- **Key language:** Do you have your (backpack)? Yes, I do. / No, I don't.
  I have (red) paint.
- **Content language:** cafeteria, classroom, library, playground; Go to the (playground).
- **Other language:** ceiling, clap, door, floor, hands, home, knee, school, window; I have (blue) here. I'm good at (home). Point to the (ceiling). I have (paints). My wheel is (orange). I'm on (blue). I like the (blue) wheel. Our Ferris Wheel is (fantastic)!

Unit objectives

- Identify and name classroom objects
- Sing the language song *Do you have your backpack?*
- Ask and say what classroom objects you have
- Understand and act out the story *Fun with paint!*
- Sing and act out the story song *The paint song*
- Sing the values song *Be good at home*
- Recognize the value of good behavior
- Identify and name places at school
- Sing and act out the traditional song *Wind the bobbin up*
- Review your learning and progress
- Participate in a collaborative project

Story

CD1 Track 24

Picture 1

Narrator: It's time for school. Dylan's excited.
Dylan: Hurray! Hurray! It's a school day!
Mommy: Yes, Dylan. Let's get ready. Be good.
Mimi: Do you have your backpack, Dylan?
Dylan: Yes, I do.
Mimi: Do you have your pencil case?
Dylan: Yes, I do. And I have a pencil, crayons, scissors and glue.
Mommy: Now remember, Dylan. Be good.
Dylan: Yes, Mommy.

Picture 2

Mrs. Cat: Good morning, children.
Children: Good morning, Mrs. Cat.
Mrs. Cat: Today please paint a picture of your favorite place.
Children: Oooh! Hurray!
Dylan: Yippee!
Mrs. Cat: Do you have paper, Dylan?
Dylan: Yes, I do.
Mrs. Cat: Do you have paints?
Dylan: Yes, I do.
Mrs. Cat: Great. You can start!

Picture 3

Dylan: This is fun! Look, Mimi. I have red paint here. And I have blue paint there.
Mimi: Oh, Dylan. You have red and blue paint everywhere! Remember, be good.
Dylan: Yes, Mimi.

Picture 4

Dylan: And look, Mimi. I have yellow paint here. And I have green paint there.
Mimi: Oh, Dylan. You have yellow and green paint everywhere! Remember, be good.
Dylan: Yes, Mimi.

Picture 5

Dylan: And look, Mimi. I have orange paint here. And I have pink paint there.
Mimi: Oh, Dylan. You have orange and pink paint everywhere! Remember, be good.
Dylan: Yes, Mimi.

Picture 6

Mrs. Cat: OK, everyone. It's time to stop. Show me your pictures, please. What a beautiful picture, Mimi. Great job!
Dylan: And look at my picture, Mrs. Cat. It's the Ferris Wheel!
Mrs. Cat: Oh, it's fantastic, Dylan! Now wash your hands, please. Good boy.
Dylan: You see, Mimi. I am good!
Mimi: Yes, Dylan, you are good. And your picture is fantastic too!

Songs 

Language song

Do you have your backpack? CD1 Track 22

Do you have your backpack, backpack? (Shrug and place hands close to shoulders)
Yes, I do. Hurray! (Thumbs up and arms in the air for hooray)
Do you have your pencil case, pencil case? (Shrug and zip a pencil case up)
No, I don't. Not today. (Shake head and fold arms)

Do you have your scissors, scissors? (Shrug and open and close two fingers as if cutting)
Yes, I do. Hurray! (Thumbs up and arms in the air for hooray)
Do you have your glue, glue? (Shrug and mime gluing)
No, I don't. Not today. (Shake head and fold arms)

Do you have your paints, paints? (Shrug and mime painting)
Yes, I do. Hurray! (Thumbs up and arms in the air for hooray)
Do you have your paper, paper? (Shrug and mime waving a piece of paper)
No, I don't. Not today. (Shake head and fold arms)

Story song

The paint song CD1 Track 25

I have red paint here. (Point right)
I have blue paint there. (Point left)
I have red and blue paint everywhere. (Point left, right and gesture all around)
Red and blue paint. Yeah! (Point left, right and throw arms up for yeah)

I have yellow paint here. (Point right)
I have green paint there. (Point left)
I have yellow and green paint everywhere. (Point left, right and gesture all around)
Yellow and green paint. Yeah! (Point left, right and throw arms up for yeah)

I have orange paint here. (Point right)
I have pink paint there. (Point left)
I have orange and pink paint everywhere. (Point left, right and gesture all around)
Orange and pink paint. Yeah! (Point left, right and throw arms up for yeah)

Values song

Be good at home CD1 Track 28

Be good at home (Thumbs up and mime a roof over your head)
Be good at school (Thumbs up and gesture around)
Be good with Mommy (Thumbs up and point to Mommy flashcard)
It's super cool! (Make a circle with thumb and forefinger)

Be good at home (Thumbs up and mime a roof over your head)
Be good at school (Thumbs up and gesture around)
Be good with Daddy (Thumbs up and point to Daddy flashcard)
It's super cool! (Make a circle with thumb and forefinger)

Be good at home (Thumbs up and mime a roof over your head)
Be good at school (Thumbs up and gesture around)
Be good with Teacher (Thumbs up and point to yourself)
It's super cool! (Make a circle with thumb and forefinger)

Culture song

Wind the bobbin up CD1 Track 30

Wind the bobbin up (Roll arms)
Wind the bobbin up (Roll arms)
Pull, pull, clap, clap, clap (Pull outwards and clap 3 times)

Point to the ceiling (Point up to the ceiling)
Point to the floor (Point down to the floor)
Point to the window (Point to a window)
Point to the door (Point to a door)

Clap your hands together
One, two, three (Clap 3 times)
And put your hands
On your knee (Place hands on knees)

Wind the bobbin up (Roll arms)
Wind the bobbin up (Roll arms)
Pull, pull, clap, clap, clap (Pull outwards and clap 3 times)

Classroom

Fun with paint!

Vocabulary Lesson 1

1:19 hello 1:20

Listen, point and repeat. Listen and play. Stick the classroom object stickers. Circle the classroom objects that you have. Say. Language: backpack, crayons, glue, pencil, pencil case, scissors; blue, green, orange, pink, red, yellow

Classroom

Lesson 1 Vocabulary

Learning objectives

- Identify and name classroom objects
- Listen and point to classroom objects
- Identify which classroom objects children have

Materials

- Class CDs, flashcards, *Ferris Wheel* mat, Mimi puppet

Main vocabulary

- backpack, crayons, glue, pencil, pencil case, scissors

Teacher's tip: Identifying objects by touch

As well as playing vocabulary games with the flashcards, play them using real classroom objects, either in a feely bag or in the pockets of the *Ferris Wheel* mat. Identifying objects by touch is a helpful, kinesthetic way for children to remember new words.

Circle time

Hello song & puppet (CD1 Track 2; see TB p 17 & 21)
Opening routines (see TB p 16)
Lesson aims (see TB p 18)

Introduce classroom objects.

- Use the puppet and real items in a backpack to introduce the classroom objects. Say each word and the children repeat it.
- Put the *Ferris Wheel* mat on the board or the floor with the classroom object flashcards face down (one on each color). Use the puppet to turn over and name each flashcard. The children repeat the words.

Game: ***Find the object!***

- Name the objects in turn and ask one or two children to find and touch the correct flashcards as fast as they can.

Game: ***Say the color!***

- Name the objects and children say the color of the wheel. Then do it in reverse.

Table time

Student's Book p 5

Listen, point and repeat.

- Play the audio. The children listen, point to each object as they hear it, and repeat the words.

CD1 Track 19

Mimi: Look Dylan! Backpack … pencil case … pencil … crayons … scissors … glue. Repeat, Dylan!
Dylan: Yes, Mimi. Backpack … pencil case … pencil … crayons … scissors … glue.
Mimi: Very good, Dylan. Let's name the classroom objects together!
Both: Backpack … pencil case … pencil … crayons … scissors … glue.

Listen and play.

- Use finger in air to pretend to spin wheel. Children spin their fingers, point to the color when they hear it on the audio and say the word.

CD1 Track 20

Mimi: Spin the wheel
One, two, three
Point and name
The classroom objects with me!
Mimi: Red … backpack!
Dylan: Orange … pencil!
Mimi: Yellow … crayons!
Dylan: Blue … pencil case!
Mimi: Pink … scissors!
Dylan: Green … glue

- Play the game with you and/or individual children naming colors and others responding with the words.

Stick the classroom object stickers.

- Children stick the classroom object stickers in the correct places.

Circle the classroom objects that you have.

- Children circle the classroom objects they have.

Say.

- Children name the classroom objects they have.

Activity Book p 5

Look, find and match.

- Children find and match the classroom objects.

Color the objects in your classroom.

- They color the objects that are in their classroom.

Point and say.

- Children name the objects.

Closing time

Learning review (see TB p 18)
Closing routines (see TB p 16)
Bye bye song and puppet (CD1 Track 3; see TB p 17 & 21)

Use the **Navio App** to play the vocabulary game, and encourage children to do the same at home.

Lesson 2 Language

Listen and find the new classroom objects. Listen, point and sing *Do you have your backpack?* Circle the objects Sam has. Ask and say. Language: backpack, glue, paints, paper, pencil case, scissors; Do you have your (backpack)? Yes, I do. / No, I don't.

6

Learning objectives

- Talk about classroom objects
- Identify and name two new classroom objects
- Sing the language song *Do you have your backpack?*
- Ask and say what classroom objects you have

Materials

- Class CDs, flashcards, *Ferris Wheel* mat, Mimi puppet

Main vocabulary

- backpack, crayons, glue, paints, paper, pencil, pencil case, scissors

Key language

- Do you have your (backpack)? Yes, I do. / No, I don't.

Teacher's tip: Encouraging children to speak

To help children feel confident about asking and answering questions, use the Mimi puppet to model them. Answer the questions yourself or elicit answers from confident students. If you include this activity as part of your daily routine, soon children will gain enough confidence to ask and answer questions with a friend.

Circle time

Hello song & puppet (CD1 Track 2; see TB p 17 & 21)
Opening routines (see TB p 16)
Recycling activity (six classroom objects from lesson 1) (see TB p 19)
Lesson aims (see TB p 18)

Introduce the new classroom objects.

- Lay out all eight flashcards of classroom objects on the floor or the board. Children identify the two new objects.
- Use the puppet to point to and say the words in turn. Children repeat in chorus.
- Turn the two new flashcards face down. Mix them up. Point to one and ask *Paper or paint?* Children guess. Repeat several times.

Introduce *Do you have ... ? Yes, I do. / No, I don't.*

- Children name all the classroom object flashcards.
- Give a flashcard to the puppet. Ask the puppet, e.g. *Do you have the (backpack)?* and model the response *Yes, I do.* Ask about a different flashcard and model the response *No, I don't.*
- Repeat several times with different flashcards.
- Give individual children flashcards. Use the puppet to ask questions and encourage them to respond *Yes, I do. / No, I don't.*
- Hold up different flashcards in turn. Use the puppet to get the children to ask you in chorus, e.g. *Do you have the backpack?* and respond *Yes, I do. / No, I don't.*

Table time

Student's Book p 6

Listen and find the new classroom objects.

- Play the audio. Children listen and find the two new words.
- Play the audio again. The children listen and say the words.

CD1 Track 21

One, two, Which words are new?
Paints! Paints!
Paper! Paper!

Listen, point and sing
Do you have your backpack?

CD1 Track 22

- Play the song. The children listen and point to each object as they hear it.
- Play the song again. Children sing and do the actions (see TB p 33).
- Remember that you can use the karaoke version of the song when children are confident.

Circle the objects Sam has.

- Play the first two lines of the song again. Ask *Does Sam have his backpack?* Elicit *Yes*. Demonstrate circling the backpack. Play the next two lines. Ask *Does Sam have his pencil case?* Elicit *No*. Shake your head and don't circle the pencil case.
- Play the song again, pausing after each answer. Children listen and circle the objects Sam has.

Ask and say.

- Ask *What does Anna ask Sam?* Encourage children to ask and answer the questions as in the song.

Activity Book p 6

Find and match the objects in the backpack.

- Children should draw lines to match the objects in the circles to the objects inside the backpack.

Color.

- Children color the objects in the backpack to look like the objects in the circles.

Ask and say.

- Children ask and answer about the items in their backpacks, e.g. *Do you have a pencil? Yes, I do. / Do you have paper? No, I don't.*

Closing time

Learning review (see TB p 18)
Closing routines (see TB p 16)
Bye bye song and puppet (CD1 Track 3; see TB p 17 & 21)

Use the **Navio App** to listen to the song, and encourage children to do the same at home.

Lesson 3 Story

Watch. Listen to the story *Fun with paint!* Circle the classroom objects Dylan uses to do his picture. Stick the story sticker. Language: backpack, crayons, glue, paints, paper, pencil, pencil case, scissors; colors; Do you have (paper)? Yes, I do. / No, I don't. I have (red) paint.

1:24

7

Learning objectives

- Watch, understand and enjoy the story *Fun with paint!*
- Make a prediction about the story
- Listen and identify the story frame
- Identify classroom objects used in the story

Materials

- Class CDs, printable story cards, flashcards, *Ferris Wheel* mat, Mimi puppet

Main vocabulary

- backpack, crayons, glue, paints, paper, pencil, pencil case, scissors; colors

Key language

- Do you have (paper)? Yes, I do. / No, I don't. I have (red) paint.

Teacher's tip: Engaging children in the story

As you tell the story, use eye contact to engage the children. Be ready to repeat words and ask questions to support comprehension. Show your own interest and enthusiasm in the story – it's contagious!

Circle time

Hello song & puppet (CD1 Track 2; see TB p 17 & 21)
Opening routines (see TB p 16)
Recycling activity (*Do you have … ?* and classroom objects) (see TB p 19)
Lesson aims (see TB p 18)

Introduce the story *Fun with paint!*

- Say *It's story time!* Play the *Story rhyme* (CD1 Track 4; see TB p 17).
- Say *Anna and Sam are listening to a story about Mimi and Dylan. Mimi and Dylan are at school. Who has fun with paint in the story?* Listen to children's answers and respond.

Watch or listen to the story *Fun with paint!*

CD1 Track 24

- Watch the video, play the audio, or read the story using the printable story cards. Pause, repeat words, point to the pictures, ask questions.
- Ask children *Who has fun with paint in the story? (Dylan, but also Mimi and the other classmates).*
- Repeat the story. Encourage children to join in with the words and phrases in the story.
- Ask: *Do you like the story? Do you like Mimi's picture / Dylan's picture?*

Look and find.

- Say e.g. *Find Dylan's backpack!* Children look at the story and point to the picture as fast as they can.
- Repeat with other objects and characters.

Table time

Student's Book p 7

Watch. Listen to the story *Fun with paint!*

- Read or play the story again. Children listen and follow the story by pointing to the pictures in their books.

Circle the classroom objects Dylan uses to do his picture.

- Children find the objects Dylan uses to do his picture (paints) and circle them.

Stick the story sticker.

- Children stick on the story sticker.
- Say sentences from the story in random order. Children point to the correct frames.

Activity Book p 7

Trace and say the numbers.

- Children trace and say the numbers.

Match to order the pictures.

- They match the numbers to the pictures to order them.

Circle your favorite picture.

- Children choose and circle their favorite picture.

Closing time

Learning review (see TB p 18)
Closing routines (see TB p 16)
Bye bye song and puppet (CD1 Track 3; see TB p 17 & 21)

Story questions

Picture 1
Is Dylan excited about school? *(Yes)*
What does Dylan have? *(Backpack/pencil case/pencil/crayons/scissors/glue)*

Picture 2
Who is the teacher? *(Mrs.Cat)*
Are the children going to draw? *(No)*

Picture 3
Is Dylan happy? *(Yes)*
What color paint does Dylan have? *(Red/blue)*

Picture 4
What color paint does Dylan have? *(Green/yellow)*
Where is the paint? *(Everywhere)*

Picture 5
What color paint does Dylan have? *(Orange/pink)*
Is Mimi happy? *(No)*

Picture 6
What is Dylan's picture? *(The Ferris Wheel)*
Is Dylan good? *(Yes)*

Use the **Navio App** to watch the video, and encourage children to do the same at home.

Lesson 4

Story Song

Classroom

Watch. Listen, point and sing *The paint song*. Draw a picture of your favorite place. Say the colors in your picture. Say the classroom objects you use.

Language: crayons, glue, paints, pencil, scissors; colors; I have (blue) here.

8

Learning objectives

- Watch, sing and act out the story song *The paint song*
- Listen to the story again and identify classroom objects
- Identify and say colors
- Identify and say classroom objects used

Materials

- Class CDs, printable story cards, flashcards, *Ferris Wheel* mat, Mimi puppet

Main vocabulary

- colors; crayons, glue, paints, pencil, scissors

Key language

- I have (blue) here.

Teacher's tip: Playing the story song at Table time

Play the story song again quietly during Table time while the children are drawing their pictures. Music often settles the mood and helps children concentrate. If the words of the song distract the children, play the karaoke version instead.

Circle time

Hello song & puppet (CD1 Track 2; see TB p 17 & 21)
Opening routines (see TB p 16)
Recycling activity (classroom objects) (see TB p 19)
Lesson aims (see TB p 18)

Retell the story *Fun with paint!*

- Watch the video, play the audio, or read the story using the printable story cards. Demonstrate that children should wave their arms in the air every time they hear a classroom object in the story.

Game: ***Memory game***

- Say *Dylan says "I have red paint." Can you remember what else he says?*
- Children say sentences about all the colors in Dylan's picture.

The paint song

CD1 Track 25

- Play the video or audio of the story song. Children watch/listen and say the colors in the song.
- Play the song again. Pause after each verse and invite individual children to stick the color flashcards on the board in three rows of two as per the song.
- Play the song again. Children listen, sing and act out the song (see TB p 33).

Table time

Student's Book p 8

Watch. Listen, point and sing *The paint song.*

CD1 Track 25

- Play the audio of the song. Children listen, sing and point to the colors in Dylan's picture.
- Remember that you can use the karaoke version of the song when children are confident.

Draw a picture of your favorite place. Say the colors in your picture.

- Ask *Do you want to make a picture of your favorite place?* Children draw and color or paint a picture of their favorite place and say the colors.

Say the classroom objects you use.

- Children name the objects they use to make their pictures.

Activity Book p 8

Color or paint Dylan and Mimi's pictures from the story.

- Children color or paint each picture, following the colored dots.

Ask and say.

- Ask a child *Do you have (red) in your picture?* and have them answer *Yes, I do.* or *No, I don't.*
- Children ask and answer about their pictures in pairs.

Closing time

Learning review (see TB p 18)
Closing routines (see TB p 16)
Bye bye song and puppet (CD1 Track 3; see TB p 17 & 21)

Use the **Navio App** to watch the video, and encourage children to do the same at home.

Speaking

Life skills

Watch. Listen and point. Circle the objects Uncle Dan has. Color the star if Uncle Dan is ready. Color the objects you have. Ask and say. **Language:** crayons, glue, paints, paper, pencil, pencil case, scissors; Do you have (a pencil)? Yes. / No. I have (paper). I don't have (scissors).

9

Learning objectives

- Ask and answer questions about what classroom objects you have
- Watch, understand and enjoy a video
- Identify classroom objects used in the video

Materials

- Class CDs, flashcards, *Ferris Wheel* mat, Mimi puppet

Main vocabulary

- crayons, glue, paints, paper, pencil, pencil case, scissors

Key language

- Do you have (a pencil)? Yes. / No. I have (paper). I don't have (scissors).

Teacher's tip: Speaking in groups

Life skills

As additional practice, divide the class into two groups and do the dialogue in groups. By speaking together with others, children's confidence will increase and this will help them develop the important life skill of asking and answering questions and maintaining a conversation.

Circle time

Hello song & puppet (CD1 Track 2; see TB p 17 & 21)
Opening routines (see TB p 16)
Recycling activity (story song) (CD1 Track 25; see TB p 19)
Lesson aims (see TB p 18)

Game: ***Stand up if you have (a pencil).***

- Hand out the flashcards to individual children.
- Say e.g. *Stand up if you have a pencil!* Demonstrate this.
- The child with the flashcard stands up and says *I have a pencil.*
- Repeat with the other objects.

Game: ***Guess what I have!***

- Hold one flashcard without children seeing. Say *Guess what I have!*
- Children ask you e.g. *Do you have … ?* *No, I don't. / Yes, I do.* and guess the flashcard.
- The child who guesses the flashcard correctly has the next turn. Repeat with different children.

Watch the video.

- Explain that Sam and Anna are talking to Uncle Dan. Uncle Dan is going to paint a picture. Play the video of Anna, Sam and Uncle Dan.
- Ask *What does Uncle Dan have? (paper, pencil, crayons, paints)*
- Watch again. Pause and children repeat the questions and what Uncle Dan says.

Table time

Student's Book p 9

Life skills

Watch. Listen and point.

- Children point to Anna, Sam and Uncle Dan in the photo. Play the audio or video. Children point to the objects as they hear them in the dialogue.

Circle the objects Uncle Dan has. Color the star if Uncle Dan is ready.

- Play the audio again. Pause it after each question and answer. Children circle the objects Uncle Dan has. Play the audio again to check children have circled the objects correctly.
- Ask *Is Uncle Dan ready to do a picture?* Elicit *Yes*, and demonstrate coloring the star.

CD1 Track 27

Uncle Dan:	Hello, Sam. Hello, Anna.
Sam & Anna:	Hello, Uncle Dan.
Uncle Dan:	Look. I'm ready to do a picture!
Anna:	Do you have paper?
Uncle Dan:	Yes, I do.
Sam:	Do you have a pencil case?
Uncle Dan:	No, I don't.
Anna:	Do you have a pencil?
Uncle Dan:	Yes, I do.
Sam:	Do you have crayons?
Uncle Dan:	Yes, I do.
Sam:	Do you have paints?
Uncle Dan:	Yes, I do. Look. I have paper. I have a pencil. I have crayons. I have paints. I'm ready to do a picture. Come on. Let's go!

Color the objects you have. Ask and say.

- Children color the objects they have.
- Remind children of the question *Do you have (paper)?* Children ask and answer questions about all the objects.

Activity Book p 9

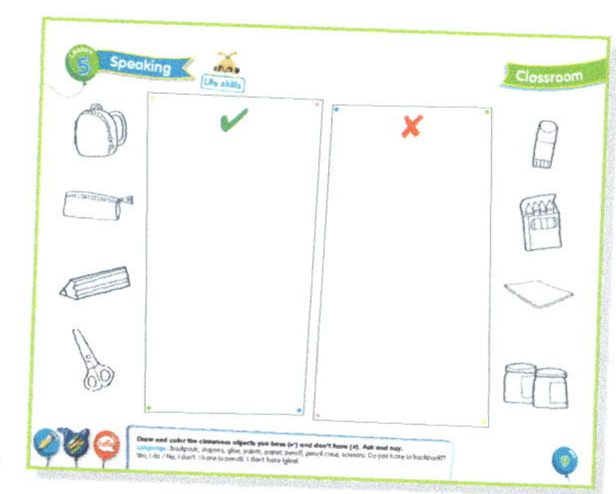

Draw and color the classroom objects you have (✓) and don't have (✗).

- Point to each object and elicit its name.
- Point to the check mark and say *I have this*. Point to the cross and say *I don't have this*. Children draw the objects in the correct place and color them.

Ask and say.

- Children talk about the objects they have and don't have.

Closing time

Learning review (see TB p 18)
Closing routines (see TB p 16)
Bye bye song and puppet (CD1 Track 3; see TB p 17 & 21)

Use the **Navio App** to watch the video, and encourage children to do the same at home.

Values Good behavior

Listen, point and sing *Be good at home*. Color the pictures of good behavior. Draw a picture of you being good at home or school. Say.

Language: home, school; Daddy, Mommy, Teacher; I'm good at (home).

SOCIAL AND EMOTIONAL LEARNING

10

Learning objectives

- Understand the value of good behavior at home and at school
- Act out the story
- Sing the values song *Be good at home*
- Identify who's being good
- Talk about your good behavior

Materials

- Class CDs, flashcards, *Ferris Wheel* mat, Mimi puppet

Main vocabulary

- home, school; Daddy, Mommy, Teacher

Key language

- I'm good at (home).

Teacher's tip: Listening to children's ideas, however they are expressed

When children describe their pictures, be ready to accept single words such as *home, school, teacher*, rather than complete sentences, when children describe their pictures to you. Alternatively, children can use their shared language to talk about when they are being good.

Circle time

Hello song & puppet (CD1 Track 2; see TB p 17 & 21)
Opening routines (see TB p 16)
Recycling activity *(Do you have a (pencil)? Yes, I do. / No, I don't.)* (see TB p 19)
Lesson aims (see TB p 18)

Watch the *Fun with paint!* story video.

- Play the story video.
- Take the parts of narrator, Mrs. Cat and Mommy yourself. Encourage children to join in acting out the story in two groups (Mimi, Dylan).
- Ask e.g. *Is Mimi good? (Yes.) Is Dylan good? (Yes). Are you good at school? Are you good at home? Is it important to be good? What does being good mean?*

***Be good at home* song**

CD1 Track 28

- Use the Mimi puppet to say *Listen and find out: Where are Dylan and Mimi good? Who are they good with?*
- Play the audio. Children name the places (school, home) and people (Mommy, Daddy, Teacher).
- Play the audio again. Children sing the song and do the actions (see TB p 33).

Table time

Student's Book p 10

Listen, point and sing *Be good at home*.

CD1 Track 28

- Focus children on the pictures. Point to them one by one and ask *Where are they? Is it good behavior?* Play the song. Children listen, point to the pictures of Mimi and Dylan being good, and sing.

Color the pictures of good behavior.

- Children color the correct pictures.

Draw a picture of you being good at home or school. Say.

- Children draw a picture of themselves being good at home or school.
- Children show you and each other their pictures and say *I'm good at (home)* or *I'm good with my (mommy).*

Activity Book p 10

Circle the pictures of good behavior.

- Children circle the pictures that show good behavior.

Talk about you.

- Children talk about when they are good, e.g. *I'm good (at home/with my daddy).*

Closing time

Learning review (see TB p 18)
Closing routines (see TB p 16)
Bye bye song and puppet (CD1 Track 3; see TB p 17 & 21)

Use the **Navio App** to listen to the song, and encourage children to do the same at home.

Lesson 7

Content

Listen and point. Follow and draw the paths from the children to the places at school. Say the places.

Language: cafeteria, classroom, library, playground; Go to the (playground).

11

Learning objectives

- Identify and name places at school, and understand what we do in each place
- Listen and identify places at school
- Give instructions
- Talk about you in your favorite place at school

Materials

- Class CDs, printable content flashcards, *Ferris Wheel* mat, Mimi puppet

Main vocabulary

- cafeteria, classroom, library, playground

Key language

- Go to the (playground).

Teacher's tip: Discovering places at school

If possible, take the children around the school to the places in the lesson. In each place, ask *Where are we?* When a child gives the correct answer, say *Yes! It's time for/to …* After the last place, say *It's time for lessons. Let's go to the classroom!* and take the children back to their classroom. This will help children associate the new words with their own familiar environment, and make English more "real" to them.

Circle time

Hello song & puppet (CD1 Track 2; see TB p 17 & 21)
Opening routines (see TB p 16)
Recycling activity (see TB p 19)
Lesson aims (see TB p 18)

Introduce content vocabulary.

- Use the printable flashcards and the puppet to introduce the new words *(cafeteria, classroom, library, playground)*. Children repeat the words.
- Play one or two flashcard games with the *Ferris Wheel* mat and/or the puppet (see TB p 20 & 21).
- Say *In our school we have …* and children name the places.

Mime and say.

- Lay out the flashcards.
- Mime running and playing with a ball. Children name the place: *playground*.
- Repeat with the other places. Mime eating (cafeteria), using a pencil (classroom), hands open as a book (library) and children name the places.
- Reverse the procedure. Point to the places in turn and children do the mimes.

Game: ***Go to the playground.***

- Stick the flashcards on different walls in the classroom.
- Name the places e.g. *playground* and children point to the flashcards.
- Ask pairs or groups of children to stand up in turn. Say e.g. *It's time for lunch. Go to the cafeteria!* Children walk to the correct flashcard.

Table time

Student's Book p 11

Listen and point.

- Say *Sam, Anna and their friends David and Nicola are at school.* Explain that the teacher is telling them where to go. Play the audio. Children point to the places as they hear them.

CD1 Track 29

Sam! It's time to play. Go to the playground, please!
Anna! It's time for lunch. Go to the cafeteria, please!
David! It's time for lessons. Go to the classroom, please!
Nicola! It's time to get a book. Go to the library, please!

Follow and draw the paths from the children to the places at school.

- Play the audio again. Children listen and follow the maze lines to each place with their finger. Use the pause button as necessary.
- Demonstrate that children should draw the path to each place.
- When they have finished, play the audio again. Children repeat the instructions, e.g. *Go to the classroom!* Check they have drawn the lines correctly.

Say the places.

- Children point and name each place.

Activity Book p 11

Match the children to the places at school.

- Children draw lines from the children to the places.

Draw and color a picture of you in your favorite place in school.

- They draw themselves in one of the four pictures.

Say.

- Children show each other their picture and say, e.g. *I'm in the (cafeteria).*

Closing time

Learning review (see TB p 18)
Closing routines (see TB p 16)
Bye bye song and puppet (CD1 Track 3; see TB p 17 & 21)

Use the **Navio App** to play the vocabulary and language games, and encourage children to do the same at home.

Lesson 8 **Culture**

Watch. Listen, point and sing *Wind the bobbin up*. Color the ceiling. Say.
Language: ceiling, clap, door, floor, hands, knee, window; Point to the (ceiling).

12

Learning objectives

- Watch, sing and act out the traditional song *Wind the bobbin up*
- Play an action game
- Identify and say parts of a classroom

Materials

- Class CDs, flashcards, *Ferris Wheel* mat, Mimi puppet

Main vocabulary

- ceiling, clap, door, floor, hands, knee, window

Key language

- Point to the (ceiling).

Teacher's tip: Enjoying traditional songs

Traditional songs develop an affinity with culture from the English-speaking world as well as an awareness of the rhythm and sounds of English, and listening and attention skills. Do not worry if children do not understand every word of the song; the most important thing is their pleasure and enthusiasm in joining in.

Circle time

Hello song & puppet (CD1 Track 2; see TB p 17 & 21)
Opening routines (see TB p 16)
Recycling activity (see TB p 19)
Lesson aims (see TB p 18)

Game: *Mimi says (point to the window).*

- Say in turn *Point to the ceiling / floor / window / door* and children respond.
- Use the puppet to give instructions in random order, e.g. *Mimi says point to the … window!* Speed up as children get more confident in responding.

***Wind the bobbin up* song**

CD1 Track 30

- Say *Stand up. Let's learn the song "Wind the bobbin up."*
- Pre-teach actions for the song (see TB p 33).
- Play the audio. Children listen and do the actions for the song with you.
- Repeat. Children join in singing and doing the actions for the song.

(Note: A "bobbin" is a traditional reel for winding wool.)

Watch the *Wind the bobbin up* song video.

- Children watch the video and join in singing the song and doing the actions with Anna and Sam.

Table time

Student's Book p 12

Watch. Listen, point and sing *Wind the bobbin up.*

CD1 Track 30

- Play the song. Children listen, sing and point to the ceiling, floor, window and door in the picture.

Color the ceiling, floor, window and door. Say.

- Children color the ceiling, floor, window and door in the picture. If you like, turn this into a color dictation, e.g. *Color the ceiling blue.*
- Children point and name the places.

Activity Book p 12

Match the children doing the actions for *Wind the bobbin up.*

- Children match the pictures that show the same action.

Point and say.

- Children point to each picture and say the action.

Closing time

Learning review (see TB p 18)
Closing routines (see TB p 16)
Bye bye song and puppet (CD1 Track 3; see TB p 17 & 21)

Use the **Navio App** to watch the video, and encourage children to do the same at home.

Review

Classroom

I can …

Vocabulary

Story

Speaking

Content

Trace and color the classroom objects you know. Listen, point and say. Ask and say. Complete the faces to show what you can do. Language: backpack, crayons, glue, paints, paper, pencil, pencil case, scissors; Do you have (glue)? Yes, I do. / No, I don't. I have (crayons). I don't have (paints).

13

Learning objectives

- Review what you have learned in this unit
- Complete a self-evaluation
- Point to and say classroom objects you have

Materials

- Class CDs, flashcards, *Ferris Wheel* mat, Mimi puppet

Main vocabulary

- backpack, crayons, glue, paints, paper, pencil, pencil case, scissors

Key language

- Do you have (glue)? Yes, I do. / No, I don't. I have (crayons). I don't have (paints).

Teacher's tip: Self-evaluation

Be prepared for children to take time to understand the concept of reviewing their learning. Model out loud the thinking processes involved and give encouragement as children identify what they have learned and achieved in this unit.

Circle time

Hello song & puppet (CD1 Track 2; see TB p 17 & 21)
Opening routines (see TB p 16)
Recycling activity (see TB p 19)
Lesson aims (see TB p 18)

Classroom object flashcard games

- Choose one or two flashcard games with the *Ferris Wheel* mat and/or the puppet to review main vocabulary (see TB p 20 & 21).

Sing *Do you have your backpack?*

CD1 Track 22

- Play the audio. Children sing and do the actions.
- Children ask and answer questions about classroom objects they have.

Game: *Guess the object.*

- Hide a classroom object behind your back. Children guess the object by asking *Do you have a (pencil case)?*

Game: *Where's Mimi?*

- Choose one of the school area flashcards . Put it face down on the floor. Put Mimi on top. Ask *Where's Mimi?*
- Children name the school areas until they guess the correct one.

Watch the story video.

- Children watch the story video. Ask *What color paints does Dylan have in his picture? Is Dylan good in the story?*

Table time

Student's Book p 13

Trace and color the classroom objects you know.

- Explain and demonstrate the activity.

Listen, point and say.

- Play the audio. Children listen, point to the objects, and say the words.

CD1 Track 31

Mimi: I'm the teacher! Can you remember the classroom objects, Dylan?
Dylan: Yes, I can. Backpack.
Mimi: Backpack.
Dylan: Pencil case.
Mimi: Pencil case.
Dylan: Pencil.
Mimi: Pencil.
Dylan: Crayons.
Mimi: Crayons.
Dylan: Scissors.
Mimi: Scissors.
Dylan: Glue.
Mimi: Glue.
Dylan: Paper.
Mimi: Paper.
Dylan: Paints.
Mimi: Paints. Great job, Dylan! Very good!

Ask and say.

- Ask children questions about the classroom objects they have. Encourage the children to ask you or the puppet similar questions.

Complete the faces to show what you can do.

- Explain the four pictures: *I can name classroom objects; I can understand the story; I can ask and answer questions about classroom objects; I can identify places at school.*
- Demonstrate that children should complete the face with a smile or downturned mouth depending on how well they think they have done in the unit.
- Monitor and encourage children to think positively about their progress.

Activity Book p 13

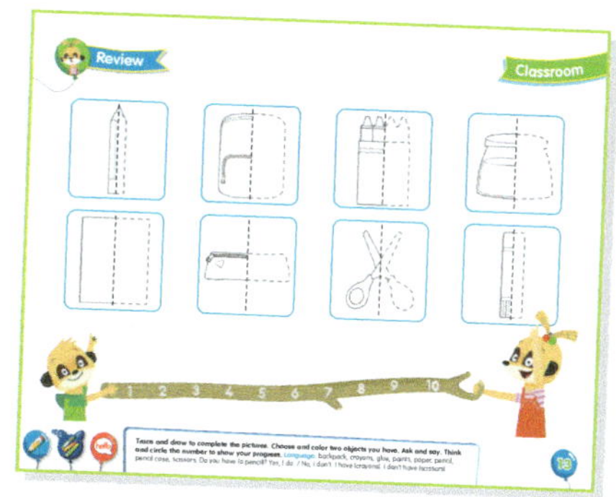

Trace and draw to complete the pictures. Choose and color two objects you have.

- Children complete the pictures and color two objects they have.

Ask and say. Think and circle the number to show your progress.

- Children ask and answer about what they have. They then circle the number to show their progress.

Closing time

Learning review (see TB p 18)
Closing routines (see TB p 16)
Bye bye song and puppet (CD1 Track 3; see TB p 17 & 21)

Use the **Navio App** to review what children have learned in this unit, and encourage them to do the same at home.

Project

COOPERATIVE LEARNING

Classroom

1

2

3

Name the classroom objects you need. Make the Ferris Wheel. Say the colors. Draw a picture of you to go on the Ferris Wheel. Language: Ferris Wheel; crayons, glue, paints, paper, pencil; colors; I have (paints). My wheel is (orange). I'm on (blue). I like the (blue) wheel. Our Ferris Wheel is (fantastic)!

14

Classroom

Learning objectives

- Work together to do a collaborative project
- Name classroom objects and colors
- Draw and color a picture of yourself

Materials

- Class CDs, Mimi puppet, photocopiable templates: Ferris Wheel pods, crayons, finger paints, pencil, scissors, small pieces of paper and glue, or sticky notes

Main vocabulary

- Ferris Wheel; crayons, glue, paints, paper, pencil; colors

Key language

- I have (paints). My wheel is (orange). I'm on (blue). I like the (blue) wheel. Our Ferris Wheel is (fantastic)!

Teacher's tip: Helping children draw and color correctly

A good way to help children hold the crayon properly as they color or draw is to give them a small balloon filled up with flour for them to hold with their baby and ring finger as they hold the crayon with their other fingers (middle, pointer, and thumb).

Circle time

Hello song & puppet (CD1 Track 2; see TB p 17 & 21)
Opening routines (see TB p 16)
Recycling activity (see TB p 19)
Lesson aims (see TB p 18)

Prepare for your project.

- Say *Let's do a project! Let's make a Ferris Wheel for our class with pictures of everyone to go on the Wheel!* Explain that children should work together in groups for this project.
- Show children the six copies of the pod template you have prepared as the basis of the wheel.
- Demonstrate using finger paint to paint the pods.
- Demonstrate drawing a picture of your face on a sticky note to stick on the pod.

Table time

COOPERATIVE LEARNING

Student's Book p 14

Name the classroom objects you need.

- Say e.g. *We're going to make a Ferris Wheel like this. Look at what we need for our project.* Hold up the objects and elicit the words: *paints, crayons, pencil, pieces of paper, glue, paper* (templates).
- Say the words again. Children listen and point to the pictures in their books.

Make the Ferris Wheel. Say the colors.

- Divide the children into six groups or tables. Hand out one large pod template to each group or table. Assign or have children choose a color for their pod.
- Make sure children have finger paints of that color available, as well as scissors and sticky notes.
- Children paint their pod. Ask them what color it is.

Draw a picture of you to go on the Ferris Wheel.

- When they are ready, children use crayons to draw a picture of their face on a piece of paper or sticky note and stick it on the pod. If you like, you can write the first names of the children on the sticky notes under their pictures.
- Arrange the pods to make a Ferris Wheel on the classroom noticeboard. Use thick black felt-tip pen or strips of white card to draw the structure and spokes of the wheel.
- Ask children *Do you like our Ferris Wheel?* Make the point that everyone helped make the Ferris Wheel and that they couldn't have made such a beautiful Ferris Wheel on their own.

Alternative version of project

- Children could use crayons instead of finger paints to color the pods.

Activity Book p 14

Use finger paints to paint the classroom objects.

- Children paint the objects.

Point and say the colors.

- Point to the objects and elicit the colors.

Talk about the classroom objects you have and don't have.

- Remind children of the question *Do you have (a backpack)?* They talk about the things they have and don't have.

Closing time

Learning review (see TB p 18)
Closing routines (see TB p 16)
Bye bye song and puppet (CD1 Track 3; see TB p 17 & 21)

My body
I can dance!

Vocabulary and language

- **Main vocabulary:** arms, feet, fingers, hands, head, legs, toes, tummy
- **Key language:** I can/can't move my (head). Can you? Can you move your (head)? Yes, I can. / No, I can't.
- **Content language**: climb, hop, jump, run; Can you (run)? Yes, I can. / No, I can't. I can/can't (climb).
- **Other language**: coat, pasta, scissors, shoes, thumb; Move your (head). I can/can't put on my shoes/coat. I can/can't cut with scissors; stand up, sit down, turn round, keep moving; I have (arms). How many (legs) do you have? (Two).

Unit objectives

- Identify and name parts of the body
- Sing the language song *I can move my head*
- Ask and say what you can do
- Understand and act out the story *I can dance!*
- Sing and act out the story song *I can dance. You can dance too!*
- Sing the values song *I can do it if I try*
- Recognize the value of making an effort
- Identify and name ways you use your body to be active
- Sing and act out the traditional song *One finger, one thumb, keep moving*
- Review your learning and progress
- Participate in a collaborative project

Story

CD1 Track 37

Picture 1

Narrator: Mommy and Daddy are learning to dance.
Monkey: Move your arms like this. Move your legs like this. Move your head like this. Move your feet like this.
Mommy: This is great!
Daddy: I can dance!

Picture 2

Narrator: Mimi and Dylan want to learn to dance too.
Daddy: Come on, Mimi.
Mommy: Come on, Dylan.
Daddy: Can you move your arms like this?
Dylan: Yes, I can. Hurray!
Mimi: Oh. No, I can't.
Mommy: Can you move your legs like this?
Dylan: Yes, I can. Hurray!
Mimi: Oh. No, I can't.

Picture 3

Narrator: Dylan is happy.
Dylan: Look at me! I can move my arms like this. I can move my legs like this. I can move my head like this. I can move my feet like this. I can dance!
Narrator: But Mimi is sad.
Mimi: Oh. Oh no. I can't dance.

Picture 4

Narrator: Two little birds are watching.
Bird 1: Don't be sad, Mimi. Listen to the music.
Bird 2: You can dance if you try, Mimi!
Mimi: Oh, but I can't!

Picture 5

Bird 1: Listen to the music!
Bird 2: Dance to the beat!
Bird 1: You can dance if you try, try, try!
Bird 2: Come on, Mimi. That's it!

Picture 6

Mimi: Oh! Look at me! I can dance! I can move my arms like this. I can move my legs like this.
Dylan: Fantastic, Mimi!
Daddy: Excellent, Mimi!
Mommy: Good job, Mimi!
Mimi: I can dance now! Thank you, little birds!

Songs

Language song

I can move my head CD1 Track 35

I can move my head (Move head slowly from side to side)
I can move my hands, too (Move hands slowly up and down)
But I can't move my tummy (Touch tummy and wave index finger to say "no")
Can you? Can you? (Hold out arms questioningly)
Yes, I can! Look! (Nod and wiggle your tummy)

I can move my arms (Wave arms about slowly)
I can move my legs, too (Move legs alternately)
But I can't move my tummy (Touch tummy and wave index finger to say "no")
Can you? Can you? (Hold out arms questioningly)
Yes, I can! Look! (Nod and wiggle your tummy)

I can move my fingers (Wiggle fingers)
I can move my toes, too (Wiggle toes around)
But I can't move my tummy (Touch tummy and wave index finger to say "no")
Can you? Can you? (Hold out arms questioningly)
Yes, I can! Look! (Nod and wiggle your tummy)
Yes, I can! Look! (Nod and wiggle your tummy)

Story song

I can dance. You can dance too! CD1 Track 38

I can dance (Point to self)
You can dance too (Point to children)
Listen to the music (Cup your ear)
Here's what we do: (Arms wide)
Move your arms, Move your arms (Move arms)
Move your legs, Move your legs (Move legs)
Listen to the music (Cup your ear)
Dance to the beat (Dance)
Move your head, Move your head (Move head)
Move your feet, Move your feet (Move feet)
Listen to the music (Cup your ear)
Dance to the beat (Dance)
(Chorus)

Values song

I can do it if I try CD1 Track 41

I can do it if I try, try, try (Thumbs up and strong arm action)
Yes, yes, yes! Ay, ay, ay! (Nod and punch arms in air)

I can put on my coat (Mime putting coat on)
I can learn and play (Clap twice)
I can put on my coat (Mime putting coat on)
Every day (Turn around)

(Chorus)

I can put on my shoes (Mime putting shoes on)
I can learn and play (Clap twice)
I can put on my shoes (Mime putting shoes on)
Every day (Turn around)

(Chorus)

I can cut with scissors (Mime cutting with two fingers)
I can learn and play (Clap twice)
I can cut with scissors (Mime cutting with two fingers)
Every day (Turn around)

(Chorus)

Culture song

One finger, one thumb, keep moving CD1 Track 43

One finger, one thumb, keep moving (Show one finger, then one thumb, swing your arms)
One finger, one thumb, keep moving (repeat)
One finger, one thumb, keep moving (repeat)
We're all happy today! (Point to your wide smile with two fingers)
One finger, one thumb, one arm, keep moving (etc) (…and raise one arm)
One finger, one thumb, one arm, one leg, keep moving (etc) (…and put one leg forward)
One finger, one thumb, one arm, one leg, stand up, sit down, keep moving (etc) (…stand straight then mime sitting down)
One finger, one thumb, one arm, one leg, stand up, sit down, turn round, keep moving (etc) (…and turn around)

My body
I can dance!

Vocabulary Lesson 1

Listen, point and repeat. Listen and play. Stick the body stickers. Circle the parts of the body Mimi and Dylan are moving. Say. Language: arms, feet, hands, head, legs, tummy; blue, green, orange, pink, red, yellow

15

Learning objectives

- Identify and name parts of the body
- Listen and point to parts of the body
- Identify the parts of the body Mimi and Dylan are moving

Materials

- Class CDs, flashcards, *Ferris Wheel* mat, Mimi puppet

Main vocabulary

- arms, feet, hands, head, legs, tummy; blue, green, orange, pink, red, yellow

Teacher's tip: Encouraging less confident children

Encourage less confident children to participate and identify parts of the body by pairing them with a more confident partner and playing *Mirror pairs*. Children face each other so they can clearly see the actions their partner is doing and mirror them.

Circle time

Hello song & puppet (CD1 Track 2; see TB p 17 & 21)
Opening routines (see TB p 16)
Lesson aims (see TB p 18)

Introduce parts of the body.

- Children stand up. Say e.g. *Touch your head!* Do the actions with the children and encourage them to repeat the words with you. Repeat for all the words.
- Put the *Ferris Wheel* mat on the floor or the board with the body flashcards face down (one on each color). Use the puppet to turn over and name. Children repeat the words.

Game: *Touch your head!*

- Point to the flashcards in turn. Use the puppet to give instructions. Children respond. As they gain confidence, go faster and/or combine instructions, e.g. *Touch your tummy and … your feet!*

Game: *Say the color!*

- Name the parts of the body on the Ferris Wheel and children name the color. Then do it in reverse.

Table time

Student's Book p 15

Listen, point and repeat.

- Play the audio. The children listen, point to each part of the body as they hear it, and repeat the words.

CD1 Track 32

Mimi: Look, Dylan! Head … arms … legs … tummy … hands … feet. Repeat, Dylan!
Dylan: Yes, Mimi. Head … arms … legs … tummy … hands … feet.
Mimi: Very good, Dylan. Let's name the parts of the body together!
Both: Head … arms … legs … tummy … hands … feet.

Listen and play.

- Use finger in air to pretend to spin wheel. Children spin their fingers, point to the color when they hear it on the audio and say the word.

CD1 Track 33

Mimi: Spin the wheel
One, two, three
Point and name
The parts of the body with me!

Blue … arms!
Red … head!
Yellow … tummy!
Green … feet!
Pink … hands!
Orange … legs!

- Play the game with you and/or individual children naming colors and others responding with the words.

Stick the body stickers.

- Children stick the parts of the body stickers in the correct places.

Circle the parts of the body Mimi and Dylan are moving.

- Children circle the parts of the body Mimi and Dylan are moving.

Say.

- Children name the parts of the body Mimi and Dylan are moving.

Activity Book p 15

Trace Mimi. Point and say.

- Children trace the outline of Mimi. They point and say the parts of the body.

Color Mimi.

- Children color Mimi.

Closing time

Learning review (see TB p 18)
Closing routines (see TB p 16)
Bye bye song and puppet (CD1 Track 3; see TB p 17 & 21)

Use the **Navio App** to play the vocabulary game, and encourage children to do the same at home.

Listen and find the new parts of the body. Listen, point and sing *I can move my head.* Draw a picture of you. Say what you can do.

Language: arms, feet, fingers, hands, head, legs, toes, tummy; I can/can't move my (head). Can you?

16

Learning objectives

- Talk about parts of the body
- Identify and name two new parts of the body
- Sing the language song *I can move my head*
- Say what you can do

Materials

- Class CDs, flashcards, *Ferris Wheel* mat, Mimi puppet

Main vocabulary

- arms, feet, fingers, hands, head, legs, toes, tummy

Key language

- I can/can't move my (head). Can you?

Teacher's tip: Singing in groups

Once the children are familiar with the actions for the song, divide them into three groups. Each group stands up and does the actions for one of the verses. Make sure that the groups who are not singing are paying attention in order to begin when it's their turn. If necessary, stop the recording to have them practice before they do it altogether.

Circle time

Hello song & puppet (CD1 Track 2; see TB p 17 & 21)

Opening routines (see TB p 16)

Recycling activity (six body words from Lesson 1) (see TB p 19)

Lesson aims (see TB p 18)

Introduce the new parts of the body.

- All eight flashcards of parts of the body on the floor or the board.
- Children identify the two new parts of the body.
- Use the puppet to point to and say the words in turn. Children repeat in chorus.
- Turn the two new flashcards face down. Mix them up. Point to one and ask *Fingers or toes?* Children guess. Repeat several times.
- Say *Let's count our fingers!* Children hold up one hand and count to five. If appropriate, get one child to take off a shoe and sock and repeat with toes.

Introduce *I can ... / I can't ... / Can you?*

- Children stand up. Say e.g. *I can shake my head* and demonstrate this. Ask *Can you? Show me!* and children respond.
- Repeat with other actions and parts of the body *(shake my arms/legs, wave my hands, stamp my feet, wiggle my fingers/toes).*
- Point to your tummy and say *I can't wave my tummy.* Use gesture to show you can't do this. Ask *Can you?*
- Repeat with other actions for tummy, e.g. *I can't shake / stamp / wiggle my tummy. Can you?*

Game: ***Repeat if it's true!***

- Say e.g. *I can stamp my feet* and demonstrate this. Children repeat the sentence and do the action if they can.
- Say e.g. *I can't stamp my tummy.* Children cross their arms and stay silent.

Table time

Student's Book p 16

Listen and find the new parts of the body.

- Play the audio. Children listen and find the two new words.
- Play the audio again. The children listen and say the words.

CD1 Track 34

One, two,
Which words are new?
Fingers! Fingers!
Toes! Toes!

Listen, point and sing *I can move my head.*

CD1 Track 35

- Play the song. The children listen and point to each part of the body as they hear it.
- Play the song again. Children sing the song and do the actions (see TB p 55).
- Remember that you can use the karaoke version of the song when children are confident.

Draw a picture of you.

- Play the song again. Pause after each part of the body and ask the children if they can move it, e.g. *Can you move your head? Can you move your arms?* Elicit *Yes.* Demonstrate that children should draw a picture of themselves doing one or more of the actions in the song.

Say what you can do.

- Encourage children to show their pictures and say what they can do, e.g. *I can move my hands.*

Activity Book p 16

Circle what you can do.

- Demonstrate that children should look carefully at the pictures and circle the ones that show movements that they can do.

Point and say.

- Children point to the pictures they circled and say, e.g. *I can move my (head).*

Closing time

Learning review (see TB p 18)

Closing routines (see TB p 16)

Bye bye song and puppet (CD1 Track 3; see TB p 17 & 21)

Use the **Navio App** to listen to the song, and encourage children to do the same at home.

Lesson 3

Story

1:37

Watch. Listen to the story *I can dance!* Circle who helps Mimi learn to dance. Stick the story sticker. Language: arms, feet, head, legs; Can you move your (head)? Yes, I can. / No, I can't. I can/can't dance. I can/can't move my (arms).

Learning objectives

- Watch, understand and enjoy the story *I can dance!*
- Make a prediction about the story
- Say a chant and do actions
- Identify and name the characters who can dance

Materials

- Class CDs, printable story cards, flashcards, *Ferris Wheel* mat, Mimi puppet

Main vocabulary

- arms, feet, head, legs

Key language

- Can you move your (head)? Yes, I can. / No, I can't. I can/can't dance. I can/can't move my (arms).

Teacher's tip: Saying the frame number

Encourage children to call out the numbers each time the frame changes. This way you can be sure the class is focusing on the correct picture.

Circle time

Hello song & puppet (CD1 Track 2; see TB p 17 & 21)
Opening routines (see TB p 16)
Recycling activity (*I can/can't* … and parts of the body) (see TB p 19)
Lesson aims (see TB p 18)

Introduce the story *I can dance!*

- Say *It's story time!* Play the *Story rhyme* (CD1 Track 4; see TB p 17).
- Say *Anna and Sam are listening to a story about Mommy, Daddy, Mimi and Dylan. Who can dance? Who can't dance?* Demonstrate what you mean and encourage children to guess. Respond e.g. *Yes, maybe. Let's listen and find out!*

Watch or listen to the story.

CD1 Track 37

- Watch the video, play the audio, or read the story using the printable story cards. Pause, repeat words, point to the pictures, ask questions.
- Ask children *Who can dance in the story? (Mommy, Daddy, Dylan and Mimi) Who can't dance at first? (Mimi) Who helps Mimi? The little (bird).*
- Repeat the story. Encourage children to join in with the words and phrases in the story.

Do a dance chant.

- Ask *Do you want to learn to dance?* Lay out the flashcards in the order of the dance movements in the story.
- Use percussion. Do actions and chant *Move your arms like this. Move your legs like this. Move your head like this. Move your feet like this.* Children join in.

Table time

Student's Book p 17

Watch. Listen to the story *I can dance!*

- Read or play the story again. Children listen and follow by pointing to the pictures in their books.

Circle who helps Mimi learn to dance.

- Children circle who helps Mimi learn to dance.

Stick the story sticker.

- Children stick on the story sticker.
- Ask *Who can dance at the end of the story?*

Activity Book p 17

Trace and color Mimi. Point and say. Trace the ✔ or ✘ to show if Mimi can or can't dance.

- Children trace and color Mimi. They point and say what she can do, then trace the check mark.

Closing time

Learning review (see TB p 18)
Closing routines (see TB p 16)
Bye bye song and puppet (CD1 Track 3; see TB p 17 & 21)

Story questions

Picture 1
Are Mommy and Daddy learning to sing? *(No)*
Can Daddy dance? *(Yes)*

Picture 2
Can Dylan move his arms? *(Yes)*
Can Mimi move her legs? *(No)*

Picture 3
What can Dylan move? *(His arms/legs/head/feet)*
Can Dylan dance? *(Yes)*

Picture 4
Who is watching Mimi dance? *(Two birds)*
Is Mimi happy? *(No)*

Picture 5
Do the birds help Mimi dance? *(Yes)*
Does Mimi try? *(Yes)*

Picture 6
What can Mimi move? *(Her arms/legs)*
Can Mimi dance? *(Yes)*

Use the **Navio App** to watch the video, and encourage children to do the same at home.

Lesson 4

Story Song

My body

Watch. Listen, point and sing *I can dance. You can dance too.* Match and color. Say. Language: arms, feet, head, legs; Move your (head). I can (dance).

18

Learning objectives

- Watch, sing and act out the story song *I can dance. You can dance too!*
- Listen to the story again and identify body parts
- Name parts of the body
- Ask and answer about which parts of the body you can move

Materials

- Class CDs, printable story cards, flashcards, *Ferris Wheel* mat, Mimi puppet

Main vocabulary

- arms, feet, head, legs

Key language

- Move your (head). I can (dance).

Teacher's tip: Calming technique

Introduce a calming technique to regain children's attention after the lively activity of the story song, e.g. ask the children to sit down very slowly while you count down from six. By the time you reach *one* the children should be seated and calm enough to move on to the next activity.

Circle time

Hello song & puppet (CD1 Track 2; see TB p 17 & 21)
Opening routines (see TB p 16)
Recycling activity (parts of the body) (see TB p 19)
Lesson aims (see TB p 18)

Retell the story *I can dance!*

- Play the audio, video or read the story using the printable story cards.
- Demonstrate that children should wave their arms in the air every time they hear a body word in the story.

Dance chant

- Say *Move your …* and move your arms. Children supply the word *(arms)*.
- Repeat with other parts of the body from the dance chant in lesson 3 (legs, head, feet).
- Children stand in a circle, say the chant and do the actions.

***I can dance. You can dance too!* song**

CD1 Track 38

- Play the video or audio of the story song. Children watch/listen and move their arms, legs, head and feet as per the song.
- Play the song again. Children listen, watch, sing and dance.
- Ask questions, e.g. *Can you move your feet? Can you dance?* and children respond *Yes, I can. / No, I can't.*

Ask Mimi and Dylan.

- Hold up the puppet. Ask Mimi questions and encourage children to join in, e.g. *Can you dance / move your (arms), Mimi? / Yes, I can.*
- Repeat using the flashcard of Dylan.

Table time

Student's Book p 18

Watch. Listen, point and sing *I can dance. You can dance too!*

CD1 Track 38

- Play the audio of the song. Children listen, sing and point to the parts of the body on the pictures of Mommy, Daddy, Mimi and Dylan dancing.
- Remember that you can use the karaoke version of the song when children are confident.

Match and color.

- Children match the body parts to the characters. They color them to match.

Say.

- Children point and name the body parts.

Activity Book p 18

Draw and color a picture of you dancing.

- Children draw a picture of themselves dancing in the space provided and color it.

Point and say.

- They point to the relevant part of the body and say what they can do.

Closing time

Learning review (see TB p 18)
Closing routines (see TB p 16)
Bye bye song and puppet (CD1 Track 3; see TB p 17 & 21)

Use the **Navio App** to watch the video, and encourage children to do the same at home.

Lesson 5 Speaking

Life skills

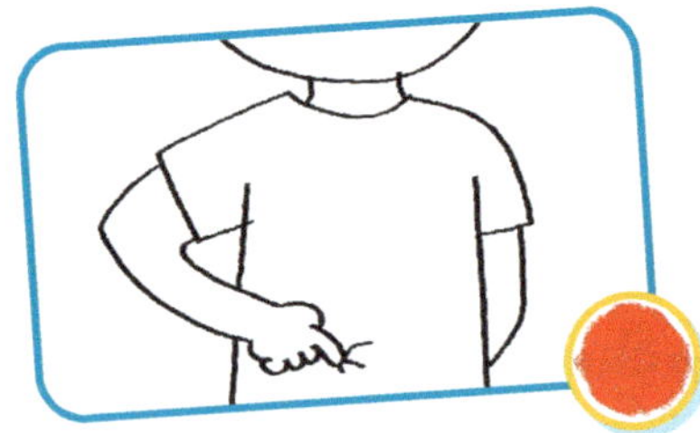

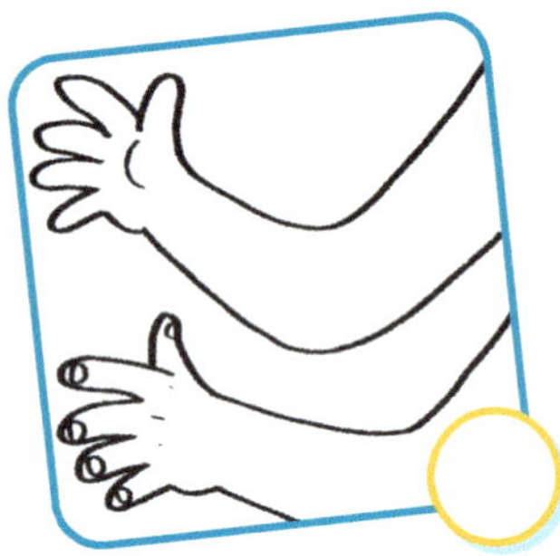

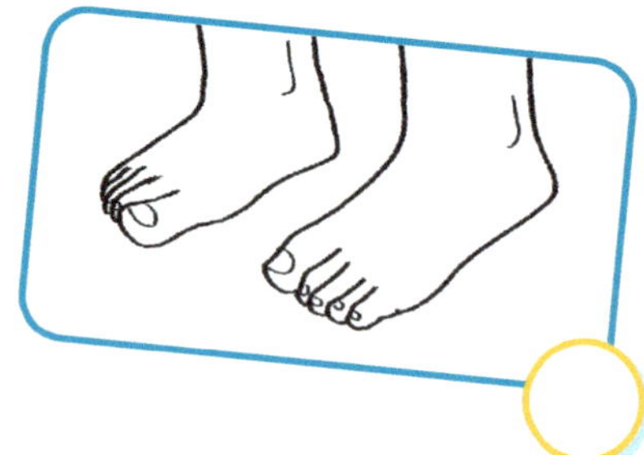

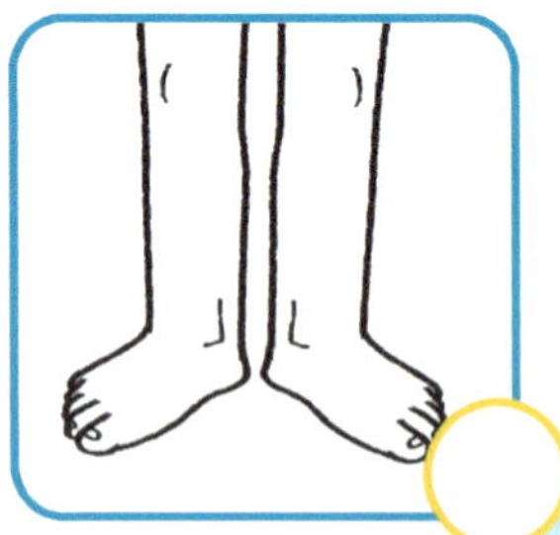

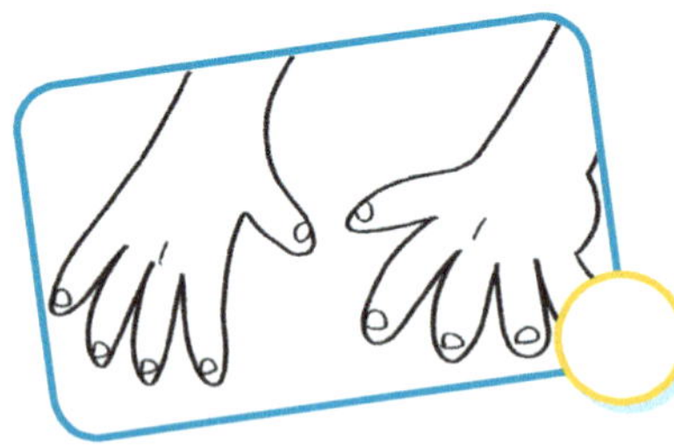

Watch. Listen and point. Color the circles green to show what Uncle Dan can do and red to show what he can't do. Color the pictures to show what you can do. Ask and say. Language: arms, feet, hands, head, legs, tummy; Can you move your (head)? Yes, I can. / No, I can't. What can you do? I can move my (head).

19

Learning objectives

- Ask and answer questions about what you can do
- Watch, understand and enjoy a video
- Identify parts of the body you can move

Materials

- Class CDs, flashcards, *Ferris Wheel* mat, Mimi puppet

Main vocabulary

- arms, feet, hands, head, legs, tummy

Key language

- Can you move your (head)? Yes, I can. / No, I can't.

Teacher's tip: Building confidence in asking questions

Life skills

Use the Mimi puppet to build children's confidence in asking questions. Point to parts of the puppet's body in turn and get children to ask with you in chorus e.g. *Can you move your head, Mimi?* By asking questions with others, children's confidence will increase, and they will develop appropriate intonation.

Circle time

Hello song & puppet (CD1 Track 2; see TB p 17 & 21)
Opening routines (see TB p 16)
Recycling activity (story song) (CD1 Track 38; see TB p 19)
Lesson aims (see TB p 18)

Game: ***Guess the flashcard.***

- Give out the body flashcards to individual children without others seeing.
- Children take turns moving the part of the body depicted on their flashcard. Other children guess.

Watch the video.

- Explain that Sam and Anna are talking to Uncle Dan. Uncle Dan is learning to dance. Play the video.
- Ask *Can Uncle Dan move his … (head, hands, arms legs, tummy, feet)?* Children respond *Yes* or *No.*
- Watch again. Pause and children repeat the questions and what Uncle Dan says.
- Ask *Can Uncle Dan dance? Yes!*

Table time

Student's Book p 19 — Life skills

Watch. Listen and point.

- Children point to Anna, Sam and Uncle Dan in the photo. Play the audio or video. Children point to the parts of the body as they hear them in the dialogue.

Color the circles green to show what Uncle Dan can do and red to show what he can't do.

- Play the audio again. Pause after the first question and answer. Elicit that Uncle Dan can move his head and point to the example green spot. Explain if he can't do something they color the spot red. Play the rest of the audio. Children color the spots.
- Play the audio again to check they have colored correctly. (Green: head, arms; Red: tummy, feet)

CD1 Track 40

Uncle Dan: Look at me, Sam and Anna. I can dance!
Sam: Can you move your head?
Uncle Dan: Yes, I can.
Anna: Can you move your arms?
Uncle Dan: Yes, I can.
Sam: Can you move your tummy?
Uncle Dan: Oh no! No, I can't.
Anna: Can you move your feet?
Uncle Dan: Oops! No, I can't. Oh no, I can't dance!
Anna: Try again.
Uncle Dan: Oh, OK. Here we go! Hey, this is great! Sam, what can you do?
Sam: I can move my arms.
Uncle Dan: Anna, what can you do?
Anna: I can move my legs.
Uncle Dan: So we can all dance! Hurray!

Color the pictures to show what you can do. Ask and say.

- Children color the parts of the body they can move.
- Remind children of the question *Can you move your (head)?* Children ask and answer questions.

Activity Book p 19

Match to show what you can (✔) and can't (✘) do.

- Children match the pictures to the check or the cross, depending on whether they can or can't do the action.

Ask and say.

- They ask and answer about what they can and can't do.

Closing time

Learning review (see TB p 18)
Closing routines (see TB p 16)
Bye bye song and puppet (CD1 Track 3; see TB p 17 & 21)

Use the **Navio App** to watch the video, and encourage children to do the same at home.

Lesson 6 Values Making an effort

Listen, point and sing ***I can do it if I try.*** **Match. Color what you can do if you try. Say.** Language: coat, scissors, shoes; I can/can't put on my (shoes). I can/can't cut with scissors.

SOCIAL AND EMOTIONAL LEARNING

20

Learning objectives

- Understand the value of making an effort
- Act out the story
- Sing the values song *I can do it if I try*
- Identify and say what you can do if you try

Materials

- Class CDs, flashcards, *Ferris Wheel* mat, Mimi puppet

Main vocabulary

- coat, scissors, shoes

Key language

- I can/can't put on my shoes/ coat. I can/can't cut with scissors.

Teacher's tip: Encouraging children's belief in their ability to learn

It's important that children believe in their ability to learn and master different skills. For some children, this comes naturally, but others need to be coached. Use positive reinforcement and praise so that children can see the value of their efforts. If children are having difficulty with something, encourage them to persevere by singing the line from the song: *I can do it if I try*.

Circle time

Hello song & puppet (CD1 Track 2; see TB p 17 & 21)
Opening routines (see TB p 16)
Recycling activity *(Can you … ? Yes, I can. / No, I can't.)* (see TB p 19)
Lesson aims (see TB p 18)

Watch the *I can dance!* story video.

- Play the story video.
- Take the parts of the narrator, monkey, Mommy, Daddy and the birds yourself. Encourage children to join in acting out the story in two groups (Mimi, Dylan).
- Ask e.g. *Can Mimi dance (at first)? (No). Can Dylan dance? (Yes). What does the little bird say to Mimi? (You can dance if you try).*
- Explain or children guess the meaning of "try." Ask e.g. *Do you try when you can't do something? Is it important to try? Why?*

***I can do it if I try* song**

CD1 Track 41

- Use the Mimi puppet to say *Listen and find out. What can Mimi and Dylan do if they try?*
- Play the audio. Do actions to support children's understanding of the song (see TB p 55).
- Repeat the actions and words. Children join in.
- Play the audio again. Children sing the song and do the actions.

Table time

Student's Book p 20

Listen, point and sing *I can do it if I try*.

CD1 Track 41

- Focus children on the pictures. Point to them one by one and ask *What's Mimi doing? Can she do it?* Play the song. Children listen, point to the pictures of Mimi succeeding in the activities, and sing.

Match.

- Children match the pictures of Mimi making an effort with the picture of her succeeding at each activity.

Color what you can do if you try. Say.

- Children color the pictures of the things they can do if they try.
- Children say what they can do, e.g *I can (put on my shoes).*

Activity Book p 20

Match the missing objects to the children. Color to show what you can do if you try.

- Children match the objects to the children. They color the pictures that show things they can do if they try.

Point and say.

- They point to each picture in turn and say what each one shows, i.e. *I can put on my coat. I can cut with scissors. I can put on my shoes.*

Closing time

Learning review (see TB p 18)
Closing routines (see TB p 16)
Bye bye song and puppet (CD1 Track 3; see TB p 17 & 21)

Use the **Navio App** to listen to the song, and encourage children to do the same at home.

Listen and point. Trace the ✔ or ✘ to show what Sam and Anna can and can't do. Color the pictures to show what you can do. Ask and say.

Language: climb, hop, jump, run; Can you (run)? Yes, I can. / No, I can't. I can/can't (climb).

21

Learning objectives

- Identify and name actions children do, and say what you can/can't do
- Listen and identify the actions
- Ask and answer about actions

Materials

- Class CDs, printable content flashcards, *Ferris Wheel* mat, Mimi puppet

Main vocabulary

- climb, hop, jump, run

Key language

- Can you (run)? Yes, I can. / No, I can't. I can/can't (climb).

Teacher's tip: Being active

Tell the children that it's important to be active and move their bodies every day. Play a jumping game by calling out numbers from 1–6 at random and have the children jump that number of times. Once you have finished, show children how to place a hand on their heart to show that it's beating faster. Establish that being active and making their heart beat faster by moving their bodies is good for them.

Circle time

Hello song & puppet (CD1 Track 2; see TB p 17 & 21)
Opening routines (see TB p 16)
Recycling activity (see TB p 19)
Lesson aims (see TB p 18)

Introduce content vocabulary.

- Use the printable flashcards to introduce the new words *(run, jump, hop, climb).*
- Say the words and mime doing the actions. Children repeat the words and mime doing the actions with you.
- Say *We use our bodies to be active. We can …* and children name the actions as you point to the flashcards.

Show what you can do.

- Use the puppet to ask children, e.g. *Can you jump?* Children do the actions and say *Yes, I can.*
- Repeat for all the actions.

Game: ***Jump to Mimi.***

- Stick the flashcards of Mommy, Daddy, Mimi and Dylan on different walls in the classroom.
- Give instructions to pairs or groups of children in turn, e.g. *Jump to Mimi!* and children respond.

Table time

Student's Book p 21

Listen and point.

- Say *Sam and Anna are playing.* Explain that the teacher is asking them what they can do. Play the audio. Children listen and point to the actions as they hear them. Use the pause button as necessary.

CD1 Track 42

Woman: We use our bodies to be active. Can you run, Anna?
Anna: Yes, I can.
Sam: I can run too.
Woman: Can you jump, Sam?
Sam: Yes, I can.
Anna: I can jump too.
Woman: Can you hop, Anna?
Anna: Yes, I can.
Woman: Can you climb, Sam?
Sam: No, I can't!

Trace the ✔ or ✘ to show what Sam and Anna can and can't do.

- Play the audio again, pausing after each question and answer. Children listen and trace the check or cross to show what Sam and Anna can or can't do.
- Play the audio again. Children point to the photos and repeat the questions and answers.

Color the pictures to show what you can do. Ask and say.

- Children color the pictures of the actions that they can do.
- Children ask and answer questions about the actions.

Activity Book p 21

Match the children doing the same actions.

- Children draw lines to match the children doing the same action.

Color the circles green to show what you can do and red to show what you can't do. Ask and say.

- Children color a circle green if they can do the action and red if they can't. They ask and answer questions about what they can and can't do.

Closing time

Learning review (see TB p 18)
Closing routines (see TB p 16)
Bye bye song and puppet (CD1 Track 3; see TB p 17 & 21)

Use the **Navio App** to play the vocabulary and language games, and encourage children to do the same at home.

Lesson 8 Culture

My body

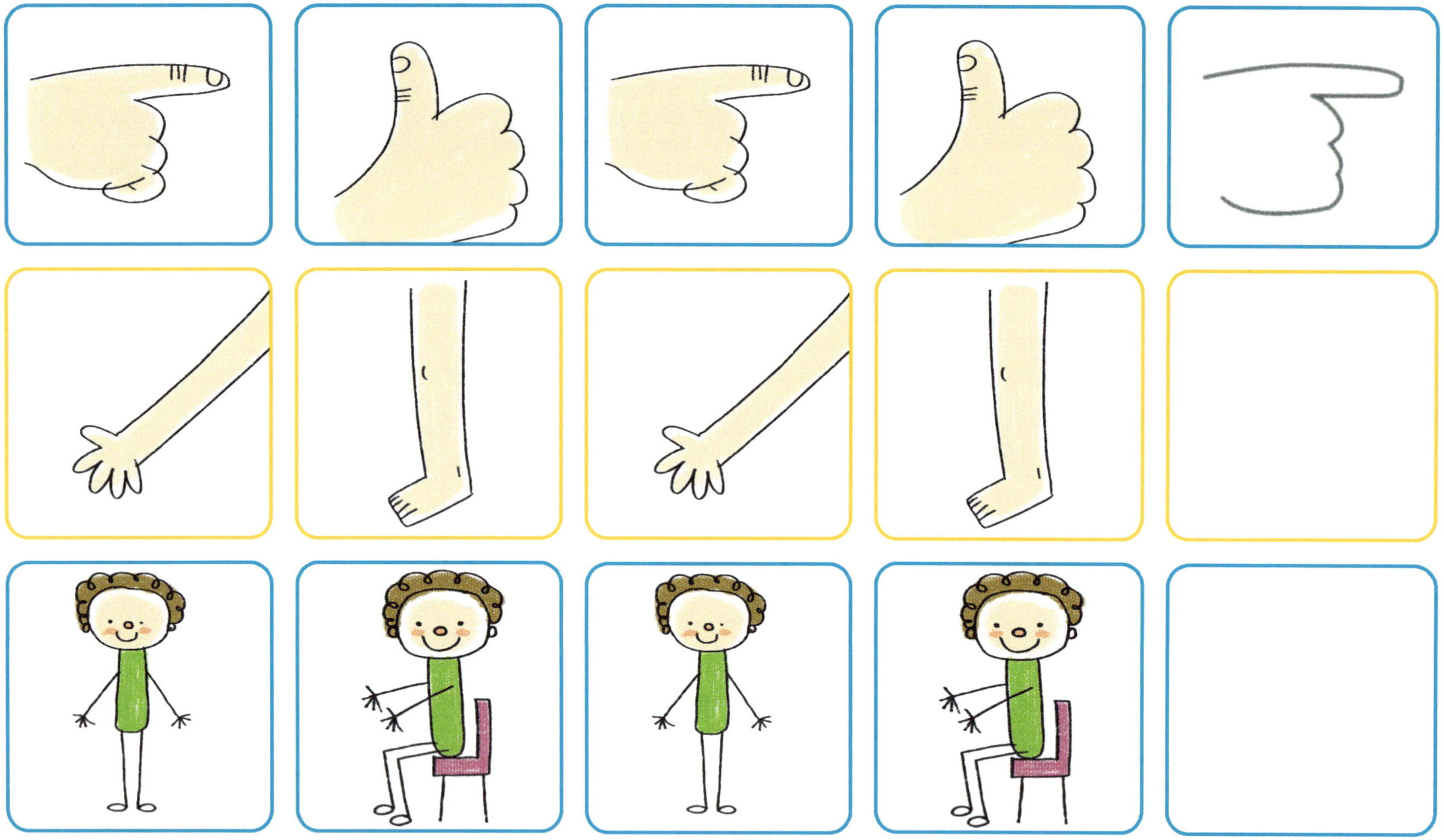

Watch. Listen, point and sing *One finger, one thumb, keep moving.* Draw the next picture in the sequence. Say.

Language: arm, finger, leg, thumb; stand up, sit down, turn round, keep moving

22

Learning objectives

- Watch, sing and act out the traditional song *One finger, one thumb, keep moving*
- Play an action game
- Identify and say parts of the body and actions

Materials

- Class CDs, flashcards, *Ferris Wheel* mat, Mimi puppet

Main vocabulary

- arm, finger, leg, thumb

Key language

- stand up, sit down, turn round, keep moving

Teacher's tip: Using actions from the song in a game

To reinforce the new actions from the song, include them in the game *Mimi says*. Have the puppet give different instructions to the children mixing body parts with actions, e.g. *Mimi says turn around. Mimi says show me your thumb.* etc.

Circle time

Hello song & puppet (CD1 Track 2; see TB p 17 & 21)
Opening routines (see TB p 16)
Recycling activity (see TB p 19)
Lesson aims (see TB p 18)

Game: *Mimi says (show me your thumb).*

- Say *Show me your thumb!* and demonstrate what you mean.
- Repeat with other parts of the body in the song (finger, arm, leg, head).
- Use the puppet to give instructions in random order. Speed up as children get more confident in responding.

***One finger, one thumb, keep moving* song**

CD1 Track 43

- Say *Stand up. Let's learn the song "One finger, one thumb, keep moving."*
- Pre-teach actions for the song (see TB p 55).
- Play the audio. Children listen and do the actions for the song with you.
- Repeat. Children join in singing and doing the actions for the song.

Watch the *One finger, one thumb, keep moving* song video.

- Children watch the video and join in singing the song and doing the actions with Anna and Sam.

Table time

Student's Book p 22

Watch. Listen, point and sing *One finger, one thumb, keep moving.*

CD1 Track 43

- Play the audio of the song. Children listen, sing and point to the pictures in the sequences as they hear them in the song.

Draw the next picture in the sequence. Say.

- Focus on the first row of pictures. Point to them one by one, saying the word each time. Point to the empty box at the end and ask *What is here?* Elicit *finger,* and demonstrate that children should draw a finger in the box.
- Repeat for the other sequences. Children draw pictures to complete the three sequences (Row 2: arm; Row 3: stand up).
- Children point to the pictures and say the words and actions.

Activity Book p 22

Circle the parts of the body in *One finger, one thumb, keep moving.*

- Children circle the body parts mentioned in the song (finger, thumb, arm, leg).

Point and say.

- Children point to the body parts they circled and say the name of the body part.

Closing time

Learning review (see TB p 18)
Closing routines (see TB p 16)
Bye bye song and puppet (CD1 Track 3; see TB p 17 & 21)

Use the **Navio App** to watch the video, and encourage children to do the same at home.

Review

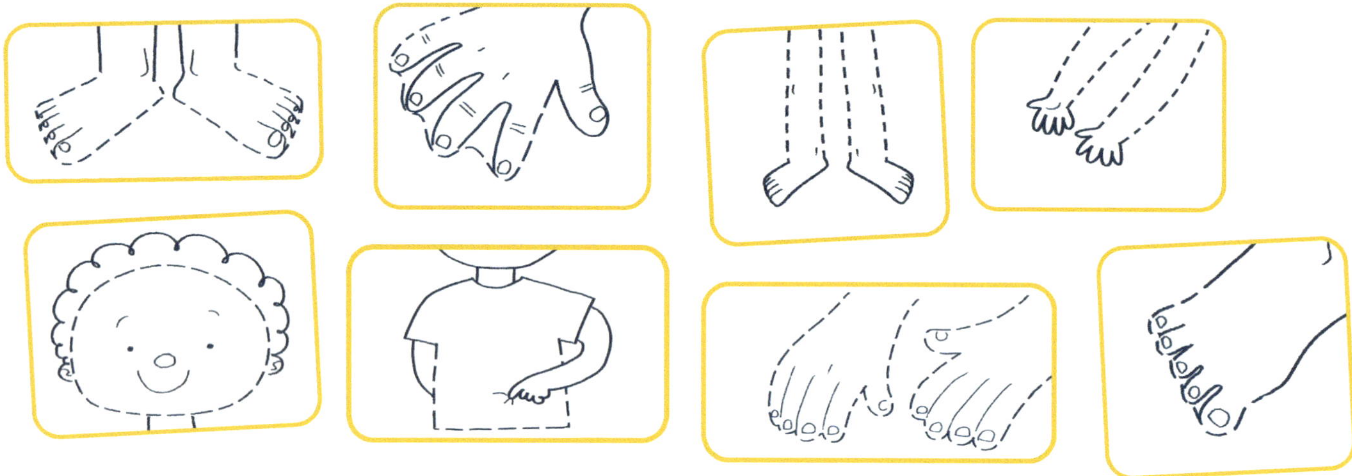

I can …

Vocabulary

Story

Speaking

Content

Trace and color the parts of the body you know. Listen, point and say. Ask and say what you can do. Complete the faces to show what you can do. Language: arms, feet, fingers, hands, head, legs, toes, tummy; Can you move your (head)? Yes, I can. / No, I can't. What can you do? I can/can't move my (legs).

23

Learning objectives

- Review what you have learned in this unit
- Complete a self-evaluation
- Talk about what you can do

Materials

- Class CDs, flashcards, *Ferris Wheel* mat, Mimi puppet

Main vocabulary

- arms, feet, fingers, hands, head, legs, toes, tummy

Key language

- Can you move your (head)? Yes, I can. / No, I can't. I can/can't move my (legs).

Teacher's tip: Guiding children

When children complete their self-evaluation, guide them by asking questions: *Do you know all the words? If you know the word, do you draw a happy or a sad face? Good! A happy face!* It's important that children understand why they are drawing a happy or a sad face. If they draw a sad face, tell them they will soon learn everything if they try and that you will help them.

Circle time

Hello song & puppet (CD1 Track 2; see TB p 17 & 21)
Opening routines (see TB p 16)
Recycling activity (see TB p 19)
Lesson aims (see TB p 18)

Parts of the body flashcard games

- Choose one or two flashcard games with the *Ferris Wheel* mat and/or the puppet to review main vocabulary (see TB p 20 & 21).

Sing *I can move my head.*

CD1 Track 35

- Play the audio. Children sing and do the actions.
- Children say and show actions they can do.

Game: ***Thumb to thumb***

- Choose a child to be your partner in the game. Say *Thumb to thumb!* and demonstrate touching your thumb to the child's thumb.
- Put the children in pairs. Use the puppet to give instructions using all the parts of the body (finger to finger, arm to arm, etc.)

Game: ***Can you jump?***

- Put the children into pairs. Show one of the action flashcards and use the puppet to demonstrate asking the question, e.g. *Can you jump?* One of the pair repeats the question and the other does the actions and says *Yes, I can.* Change roles and repeat.

Watch the story video.

- Children watch the story video. Ask *Who can dance in the story? Who helps Mimi?*

Table time

Student's Book p 23

Trace and color the parts of the body you know.

- Explain and demonstrate the activity.

Listen, point and say.

- Play the audio. Children listen, point to the parts of the body, and say the words.

CD1 Track 44

Mimi: I'm the teacher! Can you remember the parts of the body, Dylan?
Dylan: Yes, I can. Head.
Mimi: Head.
Dylan: Arms.
Mimi: Arms.
Dylan: Legs.
Mimi: Legs.
Dylan: Tummy.
Mimi: Tummy.
Dylan: Hands.
Mimi: Hands.
Dylan: Feet.
Mimi: Feet.
Dylan: Fingers.
Mimi: Fingers.
Dylan: Toes.
Mimi: Toes. Great job, Dylan! Very good!

Ask and say what you can do.

- Ask children questions about what they can do. Have them ask you or the puppet similar questions.

Complete the faces to show what you can do.

- Explain the four pictures: *I can name parts of the body; I can understand the story; I can ask and answer questions about what I can do; I can identify things I do to be active.*
- Children complete with a smile or frown depending on how well they think they have done.

Activity Book p 23

Choose and draw your face on four of the bodies to show what you can do. Ask and say.

- Children draw their faces on four actions they can do. They then ask and answer about what they can and can't do.

Think and circle the number to show your progress.

- Children circle the number that shows their progress.

Closing time

Learning review (see TB p 18)
Closing routines (see TB p 16)
Bye bye song and puppet (CD1 Track 3; see TB p 17 & 21)

Use the **Navio App** to review what children have learned in this unit, and encourage them to do the same at home.

Project

COOPERATIVE LEARNING

My body

1

2

3

Learn a dance. Make a pasta picture of you dancing. Say. Language: arms, feet, fingers, hands, head, legs, toes, tummy; pasta; What can you do? I can move my (arms). I can dance. Can you move your (head)? Yes, I can. / No, I can't. I have (arms). How many (legs) do you have? (Two).

24

Learning objectives

- Work together to do a collaborative project
- Name parts of the body
- Learn a dance
- Make a pasta picture
- Count your fingers and say how many

Materials

- Class CDs, Mimi puppet, photocopiable templates: pasta dancer, crayons, glue, pasta

Main vocabulary

- pasta; arms, feet, fingers, hands, head, legs, toes, tummy

Key language

- I can move my (arms). I can (dance). Can you move your (head)? Yes, I can. / No, I can't. I have (arms). How many (legs) do you have? (Two).

Teacher's tip: Cleaning up

COOPERATIVE LEARNING

Once the children have finished making their pasta picture, point out the importance of cleaning up. Provide a box for any left over pasta and encourage children to make sure there are no pasta pieces on the floor or tables at the end of the lesson. If you like, children can sing a version of the *Clean up song* (CD1 Track 9; see TB p 17) as they do this: *Let's clean up, let's clean up, And put the pasta in the box.*

Circle time

Hello song & puppet (CD1 Track 2; see TB p 17 & 21)
Opening routines (see TB p 16)
Recycling activity (see TB p 19)
Lesson aims (see TB p 18)

Prepare for your project.

- Say *Let's do a project. Let's make a picture of us all dancing together!* Explain that children should work together in groups for this project.
- Show children the templates of the dancing person. Point to the picture and children name the parts of the body.
- Demonstrate using crayons to color the head, hair etc of the person to look like you.
- Demonstrate gluing pieces of pasta on the template for the legs, arms and other body parts.

Table time

COOPERATIVE LEARNING

Student's Book p 24

Learn a dance.

- If possible, bring some music to the class.
- Say *Let's learn a dance!* Have children stand up.
- Say and do some actions, e.g. *Move your arms. Now move your legs. Move your head like this.* Have the children copy your actions to create a dance.
- Now play the music and have the children do the dance in time to the music.

Make a pasta picture of you dancing. Say.

- Say *We're going to make a poster of us all dancing together like this. Look at what we need for our project.* Hold up the objects and elicit the words: *crayons, glue, pasta, paper* (the templates).
- Say the words again. Children listen and point to the pictures in their books.
- Give a template to each child.
- Make sure children have pasta shapes (thin macaroni) and glue available.
- Children draw and color the head, face, hands and hair of the person to look like themselves.
- Children then glue pasta on the lines on their template to make the shape of a body dancing.
- Ask children to take turns showing and naming the parts of the body on their pictures and saying, e.g. *I can move my (head).* Encourage them to ask questions, e.g. *Can you move your (head)? How many (legs) do you have?*
- If you like, write the first names of children under their completed pictures and display them on the class noticeboard.
- Ask children *Do you like our pasta pictures?*
- Play the story song again (see lesson 4). Children sing, do the actions, and point to their pictures.
- Make the point that everyone worked together to do the dance and to make the pictures, and that all the pictures together show how they as a class can do the dance.

Activity Book p 24

Trace and paint the hands.

- Hand out pencils and paint to children. They trace the right hand and then paint both hands in a color of their choice.

Count your fingers and circle the correct number. Say.

- Point to each finger in turn. Encourage children to count with you to ten. Children circle the correct number.
- Children talk about the color of the hands, e.g. *The hands are (blue).*

Closing time

Learning review (see TB p 18)
Closing routines (see TB p 16)
Bye bye song and puppet (CD1 Track 3; see TB p 17 & 21)

Clothes

Let's dress up!

Vocabulary and language

- **Main vocabulary:** coat, dress, pants, shirt, shoes, skirt, socks, sweater
- **Key language:** This is my (skirt). These are my (shoes). I'm wearing my (sweater).
- **Content language:** boots, gloves, hat, sandals, scarf, shorts; cold, hot; It's (cold). I'm wearing (a scarf).
- **Other language:** clothespin, clothes line, family, friends, learn, play, share, stamps, string, T-shirt; I'm wearing a (white) (hat). (green and brown) (shorts). I (play) with my (friends). This is the way I put on my (shoes). Our clothes are (fantastic)!

Unit objectives

- Identify and name clothes
- Sing the language song *My clothes*
- Say what you're wearing
- Understand and act out the story *Let's dress up!*
- Sing and act out the story song *Let's wear funny clothes today!*
- Sing the values song *When we play together*
- Recognize the value of cooperating
- Identify and name clothes to wear when it's hot and cold
- Sing and act out the traditional song *This is the way I put on my shirt*
- Review your learning and progress
- Participate in a collaborative project

Story

CD2 Track 6

Picture 1

Narrator: Mimi and Dylan find a big box of clothes.
Mimi: Oh look, Dylan. This is a shirt. And this is a hat.
Dylan: And look, Mimi. These are pants. And these are shoes.
Mimi: Let's dress up!
Dylan: Oh yes. Great idea! Put on these shoes, Mimi!
Mimi: Put on this hat, Dylan!

Picture 2

Mimi: Look at me! I'm wearing green and brown shorts. I'm wearing a green and yellow shirt. I'm wearing a green hat. And I'm wearing brown shoes. I'm an explorer!
Dylan: Oh great, Mimi! And look at me! I'm wearing blue and white pants. I'm wearing a white shirt. And I'm wearing a big, white hat. I'm a chef!
Mimi: Oh you look great, Dylan!

Picture 3

Mommy: Mimi! Dylan! It's time to go out. Put on your blue skirt, Mimi.
Mimi: No, Mommy. Please. I'm wearing green and brown shorts today.
Mommy: And put on your red shoes,
Mimi: No, Mommy. Please. I'm wearing brown shoes today. I'm an explorer!

Picture 4

Mommy: Put on your green pants, Dylan.
Dylan: No, Mommy. Please. I'm wearing blue and white pants today.
Mommy: And put on your orange shirt.
Dylan: No, Mommy. Please. I'm wearing a white shirt today. I'm a chef!

Picture 5

Mommy: Mimi and Dylan … costume party … now … very kind … thank you.
Mimi: Can we go, Mommy?
Dylan: Oh please!
Mommy: Yes, of course! You're wearing the perfect clothes!

Picture 6

Lion: Hello, Mimi. Hello, Dylan.
Mimi: Hello. Look at me. I'm wearing green and brown shorts. I'm wearing a green and yellow shirt. I'm wearing a green hat. And I'm wearing brown shoes. I'm an explorer!
Lion: Ha, ha. Oh, fantastic.
Dylan: I'm wearing blue and white pants. I'm wearing a white shirt. And I'm wearing a big white hat. I'm a chef!
Lion: Ha, ha. Oh great. And I'm Little Red Riding Hood! Please come in and join the party!

Songs

Language song

My clothes CD2 Track 4

This is my skirt. (Pull arms out to sides as if holding skirt)
This is my sweater. (Hug yourself as if the sweater is warm)
I'm wearing my skirt and my sweater today. (Point down for "today")
I'm wearing my skirt and my sweater. Hurray! (Wave arms in the air for "hurray")
These are my shoes. (Pretend to tie shoelaces)
These are my socks. (Pretend to pull up socks)
I'm wearing my shoes and my socks today. (Point down for "today")
I'm wearing my shoes and my socks. Hurray! (Wave arms in the air for "hurray")
This is my shirt. (Pretend to button up shirt)
These are my pants. (Gesture down legs)
I'm wearing my shirt and my pants today. (Point down for "today")
I'm wearing my shirt and my pants. Hurray! (Wave arms in the air for "hurray")

Story song

Let's wear funny clothes today! CD2 Track 7

Let's dress up! Let's play! (Mime getting dressed)
Let's wear funny clothes today! (Wiggle down)
Green and brown shorts (Point to pretend shorts)
A green hat and a yellow shirt. (Mime putting on a hat and buttoning a shirt)
Look at me! Look at me! (Twirl around)
I'm an explorer. Hee, hee, hee. (Point to self)
Let's dress up! Let's play! (Mime getting dressed)
Let's wear funny clothes today! (Wiggle down)
Blue and white pants (Point to pretend pants)
A white hat and a white shirt (Mime putting on a hat and buttoning a shirt)
Look at me! Look at me! (Twirl around)
I'm a chef. Hee, hee, hee. (Point to self)
Let's dress up! Let's play! (Mime getting dressed)
Let's wear funny clothes today! (Wiggle down)

Values song

When we play together CD2 Track 10

When we play together (Clap with partner)
We're happy, we're happy. (Point to smile with two fingers)
I play with my friends. (Clap to left)
I play with my family. (Clap to right)
When we play together we're ha-ha-happy (Clap with partner and smile)
When we learn together (A finger on either side of head)
We're happy, we're happy. (Point to smile with two fingers)
I learn with my friends. (Gesture to left)
I learn with my family. (Gesture to right)
When we learn together we're ha-ha-happy. (Fingers on head & smile)
When we share together (Mime giving each other something)
We're happy, we're happy. (Point to smile with two fingers)
I share with my friends. (Gesture to left)
I share with my family. (Gesture to right)
When we share together we're ha-ha-happy. (Mime giving something & smile)

Culture song

This is the way I put on my shirt CD2 Track 12

This is the way I put on my shirt (Mime putting on shirt on)
Put on my shirt, put on my shirt
This is the way I put on my shirt
Early in the morning. (March)
This is the way I put on my pants (Mime putting on pants)
Put on my pants, put on my pants
This is the way I put on my pants
Early in the morning. (March)
This is the way I put on my shoes (Mime tying shoelaces)
Put on my shoes, put on my shoes
This is the way I put on my shoes (Mime tying shoelaces on the other foot)
Early in the morning. (March)
This is the way I put on my coat (Mime putting on coat)
Put on my coat, put on my coat
This is the way I put on my coat
Early in the morning. (March)

Clothes
Let's dress up!

Listen, point and repeat. Listen and play. Stick the clothes stickers. Circle the clothes Mimi and Dylan are wearing. Say. **Language:** coat, dress, pants, shirt, skirt, sweater; blue, green, orange, pink, red, yellow

Learning objectives

- Identify and name clothes
- Listen and point to clothes
- Identify the clothes Mimi and Dylan are wearing

Materials

- Class CDs, flashcards, *Ferris Wheel* mat, Mimi puppet

Main vocabulary

- coat, dress, pants, shirt, skirt, sweater; blue, green, orange, pink, red, yellow; numbers

Teacher's tip: Dressing up

If possible, bring in some oversized old clothes and play a dressing up game. Choose a different volunteer each time and say e.g. *Put on your shirt.* The element of play will help fix the words in children's memories. Leave the clothes in a dressing up box either for any fast finishers to play with in pairs or as a resource for your English Language Area (see TB p 25).

Circle time

Hello song & puppet (CD1 Track 2; see TB p 17 & 21)
Opening routines (see TB p 16)
Lesson aims (see TB p 18)

Introduce clothes.

- Use the puppet to introduce the new vocabulary by pointing to your and the children's clothes. Say the words and encourage children to repeat them with you. Repeat for all the words.
- Put the *Ferris Wheel* mat on the floor or board with the clothes flashcards face down (one on each color). Use puppet to turn over and name. Children repeat the words.

Game: *Put on your shirt!*

- Point to the flashcards in turn. Use the puppet to give instructions. Children mime putting on the clothes.

Game: *Say the color!*

- Name the clothes on the Ferris Wheel and children name the color. Then do it in reverse.

Game: *Guess the clothes!*

- Turn the flashcards face down and mix them up so that they are on different colors of the wheel.
- Point to one flashcard. Children guess what it is. Then say *Let's find out!* Turn the flashcard over and children say the word. Repeat with all the flashcards.

Table time

Student's Book p 25

Listen, point and repeat.

- Play the audio. The children listen, point to each item of clothing as they hear it, and repeat the words.

CD2 Track 1

Mimi: Look, Dylan! Pants … skirt … dress … sweater … coat … shirt. Repeat, Dylan!
Dylan: Yes, Mimi. Pants … skirt … dress … sweater … coat … shirt.
Mimi: Very good, Dylan. Let's name the clothes together!
Both: Pants … skirt … dress … sweater … coat … shirt.

Listen and play.

- Use finger in air to pretend to spin wheel. Children spin their fingers, point to the color when they hear it on the audio and say the word.

CD2 Track 2

Mimi: Spin the wheel
One, two, three
Point and name
The clothes with me!

Yellow … sweater!
Pink … coat!
Blue … skirt!
Green … shirt!
Red … pants!
Orange … dress!

- Play the game with you and/or individual children naming colors and others responding with the words.

Stick the clothes stickers.

- Children stick the clothes stickers in the correct places.

Circle the clothes Mimi and Dylan are wearing.

- Children circle the clothes Mimi and Dylan are wearing.

Say.

- Children name the clothes Mimi and Dylan are wearing (sweater, skirt; shirt, pants).

Activity Book p 25

Color the clothes following the key.

- Say the numbers and children name the colors in the key. Reverse and repeat.
- Children color the clothes following the key.

Point and say.

- Children point and name the clothes.

Closing time

Learning review (see TB p 18)
Closing routines (see TB p 16)
Bye bye song and puppet (CD1 Track 3; see TB p 17 & 21)

Use the **Navio App** to play the vocabulary game, and encourage children to do the same at home.

Listen and find the new clothes. Listen, point and sing *My clothes.* Draw your clothes. Say what you're wearing. Language: pants, shirt, shoes, skirt, socks, sweater; This is my (skirt). These are my (shoes). I'm wearing my (sweater).

26

Learning objectives

- Talk about clothes
- Identify and name two new clothes
- Sing the language song *My clothes*
- Say what you're wearing

Materials

- Class CDs, flashcards, *Ferris Wheel* mat, Mimi puppet

Main vocabulary

- pants, shirt, shoes, skirt, socks, sweater

Key language

- This is my (skirt). These are my (shoes). I'm wearing my (sweater).

Teacher's tip: Reducing the volume to encourage singing

Once the children are familiar with the song, play the track as normal, but turn down the volume for the last line in each verse to encourage children to sing more. Put your hand to your ear and use gesture to make this clear. Repeat, turning down the volume of the penultimate and last line in each verse.

Circle time

Hello song & puppet (CD1 Track 2; see TB p 17 & 21)
Opening routines (see TB p 16)
Recycling activity (six clothes words from Lesson 1) (see TB p 19)
Lesson aims (see TB p 18)

Introduce the new clothes words.

- All eight flashcards of clothes on the floor or board. Children identify the two new clothes. Use the puppet to point to and say the words in turn. Children repeat in chorus.
- Turn the two new flashcards face down. Mix them up. Point to one and ask *Shoes or socks?* Children guess. Repeat several times.
- Say the words in turn. Children respond by touching their shoes or their socks. Repeat several times going faster and faster as children gain confidence.

Introduce *This is my … / These are my …*

- Children stand up. Have them point to their clothes and say, e.g. *This is my sweater. / These are my socks.*
- Hold up the flashcard of Mommy. Point to her clothes and ask *What does Mommy say?* Children join in with you, e.g. *This is my dress. / These are my shoes.*
- Repeat with the flashcards of Daddy, Mimi and Dylan. (Note: do not attempt to explain the difference between "this" and "these" at this stage.)

Game: *Repeat if it's true!*

- Say e.g. *I'm wearing my shirt today* and touch the collar, button and sleeves to show this. Demonstrate that children should repeat the sentence and do similar actions if they're wearing a shirt and cross their arms and stay silent if not.
- Repeat with other clothes you're wearing or, alternatively, ask a child to come and stand by you and say sentences with them that refer to their clothes.

Table time

Student's Book p 26

Listen and find the new clothes.

- Play the audio. Children listen and find the two new words. Play the audio again. The children listen and say the words.

  CD2 Track 3

  One, two, Which words are new?
  Shoes! Shoes!
  Socks! Socks!

Listen, point and sing *My clothes*.

CD2 Track 4

- Play the song. The children listen and point to Sam and Anna's clothes as they hear them in the song.
- Play the song again. Children point to their clothes (real or pretend) and sing the song (see TB p 77).
- Remember that you can use the karaoke version of the song when children are confident.

Draw your clothes.

- Demonstrate that children should draw a picture of themselves wearing clothes of their choice.

Say what you're wearing.

- Encourage children to show their pictures and say, e.g. *I'm wearing my pants.*

Activity Book p 26

Follow and draw the paths from the children to the clothes.

- Demonstrate following the paths with your finger. The children do the same. Elicit that the clothes in the wardrobes are the same as the children are wearing. The children draw along the paths to match the children to the clothes.

Color the clothes.

- Children color the clothes to look the same as those the children are wearing.

Point and say.

- Children point and say, e.g. *This is my shirt. / These are my shoes. / I'm wearing my (sweater).*

Closing time

Learning review (see TB p 18)
Closing routines (see TB p 16)
Bye bye song and puppet (CD1 Track 3; see TB p 17 & 21)

Use the **Navio App** to listen to the song, and encourage children to do the same at home.

Watch. Listen to the story *Let's dress up!* Circle the clothes Mimi and Dylan wear to the party. Stick the story sticker. Language: hat, pants, shirt, shoes, shorts; colors; This is a (shirt). These are (shoes). I'm wearing (a white) (hat).

Learning objectives

- Watch, understand and enjoy the story *Let's dress up!*
- Make a prediction about the story
- Identify the clothes Mimi and Dylan are wearing
- Look and find the clothes in the story

Materials

- Class CDs, printable story cards, flashcards, *Ferris Wheel* mat, Mimi puppet

Main vocabulary

- hat, pants, shirt, shoes, shorts; colors

Key language

- This is a (shirt). These are (shoes). I'm wearing (a white) (hat).

Teacher's tip: Maintaining focus

Maintain eye contact with the children during the story telling. Be ready to ask questions to focus their attention.

Circle time

Hello song & puppet (CD1 Track 2; see TB p 17 & 21)
Opening routines (see TB p 16)
Recycling activity (*I'm wearing* … and clothes) (see TB p 19)
Lesson aims (see TB p 18)

Introduce the story *Let's dress up!*

- Say *It's story time!* Play the *Story rhyme* (CD1 Track 4; see TB p 17).
- Say *Anna and Sam are listening to a story about Mimi and Dylan. What are they wearing?*

Watch or listen to the story.

CD2 Track 6

- Watch the video, play the audio, or read the story using the printable story cards. Pause, repeat words, point to the pictures, ask questions.
- Ask children *What's Mimi wearing? (dress, hat, shoes) What's Dylan wearing? (pants, hat, shirt) Where do they go? (a party).*
- Repeat the story. Encourage children to join in with the words and phrases in the story.
- Ask *Do you want to go to a costume party?*

Look and find.

- Say e.g. *Find the green hat.* Children point to the picture. Repeat with other clothes.

Table time

Student's Book p 27

Watch. Listen to the story *Let's dress up!*

- Read or play the story again. Children listen and follow the story by pointing to the pictures.

Story questions

Picture 1
What do Mimi and Dylan find in the box? *(Clothes)*
What does Mimi put on? *(Shoes)*

Picture 2
What does Mimi put on? *(Green and brown shorts, green and yellow shirt, green hat, brown shoes)*
What does Dylan put on? *(Blue and white pants, white shirt, white hat)*

Picture 3
What does Mommy want Mimi to put on? *(Blue skirt/red shoes)*
What color shoes is Mimi wearing? *(Brown)*

Picture 4
What does Mommy want Dylan to put on? *(Green pants/orange shirt)*
What color shirt is Dylan wearing? *(White)*

Picture 5
Where are Mimi and Dylan going? *(A party)*
What kind of party is it? *(Costume party)*

Picture 6
What is Mimi? *(An explorer)*
What is Dylan? *(A chef)*

Circle the clothes Mimi and Dylan wear to the party.

- Children find the clothes Mimi and Dylan wear to the party and circle them.

Stick the story sticker.

- Children stick on the story sticker.
- Say sentences from the story in random order. Children listen and point to the correct frames.
- Ask *Who's (a chef)?* and children respond.

Activity Book p 27

Trace and say the numbers. Match to order the pictures.

- Children trace and say the numbers. Then they match them to the pictures.

Circle your favorite picture.

- Children choose and circle their favorite picture.

Closing time

Learning review (see TB p 18)
Closing routines (see TB p 16)
Bye bye song and puppet (CD1 Track 3; see TB p 17 & 21)

Use the **Navio App** to watch the video, and encourage children to do the same at home.

Lesson 4 Story Song

Clothes

Watch. Listen, point and sing *Let's wear funny clothes today!* Find and circle the clothes Mimi and Dylan wear to the party. Point and say. **Language:** hat, pants, shirt, shoes, shorts, skirt, socks, sweater; colors; (green and brown) (shorts); a (white) (hat)

2:07

hello

28

Learning objectives

- Watch, sing and act out the story song *Let's wear funny clothes today!*
- Listen to the story again and identify clothes
- Mime and say what you're wearing
- Identify and name clothes

Materials

- Class CDs, printable story cards, flashcards, *Ferris Wheel* mat, Mimi puppet

Main vocabulary

- hat, pants, shirt, shoes, shorts, skirt, socks, sweater; colors

Key language

- (green and brown) (shorts), a (white) (hat)

Teacher's tip: Learning the song in stages

Using story songs gives the children an opportunity to listen and repeat the sounds, rhythm and intonation of language before producing it in a communicative way. First, have the children join in with the chorus, then the repeated sections *(Look at me, look at me)* gradually building up to the whole story song.

Circle time

Hello song & puppet (CD1 Track 2; see TB p 17 & 21)
Opening routines (see TB p 16)
Recycling activity (clothes) (see TB p 19)
Lesson aims (see TB p 18)

Retell the story *Let's dress up!*

- Play the audio, video or read the story using the printable story cards.
- Demonstrate that children should wave their arms in the air every time they hear a clothes word in the story.

Game: *Explorer or chef?*

- Say e.g. *Green hat!* (and children say *Mimi* or *Explorer!*), *Blue and white pants!* (and children say *Dylan* or *Chef!*).
- Repeat with other clothes Mimi and Dylan wear in the story.

***Let's wear funny clothes today!* song**

CD2 Track 7

- Play the video or audio of the story song. Children watch/listen and raise their hands when they hear clothes in the song.
- Ask *Who sings verse 1? Who sings verse 2?* Children watch the video and respond.
- Play the video again. Children mime wearing the clothes in each verse and join in singing the song.
- Ask e.g. *Do you want to dress up / wear funny clothes?* and children respond.

Pretend to be Mimi and Dylan.

- Children choose if they want to be Mimi or Dylan and make two groups.
- Children take turns miming and saying with you what they're wearing for the party in chorus, e.g. *I'm wearing a white hat.*

Table time

Student's Book p 28

Watch. Listen, point and sing *Let's wear funny clothes today!*

CD2 Track 7

- Play the audio of the song. Children listen, sing and point to the clothes in the picture.
- Remember that you can use the karaoke version of the song when children are confident.

Find and circle the clothes Mimi and Dylan wear to the party.

- Children find and circle the clothes Mimi and Dylan wear to the party.

Point and say.

- Children name the clothes Mimi and Dylan wear to the party.
- Children point to other clothes in the picture and say, e.g. *This is a (skirt). / These are (shoes).*

Activity Book p 28

Trace and color the clothes Mimi and Dylan wear to the party.

Children trace and color the clothes in the correct colors.

Say.

- Children say what Mimi and Dylan are wearing, as if they are Mimi or Dylan, e.g. *I'm wearing (a green) hat.*

Closing time

Learning review (see TB p 18)
Closing routines (see TB p 16)
Bye bye song and puppet (CD1 Track 3; see TB p 17 & 21)

Use the **Navio App** to watch the video, and encourage children to do the same at home.

Lesson 5 Speaking

Life skills

Watch. Listen and point. Match and color the clothes Uncle Dan is wearing. Circle the clothes you're wearing. Say. Language: boots, coat, hat, pants, shirt, shoes, sweater; colors; What are you wearing? I'm wearing (a red) (sweater).

Learning objectives

- Talk about what clothes you're wearing
- Watch, understand and enjoy a video
- Identify the clothes you're wearing

Materials

- Class CDs, flashcards, *Ferris Wheel* mat, Mimi puppet

Main vocabulary

- boots, coat, hat, pants, shirt, shoes, sweater; colors

Key language

- What are you wearing? I'm wearing (a red) (sweater).

Teacher's tip: Scaffolding words to sentences

Life skills

Initially children may just answer with single words to describe what they are wearing. Scaffold and recast their sentences so that they gradually gain the confidence to start producing the full sentence: *I'm wearing (boots).*

Circle time

Hello song & puppet (CD1 Track 2; see TB p 17 & 21)
Opening routines (see TB p 16)
Recycling activity (story song) (CD2 Track 7; see TB p 19)
Lesson aims (see TB p 18)

Game: *Guess the flashcard.*

- Give out the clothes flashcards to individual children without others seeing.
- Children take turns miming putting on the item of clothing on their flashcard. Other children guess.

Watch the video.

- Explain that Sam and Anna are talking to Uncle Dan. Uncle Dan is acting in the theater. He's a pirate.
- Play the video of Anna, Sam and Uncle Dan.
- Ask *What's Uncle Dan wearing? (hat, shirt, pants, boots, coat)*
- Watch again. Pause and children repeat what Uncle Dan says.
- Ask *Who's Uncle Dan's friend? (Jack)*

Table time

Student's Book p 29 Life skills

Watch. Listen and point.

- Children point to Anna, Sam and Uncle Dan in the photo. Play the audio or video. Children point to the clothes as they hear them in the dialogue.

Match and color the clothes Uncle Dan is wearing.

- Point to the clothes around the photo and children say the words. Children match the clothes to the photo of Uncle Dan. They then color the clothes to match the ones Uncle Dan is wearing.
- Play the audio again. Use the pause button and children repeat the sentences *I'm wearing (a yellow shirt).* Check they have matched and colored the clothes correctly.

CD2 Track 9

Sam: Hello, Uncle Dan!
Uncle Dan: Hello!
Anna: What are you wearing for the party, Uncle Dan?
Uncle Dan: I'm wearing a yellow shirt. I'm wearing blue pants. I'm wearing black boots. And I'm wearing a red coat.
Sam: Oh fantastic!
Uncle Dan: Hey, I'm a pirate! And this is my friend, Jack.
Anna: Hello, Jack! You're amazing too!

Circle the clothes you're wearing. Say.

- Children circle the pictures of the clothes they're wearing.
- Remind children of the question *What are you wearing?* Children say what they are wearing.

Activity Book p 29

Find and color Uncle Dan's pirate clothes.

- Children color the pictures that Uncle Dan wears as a pirate (boots, pirate hat, coat).

Choose and circle clothes for you. Ask and say.

- Children circle clothes for them. They ask and say what they are wearing.

Closing time

Learning review (see TB p 18)
Closing routines (see TB p 16)
Bye bye song and puppet (CD1 Track 3; see TB p 17 & 21)

Use the **Navio App** to watch the video, and encourage children to do the same at home.

Lesson 6 Values Cooperating

2:10

hello

Listen, point and sing *When we play together*. Complete the faces to show if you cooperate with others like Mimi and Dylan. Draw a picture to show you cooperating with your friends or family. Say. Language: learn, play, share; family, friends; I (play) with my (friends).

SOCIAL AND EMOTIONAL LEARNING

30

Learning objectives

- Understand the value of cooperating
- Act out the story
- Sing the values song *When we play together*
- Identify how people cooperate and talk about how you cooperate with others

Materials

- Class CDs, flashcards, *Ferris Wheel* mat, Mimi puppet

Main vocabulary

- learn, play, share; family, friends

Key language

- I (play) with my (friends).

Teacher's tip: Working with different partners

Working with a partner helps children learn to cooperate. This in turn helps create a positive atmosphere in the classroom. Give the children as many opportunities as possible to work in pairs. Alternate between selecting the partners yourself and allowing them to choose who they work with.

Circle time

Hello song & puppet (CD1 Track 2; see TB p 17 & 21)
Opening routines (see TB p 16)
Recycling activity (*I'm wearing …*) (see TB p 19)
Lesson aims (see TB p 18)

Watch the *Let's dress up!* story video.

- Play the story video.
- Take the parts of the narrator, Mommy and the lion yourself. Encourage children to join in acting out the story in two groups (Mimi, Dylan).
- Ask e.g. *Do Mimi and Dylan play together in the story? (Yes). Are they happy? (Yes). Do they have fun? (Yes)*
- Ask e.g. *Is it important to play, learn and share things together?* (i.e. to cooperate) *Why?*

***When we play together* song**

CD2 Track 10

- Put the children in pairs. Pre-teach actions for the song (see TB p 77).
- Play the audio. Children listen and do the actions with you.
- Play the audio again. Children sing the song and do the actions.

Table time

Student's Book p 30

Listen, point and sing *When we play together.*

CD2 Track 10

- Children sing and point to the pictures.

Complete the faces to show if you cooperate with others like Mimi and Dylan.

- Children complete the faces with a ☺ or ☹ to show if they play, learn and share with others as Mimi and Dylan do in the pictures.

Draw a picture to show you cooperating with your friends or family. Say.

- Children draw a picture of themselves cooperating with friends or family.
- Children take turns showing their pictures and saying e.g. *I (play) with my (friends).*

Activity Book p 30

Circle the pictures of children cooperating.

- Children color the pictures that show children cooperating.

Talk about you.

- They talk about the ways they cooperate, e.g. *I (learn) with my (friends).*

Closing time

Learning review (see TB p 18)
Closing routines (see TB p 16)
Bye bye song and puppet (CD1 Track 3; see TB p 17 & 21)

Use the **Navio App** to listen to the song, and encourage children to do the same at home.

Lesson 7

Content

Clothes

Listen and point. Circle clothes for hot weather orange. Circle clothes for cold weather blue. Say. **Language:** boots, coat, gloves, hat, sandals, scarf, shorts, shirt; cold, hot; It's (cold). I'm wearing (a scarf).

31

Learning objectives

- Identify and name clothes we wear in different weather
- Listen and identify the clothes
- Talk about clothes we wear in different weather

Materials

- Class CDs, printable content flashcards, *Ferris Wheel* mat, Mimi puppet

Main vocabulary

- boots, coat, gloves, hat, sandals, scarf, shorts, shirt; cold, hot

Key language

- It's (cold). I'm wearing (a scarf).

Teacher's tip: Being safe in hot weather

Life skills

In addition to talking about clothes, introduce ways of keeping cool and being safe in hot weather. Draw a sun on the board and tell the children that Sam is going out in the sun. Collectively mime putting on shorts, shirt, sandals and hat, followed by sun cream on your face, arms and legs. Mime playing in the sun and say *It's too hot!* Mime moving to the shade and drinking water. Fan yourself with your hand and say *That's better!*

Circle time

Hello song & puppet (CD1 Track 2; see TB p 17 & 21)
Opening routines (see TB p 16)
Recycling activity (see TB p 19)
Lesson aims (see TB p 18)

Introduce content vocabulary.

- Use the puppet and the printable flashcards to introduce the new words (*scarf, gloves, sandals, shorts*).
- Say the words and mime putting on the clothes. Children repeat the words and mime putting on the clothes with you.
- Say *We wear shorts and sandals when it's hot. We wear a scarf and gloves when it's cold.* (Use mime to convey meaning.)

Game: ***Hot or cold!***

- Hold up one of the flashcards and say the word, e.g. *Sandals*. Children respond by saying *Hot!* or *Cold!* depending when you wear the clothes.
- Repeat for all the clothes. You may also like to include other familiar or recycled clothes, e.g. boots, hat, T-shirt, coat.

Game: ***Sort the clothes.***

- Lay out flashcards of the clothes face up on the floor in jumbled order. Designate one side of the circle as "hot" and the other as "cold."
- Invite individual children to take turns placing the flashcards on the correct side of the circle.

Table time

Student's Book p 31

Listen and point.

- Say *Sam and Anna are wearing clothes for different weather.* Say *Look at the photos of Sam and Anna.* Ask *Is it hot or cold for Sam?* (*hot*) *Is it hot or cold for Anna?* (*cold*).
- Play the audio. Children listen and point to the clothes as they hear them.

CD2 Track 11

Sam: It's hot. I'm wearing a hat. I'm wearing a shirt. I'm wearing shorts. I'm wearing sandals.
Anna: It's cold. I'm wearing a hat. I'm wearing a coat. I'm wearing a scarf. I'm wearing gloves. I'm wearing boots.

- Play the audio again. Use the pause button. Children repeat the sentences.

Circle clothes for hot weather orange. Circle clothes for cold weather blue. Say.

- Children circle the clothes for hot weather orange and clothes for cold weather blue. They point and say, e.g. *It's hot. I'm wearing a hat.*

Activity Book p 31

Draw clothes for hot and cold weather.

- Children draw clothes for hot weather under the sun. They draw clothes for cold weather under the clouds.

Choose, ask and say.

- Ask them to choose either hot or cold weather. They ask and answer about clothes for that weather.

Closing time

Learning review (see TB p 18)
Closing routines (see TB p 16)
Bye bye song and puppet (CD1 Track 3; see TB p 17 & 21)

Use the **Navio App** to play the vocabulary and language games, and encourage children to do the same at home.

Lesson 8

Culture

Watch. Listen, point and sing *This is the way I put on my shirt*. Match the photos and clothes. Say. Language: coat, pants, shirt, shoes; This is the way I put on my (shoes).

32

Learning objectives

- Watch, sing and act out the a traditional song *This is the way I put on my shirt*
- Play an action game
- Identify and say clothes
- Talk about what you're wearing

Materials

- Class CDs, flashcards, *Ferris Wheel* mat, Mimi puppet

Main vocabulary

- coat, pants, shirt, shoes

Key language

- This is the way I put on my (shoes).

Teacher's tip: Putting on a coat

Life skills

Children of this age group often need help putting on their coats. Use the opportunity to work on the life skill of putting on a coat. Show them how to make sure their coat is turned the right way before starting to put it on. Then, show them how to hold it and put one arm in first, then the other. Encourage them to work in pairs and help each other putting their coats on and fastening them. While they are doing so, encourage them to sing *This is the way I put on my coat.* (see TB p 23 (Life Skills) for an alternative way of putting on a coat.)

Circle time

Hello song & puppet (CD1 Track 2; see TB p 17 & 21)
Opening routines (see TB p 16)
Recycling activity (see TB p 19)
Lesson aims (see TB p 18)

Game: *Put on your hat!*

- Use the puppet to give instructions to put on different clothes. Children mime the actions.
- Invite individual children to take turns holding the puppet and supplying the words or giving instructions in the same way.

This is the way I put on my shirt song

CD2 Track 12

- Ask *How many clothes words can you hear in the song? What are they?*
- Play the audio. Children listen and count the clothes words. Check the answers (four: *shirt, pants, shoes, coat*).
- Play the audio again. Children join in singing and miming putting on the clothes (see TB p 77).

Watch the *This is the way I put on my shirt* song video.

- Children watch the video and join in singing the song and miming putting on the clothes with Anna and Sam.

Table time

Student's Book p 32

Watch. Listen, point and sing *This is the way I put on my shirt.*

CD2 Track 12

- Play the audio of the song. Children listen, sing and point to the the photos of each verse.

Match the photos and clothes. Say.

- Children draw lines to match the photos and clothes.
- Children point and say *This is the way I put on my (shoes).*

Activity Book p 32

Choose, draw and color your clothes.

- Children draw and color a picture of themselves wearing some of the clothes on the right.

Mime and say.

- They mime putting on the clothes they drew in their picture. As they "put on" each item of clothing they say what they are wearing.

Closing time

Learning review (see TB p 18)
Closing routines (see TB p 16)
Bye bye song and puppet (CD1 Track 3; see TB p 17 & 21)

Use the **Navio App** to watch the video, and encourage children to do the same at home.

I can …

Vocabulary

Story

Speaking

Content

Trace and color the clothes you know. Listen, point and say. Ask and say. Complete the faces to show what you can do. Language: coat, dress, gloves, pants, sandals, scarf, shirt, shoes, shorts, skirt, socks, sweater; colors; What are you wearing? I'm wearing (a blue) (skirt).

Clothes

Review Lesson

Learning objectives
- Review what you have learned in this unit
- Complete a self-evaluation
- Talk about what you're wearing

Materials
- Class CDs, flashcards, *Ferris Wheel* mat, Mimi puppet

Main vocabulary
- coat, dress, gloves, pants, sandals, scarf, shirt, shoes, shorts, skirt, socks, sweater; colors

Key language
- This is my (skirt). These are my (shoes). I'm wearing (a blue) (skirt).

Teacher's tip: Sharing self-evaluation with a friend

Once the children have completed the self-evaluation section of the review, encourage them to show it to a friend and compare their answers. Remind them to be positive about each other's efforts.

Circle time

Hello song & puppet (CD1 Track 2; see TB p 17 & 21)
Opening routines (see TB p 16)
Recycling activity (see TB p 19)
Lesson aims (see TB p 18)

Clothes flashcard games

- Choose one or two flashcard games with the *Ferris Wheel* mat and/or the puppet to review main vocabulary (see TB p 20 & 21).

Sing *My clothes.*

CD2 Track 4

- Play the audio. Children sing and do the actions.
- Children point to and say sentences about their clothes.

Game: *Giant's footsteps*

- Children line up on one side of the room. The aim is to get to the other side first.
- Show one of the clothes flashcards and say, e.g. *I'm wearing shoes.* All children wearing shoes take a giant step forward and repeat the sentence. Continue with other items until there is a winner.

Game: *This is my shirt.*

- Say *This is my shirt.* Point to your shirt. Children say *yes* and put arms in air.
- Say *These are my shoes* and point to your pants. Children fold arms and say *no.* Children play in pairs.

Watch the story video.

- Children watch the story video. Ask *What are Mimi and Dylan wearing for the party?*

Table time

Student's Book p 33

Trace and color the clothes you know.

- Explain and demonstrate the activity.

Listen, point and say.

- Play the audio. Children listen, point to the clothes, and say the words.

CD2 Track 13

Mimi: I'm the teacher! Can you remember the clothes, Dylan?
Dylan: Yes, I can. Pants.
Mimi: Pants.
Dylan: Skirt.
Mimi: Skirt.
Dylan: Dress.
Mimi: Dress.
Dylan: Sweater.
Mimi: Sweater.
Dylan: Coat.
Mimi: Coat.
Dylan: Shirt.
Mimi: Shirt.
Dylan: Shoes.
Mimi: Shoes.
Dylan: Socks.
Mimi: Socks. Great job, Dylan! Very good!

Say what you're wearing.

- Ask children to tell you or each other what they're wearing. Have them ask you or the puppet similar questions.

Complete the faces to show what you can do.

- Explain the four pictures: *I can name clothes; I can understand the story; I can talk about what I'm wearing; I can identify clothes for hot and cold weather.*
- Remind them to complete the face with a smile or frown, depending on how well they think they have done.

Activity Book p 33

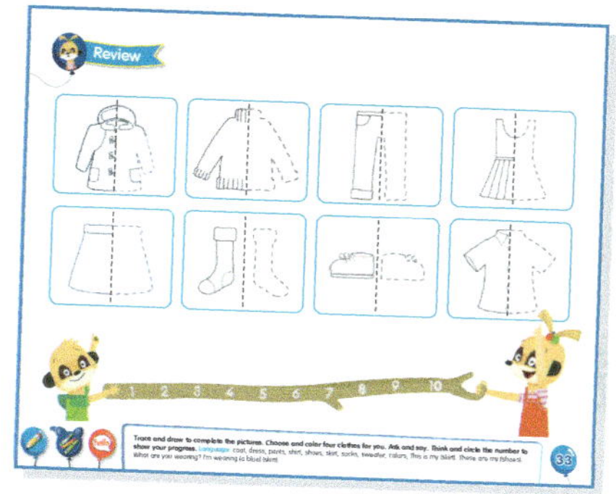

Trace and draw to complete the pictures.

- Children complete the pictures.

Choose and color four clothes for you. Ask and say.

- Children choose and color four clothes. They ask and answer about what they're wearing.

Think and circle the number to show your progress.

- They choose and circle the number.

Closing time

Learning review (see TB p 18)
Closing routines (see TB p 16)
Bye bye song and puppet (CD1 Track 3; see TB p 17 & 21)

Use the **Navio App** to review what children have learned in this unit, and encourage them to do the same at home.

Project

COOPERATIVE LEARNING

Make a shirt for hot weather or a sweater for cold weather. Hang your clothes on the correct clothes line. Say.
Language: shirt, sweater; clothespin, clothes line, stamps, string; colors; numbers; cold, hot; It's (hot). This is a (blue) (shirt). I like the (green) (shirt). How many (pink) (shirts)? (Two). I have a (blue and green) (sweater). Our clothes are (fantastic)!

34

Learning objectives

- Work together to do a collaborative project
- Talk about clothes for hot and cold weather
- Make a shirt or a sweater and hang it on a clothes line
- Choose clothes for hot and cold weather and say what you're wearing

Materials

- Class CDs, Mimi puppet, photocopiable templates: sweater and shirt, paints, string, clothespins, potatoes
- optional: crayons

Main vocabulary

- shirt, sweater, clothespin, clothes line, stamps, string; colors; numbers; cold, hot

Key language

- It's (hot). This is a (blue) (shirt). I like the (green) (shirt). How many (pink) (shirts)? (Two). I have a (blue and green) sweater. Our clothes are (fantastic)!

Teacher's tip: Being positive about one another's work

COOPERATIVE LEARNING

Once the children have finished their drawings, encourage them to look at each other's work on the display. Encourage them to say *It's great. / It's fantastic.* etc. Make sure all the comments are positive and discourage any negativity.

Circle time

Hello song & puppet (CD1 Track 2; see TB p 17 & 21)
Opening routines (see TB p 16)
Recycling activity (see TB p 19)
Lesson aims (see TB p 18)

Prepare for your project.

- Say *Let's do a project. Let's make clothes for hot and cold weather.* Explain that children should work together in groups for this project.
- Show children the shirt and sweater templates. Ask them which clothes are for hot weather, and which for cold weather.
- Tell the children that your favorite colors are (red) and (blue), so you want your (shirt) to be those colors. Demonstrate using a potato stamp and paint to create a bright pattern on your (shirt).
- Demonstrate pinning your shirt on a clothes line.

Table time

COOPERATIVE LEARNING

Student's Book p 34

Make a shirt for hot weather or a sweater for cold weather.

- Say *Look at what we need for our project.* Hold up the objects and elicit the words: *paints, potato stamps, string, clothespins, paper* (the templates).
- Say the words again. Children listen and point to the pictures in their books.
- Give each child either a shirt or a sweater template. Make sure children have paints and potato stamps available, and encourage them to make brightly-colored patterns.
- Children use stamps and paint to make patterns on their shirt or sweater. Ask them what color it is.

Hang your clothes on the correct clothes line. Say.

- When they are ready, show the children two string clothes lines: one for hot weather, and one for cold weather. Children pin their shirt or sweater on the correct clothes line.
- Children take turns asking and answering about the clothes on the line.
- Ask children *Do you like our clothes?* Make the point that everyone helped make the display and that they couldn't have made such a beautiful display on their own.

Alternative version of project

- Children could use crayons to color their shirt or sweater templates, instead of using paints and potato stamps.

Activity Book p 34

Find and glue photos of you wearing clothes for hot weather and clothes for cold weather.

- Children find and bring in photos of themselves wearing clothes for both hot and cold weather. They glue them in the space provided. Alternatively, they can draw pictures of themselves.

Ask and say.

- They take turns asking and answering about what they're wearing.

Closing time

Learning review (see TB p 18)
Closing routines (see TB p 16)
Bye bye song and puppet (CD1 Track 3; see TB p 17 & 21)

Home
Hide and seek

Vocabulary and language

- **Main vocabulary:** bathroom, bedroom, dining room, garage, house, kitchen, living room, yard
- **Key language:** Is Anna in the (yard)? Yes. / No. Where's Sam? In the (yard). Is he/she in the (yard)? Yes. / No.
- **Content language:** box, closet, shelf, recycling bin; books, clothes, paper, toys; I put (paper) in the (recycling bin).
- **Other language:** door, house, street, window; Is Dylan in the (kitchen). Yes, he is. / No, he isn't. My family is (small). I have (one brother). Round and round the (garden). Here's the (window). It's (blue). I have a (red) house. I like the (yellow) (door). How many (windows)? (Four). Our street is (fantastic)!

Unit objectives

- Identify and name rooms and places in a home
- Sing the language song *Where's Sam?*
- Ask and say where people are
- Understand and act out the story *Hide and seek*
- Sing and act out the story song *Hide and seek is lots of fun*
- Sing the values song *Some families are big*
- Recognize the value of families
- Identify and name places to put things away at home
- Say and act out the traditional rhyme *Round and round the garden*
- Review your learning and progress
- Participate in a collaborative project

Story

CD2 Track 19

Picture 1

Narrator: Mimi and Dylan are playing *Hide and Seek* with Mommy and Daddy.
Mimi: One … two … three … four … five … ! Ready or not, here I come!

Picture 2

Narrator: Mimi looks in the yard …
Mimi: I can see you, Mommy!
Mommy: Oh very good, Mimi!
Narrator: Mimi looks in the garage.
Mimi: I can see you, Daddy!
Daddy: Oh good job, Mimi!

Picture 3

Mimi: Now … Where's Dylan?
Mommy: I don't know.
Daddy: Is he in the living room? Let's look and see.
Mimi: Oh yes, he is! Look! Oh no, he isn't. This isn't Dylan. He isn't here.

Picture 4

Mimi: Oh no … Where's Dylan?
Daddy: I don't know.
Mommy: Is he in the kitchen?
Mimi: Oh yes, he is! Look! Oh no, he isn't. This isn't Dylan. He isn't here.

Picture 5

Mimi: Oh … Where's Dylan?
Mommy: I don't know.
Daddy: Is he in the dining room?
Mimi: Oh yes, he is! Look! Oh no, he isn't. This isn't Dylan. He isn't here. I don't want to play.
Mommy: Keep trying. Let's find Dylan.
Mimi: Oh alright.
Daddy: Come on, Mimi. Come with me. Let's look upstairs.

Picture 6

Mommy: Is Dylan in the bedroom?
Mimi: Oh yes, he is! Look! This is Dylan! He's here! And listen! He's asleep! Wake up, Dylan. I can see you!

Songs

Language song

Where's Sam? CD2 Track 17

Where's Sam? (Arms out questioningly)
I don't know. (Shrug)
Is he in the kitchen? Is he in the kitchen? (Mime turning on a faucet)
No, no, no! (Shake a finger)

Where's Sam? (Arms out questioningly)
I don't know. (Shrug)
Is he in the yard? Is he in the yard? (Mime watering plants)
Yes, yes, yes! (Thumbs up)

Where's Anna? (Arms out questioningly)
I don't know. (Shrug)
Is she in the bedroom? Is she in the bedroom? (Mime sleeping)
No, no, no! (Shake a finger)

Where's Anna? (Arms out questioningly)
I don't know. (Shrug)
Is she in the garage? Is she in the garage? (Mime driving)
Yes, yes, yes! (Thumbs up)

Story song

Hide and seek is lots of fun CD2 Track 20

One, two, three, four, five (Count to five on fingers)
Quick, quick, run and hide (Mime running and cover head with arms for "hide")
Ready or not, here I come (Walk in place)
Hide and seek is lots of fun. (Punch fists in the air)

Is Dylan in the living room? (March in place)
Let's look and see! (Shade eyes with one hand)
No, he isn't. Come with me! (Shake a finger and beckon)

Is Dylan in the kitchen? (March in place)
Let's look and see! (Shade eyes with one hand)
No, he isn't. Come with me! (Shake a finger and beckon)

Is Dylan in the dining room? (March in place)
Let's look and see! (Shade eyes with one hand)
No, he isn't. Come with me! (Shake a finger and beckon)

Is Dylan in the bedroom? (March in place)
Let's look and see! (Shade eyes with one hand)
Yes, he is. Listen, he's asleep! (Nod and cup ear)
Wake up, Dylan! I can see you! (Point to your eye)

Values song

Some families are big CD2 Track 23

Some families are big (Open arms out wide)
Some families are small (Bring hands close together)
Families are different (Separate hands)
And that is all. (Shrug)

Mommy, daddy, grandma, grandpa (Point around)
Brother, sister, baby too (Point around)
Whoever's in your family (Point around)
They love and care for you. (Hug yourself and point to the class)

Some families are big (Open arms out wide)
Some families are small (Bring hands close together)
My family is special (Make a heart with your hands)
I love them all. (Hug yourself)

Culture rhyme

Round and round the garden CD2 Track 25

Round and round the garden, (Walk around in a small circle)
Like a teddy bear, (Cross arms and tilt from side to side)
One step, two step, (Take one step, then another step)
And … tickle you there. (Hands on tummy and laugh)

Round and round the kitchen, (Walk around in a small circle)
Like a teddy bear, (Cross arms and tilt from side to side)
One step, two step, (Take one step, then another step)
And … tickle you there. (Hands on tummy and laugh)

Round and round the living room, (Walk around in a small circle)
Like a teddy bear, (Cross arms and tilt from side to side)
One step, two step, (Take one step, then another step)
And … tickle you there. (Hands on tummy and laugh)

Round and round the bedroom, (Walk around in a small circle)
Like a teddy bear, (Cross arms and tilt from side to side)
One step, two step, (Take one step, then another step)
And … tickle you there. (Hands on tummy and laugh)

Home
Hide and seek

Vocabulary Lesson 1

2:14 2:15 hello

Listen, point and repeat. Listen and play. Stick the home stickers. Circle your favorite place at home. Say. Language: bathroom, bedroom, dining room, house, kitchen, living room; blue, green, orange, pink, red, yellow

35

Learning objectives

- Identify and name places at home
- Listen and point to places at home
- Identify what you do at home

Materials

- Class CDs, flashcards, *Ferris Wheel* mat, Mimi puppet

Main vocabulary

- bathroom, bedroom, dining room, house, kitchen, living room; blue, green, orange, pink, red, yellow

Teacher's tip: Using mime to associate activities with rooms

Play a mime game to help associate activities with rooms in the house. First, point to the flashcards in turn, say the rooms and mime an activity for each one (watching TV, sleeping, etc.). Encourage the children to join in. Then, just say the rooms and have the children mime the activities. Finally, mime the activities yourself and have the class say the rooms.

Circle time

Hello song & puppet (CD1 Track 2; see TB p 17 & 21)
Opening routines (see TB p 16)
Lesson aims (see TB p 18)

Introduce *house* and rooms.

- Use the puppet and flashcard to introduce the word *house*. Ask children what rooms there are in a house. As they respond in their shared language, introduce the words in English. Children repeat the words.
- Put the *Ferris Wheel* mat on the floor or board with the home flashcards face down (one on each color). Use puppet to turn over and name. Children repeat the words.

Game: *Say the color!*

- Name the rooms on the Ferris Wheel and children name the color. Then do it in reverse.

Game: *Go to the kitchen!*

- Stick the flashcards at the children's height on different walls around the classroom.
- Ask two to four children to stand up. Say e.g. *Go to the kitchen!* Children respond by walking to the flashcard. Repeat with different pairs or groups of children and all the flashcards.

Table time

Student's Book p 35

Listen, point and repeat.

- Play the audio. The children listen, point to each part of the house as they hear it, and repeat the words.

CD2 Track 14

Mimi: Look, Dylan! House … living room … kitchen … bedroom … bathroom … dining room. Repeat, Dylan!
Dylan: Yes, Mimi. House … living room … kitchen … bedroom … bathroom … dining room.
Mimi: Very good, Dylan. Let's name the parts of the house together!
Both: House … living room … kitchen … bedroom … bathroom … dining room.

Listen and play.

- Use finger in air to pretend to spin wheel. Children spin their fingers, point to the color when they hear it on the audio and say the word.

CD2 Track 15

Mimi: Spin the wheel
One, two, three
Point and name
The parts of the house with me!

Orange … kitchen!
Red … house!
Yellow … bedroom!
Blue … living room!
Pink … bathroom!
Green … dining room!

- Play the game with you and/or individual children naming colors and others saying the places.

Stick the home stickers.

- Children stick the home stickers in the correct places.

Circle your favorite place at home.

- Children circle their favorite place in their home.

Say.

- Children name their favorite place at home.

Activity Book p 35

Match the meerkats to the places.

- Children look at the pictures of the characters and match them to the correct room.

Color the pictures that show what you do at home.

- They color the pictures that show activities that they do at home.

Point and say.

- Children point and name the places.

Closing time

Learning review (see TB p 18)
Closing routines (see TB p 16)
Bye bye song and puppet (CD1 Track 3; see TB p 17 & 21)

Use the **Navio App** to play the vocabulary game, and encourage children to do the same at home.

Lesson 2 Language

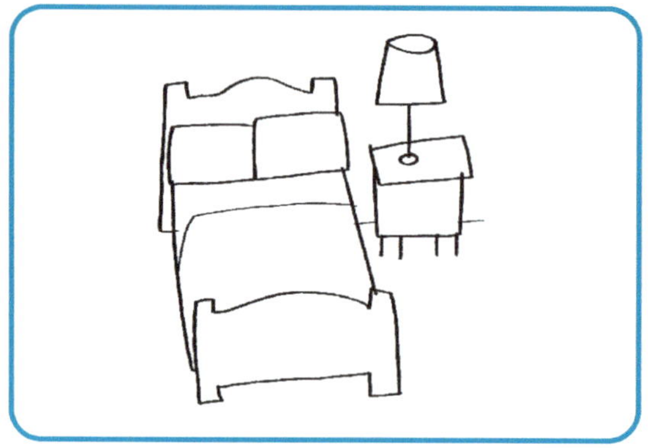

Listen and find the new places. Listen, point and sing *Where's Sam?* Match Sam and Anna to the places. Color. Ask and say. **Language:** bathroom, bedroom, garage, house, kitchen, living room, yard; Is Anna in the (yard)? Yes. / No. Where's Sam? In the (yard).

36

Learning objectives

- Talk about where things are
- Identify and name two new places at home
- Sing the language song *Where's Sam?*
- Ask and say where people are

Materials

- Class CDs, flashcards, *Ferris Wheel* mat, Mimi puppet

Main vocabulary

- bathroom, bedroom, dining room, garage, house, kitchen, living room, yard

Key language

- Is Anna in the (yard)? Yes. / No. Where's Sam? In the (yard).

Teacher's tip: Encouraging non-verbal responses

Children's comprehension level is greater than their level of production at first. Be ready to encourage and accept non-verbal responses to questions, such as nodding, shaking the head and pointing before you expect children to produce verbal answers.

Circle time

Hello song & puppet (CD1 Track 2; see TB p 17 & 21)
Opening routines (see TB p 16)
Recycling activity (six home words from Lesson 1) (see TB p 19)
Lesson aims (see TB p 18)

Introduce the new home vocabulary.

- All eight home flashcards on the floor or board. Children identify the two new places. Use the puppet to point to and say the words in turn. Children repeat in chorus.
- Turn the two new flashcards face down. Mix them up. Point to one and ask *Yard or garage?* Children guess. Repeat several times.
- Say the words in turn. Children respond by pretending to drive a car (garage) or throw a ball (yard). Repeat several times going faster and faster as children gain confidence in responding.

Introduce *Is Anna in the (yard)? Yes. / No.*

- Lay out the flashcards face up on the floor or board. Place the flashcard of Anna overlapping one of the flashcards Ask *Is Anna in the yard? (Yes). Is Anna in the kitchen? (No).* Repeat with the flashcard of Sam.
- Invite children to place the flashcards of Sam and Anna in different places and repeat the procedure.

Game: *Where's Sam?*

- Hide the flashcard of Sam face down under one of the home flashcards.
- Ask *Where's Sam?* Encourage children to guess by pointing to the flashcards and asking questions along with you, e.g. *Is Sam in the garage? Yes. / No.* Repeat with the flashcard of Anna.
- As children gain confidence, encourage them to ask questions individually. The child who guesses each time has the next turn at hiding the flashcard.

Table time

Student's Book p 36

Listen and find the new places.

- Play the audio. Children listen and find the two new places. Play the audio again. The children listen and say the words.

CD2 Track 16

One, two, Which words are new?
Garage! Garage!
Yard! Yard!

Listen, point and sing *Where's Sam?*

CD2 Track 17

- Play the song. Children listen and point to the rooms and places as they hear them in the song.
- Play the song again. Children sing the song and do the actions (see TB p 99).
- Remember that you can use the karaoke version of the song when children are confident.

Match Sam and Anna to the places.

- Play the first verse of the song again. Ask *Is Sam in the kitchen?* Elicit *No.* Play the second verse, and ask *Where's Sam?* Elicit *in the yard.* Demonstrate drawing a line to match Sam to the yard.
- Play the song again, pausing after each verse. Children listen and match Sam and Anna to the places.

Color.

- Children color the places where Sam and Anna are.

Ask and say.

- Encourage children to ask and answer the questions about where Sam and Anna are as in the song.

Activity Book p 36

Draw the boy and girl in different places.

- Ask the children to choose where to put the boy and girl, and draw each one in a different room. Make sure that children understand that there is no correct answer.

Ask and say.

- Ask questions and children respond e.g. *Is he in the bedroom? Yes. / No.*

Closing time

Learning review (see TB p 18)
Closing routines (see TB p 16)
Bye bye song and puppet (CD1 Track 3; see TB p 17 & 21)

Use the **Navio App** to listen to the song, and encourage children to do the same at home.

Lesson 3 Story

2:19

Watch. Listen to the story *Hide and seek*. Circle where Dylan is hiding. Stick the story sticker. Language: bathroom, bedroom, dining room, garage, kitchen, living room, yard; Is Dylan in the (kitchen)? Yes, he is. / No, he isn't.

37

Learning objectives

- Watch, understand and enjoy the story *Hide and seek*
- Make a prediction about the story
- Look and find the places in the story
- Identify where Dylan is hiding

Materials

- Class CDs, printable story cards, flashcards, *Ferris Wheel* mat, Mimi puppet

Main vocabulary

- bathroom, bedroom, dining room, garage, kitchen, living room, yard

Key language

- Is Dylan in the (kitchen)? Yes, he is. / No, he isn't.

Teacher's tip: Using visual clues, mime and voice to help understanding

Children will understand the gist of the story by using contextual clues and visual information to work out meaning. By using mime and pointing to key items in the printable story cards, as well as changing your voice to convey different moods and characters, you can facilitate the process.

Circle time

Hello song & puppet (CD1 Track 2; see TB p 17 & 21)

Opening routines (see TB p 16)

Recycling activity (*Is … in the … ?* and home vocabulary) (see TB p 19)

Lesson aims (see TB p 18)

Introduce the story *Hide and seek*.

- Say *It's story time!* Play the *Story rhyme* (CD1 Track 4; see TB p 17).
- Say *Anna and Sam are listening to a story about the Meerkat family. They're playing "Hide and seek."* Briefly explain the game. Ask *Where's Mommy / Daddy / Dylan?* and encourage children to guess.

Watch or listen to the story.

CD2 Track 19

- Watch the video, play the audio, or read the story using the printable story cards. Pause, repeat words, point to the pictures, ask questions.
- Ask children *Where's Mommy? (In the yard) Where's Daddy? (In the garage) Where's Dylan? (In the bedroom).*
- Repeat the story. Encourage children to join in with the words and phrases in the story.
- Ask *Do you like the story? Do you like "Hide and seek"?*

Look and find.

- Say e.g. *Find the garage!* Children look at the story and point to the picture as fast as they can.
- Repeat with other rooms and places in the story.

Table time

Student's Book p 37

Watch. Listen to the story *Hide and seek*.

- Read or play the story again. Children listen and follow by pointing to the pictures in their books.

Story questions

Picture 1
Who is counting? *(Mimi)*
Who is hiding? *(Dylan/Mommy/Daddy)*

Picture 2
Where is Daddy hiding? *(The garage)*
Where is Mommy hiding? *(The yard)*

Picture 3
Where does Mimi look for Dylan? *(The living room)*
Is Dylan in the living room? *(No)*

Picture 4
Where does Mimi look for Dylan? *(The kitchen)*
Is Dylan in the kitchen? *(No)*

Picture 5
Where does Mimi look for Dylan? *(The dining room)*
Is Dylan in the dining room? *(No)*

Picture 6
Where is Dylan? *(In the bedroom)*
Is Dylan asleep? *(Yes)*

Circle where Dylan is hiding.

- Children find the room where Dylan is hiding (bedroom) and circle it.

Stick the story sticker.

- Children stick on the story sticker.
- Ask *Is Dylan good at hiding?* and children respond.

Activity Book p 37

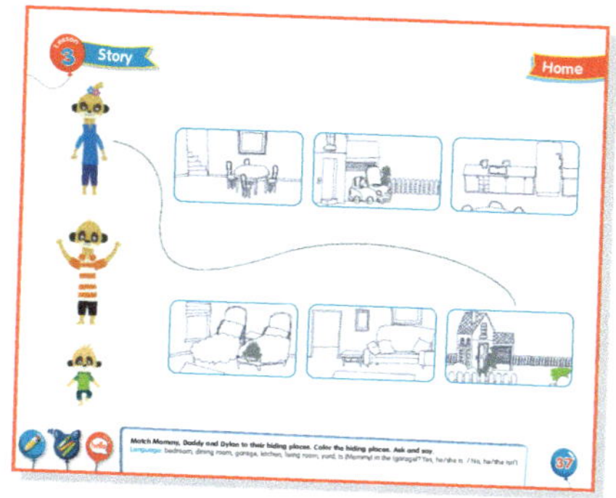

Match Mommy, Daddy and Dylan to their hiding place. Color the hiding places.

- Children match the characters to their hiding places, then color the places.

Ask and say.

- They ask and answer about where the characters are.

Closing time

Learning review (see TB p 18)

Closing routines (see TB p 16)

Bye bye song and puppet (CD1 Track 3; see TB p 17 & 21)

Use the **Navio App** to watch the video, and encourage children to do the same at home.

Lesson 4 Story Song

Home

1 2 3 4

2:20

hello

Watch. Listen, point and sing *Hide and seek is lots of fun*. Trace the numbers. Match to order the pictures. Ask and say. Language: bedroom, dining room, kitchen, living room; numbers 1–4; Is Dylan in the (kitchen)? Yes, he is. / No, he isn't. Where's Dylan? In the (bedroom).

38

Learning objectives

- Watch, sing and act out the story song *Hide and seek is lots of fun*
- Listen to the story again and identify the places
- Identify the order of places in the song
- Ask and say where people are

Materials

- Class CDs, printable story cards, flashcards, *Ferris Wheel* mat, Mimi puppet

Main vocabulary

- bedroom, dining room, kitchen, living room; numbers 1–4

Key language

- Is Dylan in the (kitchen)? Yes, he is. / No, he isn't. Where's Dylan? In the (bedroom).

Teacher's tip: Pre-teaching actions for the story song

Before introducing the story song, play an action game to teach the actions needed for the song, e.g. *Quick, quick, run and hide. Look and see. Come with me.* Introduce the actions in turn, then say them at random, varying the order and increasing the pace, and children respond.

Circle time

Hello song & puppet (CD1 Track 2; see TB p 17 & 21)
Opening routines (see TB p 16)
Recycling activity (home vocabulary) (see TB p 19)
Lesson aims (see TB p 18)

Retell the story *Hide and seek.*

- Play the audio, video or read the story using the printable story cards.
- Demonstrate that children should clap their hands once every time they hear a home word in the story.

Game: *Guess where!*

- Give home flashcards face down to individual children without others seeing. Either whisper or children have a quick look at the flashcard.
- Say e.g. *Let's guess where Alex is* naming one of the children with a flashcard. Children take turns asking you questions and guessing the room or place, e.g. *Is Alex in the yard? Yes, he/she is. / No, he/she isn't.*

***Hide and seek is lots of fun* song**

CD2 Track 20

- Play the video or audio of the story song. Children watch/listen and mime walking in place, having a look inside, and beckoning others to come.
- Play the song again. Children join in singing the song and doing the actions (see TB p 99).

Game: *Hide and seek!*

- Stick the flashcards of the places in the song at children's height on the classroom walls.
- Explain that children are going to play *Hide and seek* with the Mimi puppet.
- Divide the class into two groups. Ask one group to close their eyes or cover their eyes with their hands. Involve the other group in a whisper as you "hide" the Mimi puppet by one of the flashcards.
- Children in the first group open their eyes and ask questions to find Mimi, e.g. *Is Mimi in the bedroom? No, she isn't. / Yes, she is.*
- Groups reverse roles and repeat.

Table time

Student's Book p 38

Watch. Listen, point and sing *Hide and seek is lots of fun.*

CD2 Track 20

- Play the audio of the song again. Children listen, sing and point to the places on the page.
- Remember that you can use the karaoke version of the song when children are confident.

Trace the numbers. Match to order the pictures.

- Children trace the numbers 1–4. Play the audio of the song again, pausing after each verse. Children listen and match the numbers to the rooms to show the order Mimi looks in the rooms in the song (1 = living room, 2 = kitchen, 3 = dining room, 4 = bedroom).

Ask and say.

- Ask children *Is Dylan in the (living room)?* Encourage children to ask and answer themselves.

Activity Book p 38

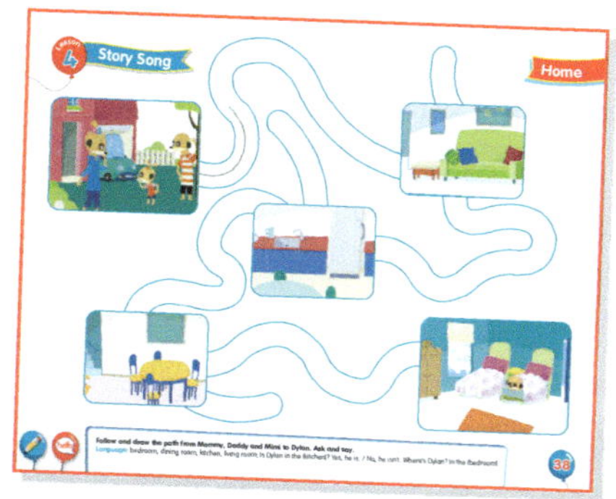

Follow and draw the path from Mommy, Daddy and Mimi to Dylan.

- Children draw the path through the maze.

Ask and say.

- They ask and say where Dylan is.

Closing time

Learning review (see TB p 18)
Closing routines (see TB p 16)
Bye bye song and puppet (CD1 Track 3; see TB p 17 & 21)

Use the **Navio App** to watch the video, and encourage children to do the same at home.

Lesson 5 Speaking

Life skills

2:22

Watch. Listen and point. Check (✓) where Kitty and Bruno are. Draw Kitty and Bruno in your favorite place in your house. Ask and say. **Language:** garage, house, yard; cat, dog; Is he/she in the (house)? Yes, he/she is. / No, he/she isn't; He's/She's in the (house). He/She isn't in the (garage).

39

Learning objectives
- Ask and answer questions about where people/things are
- Watch, understand and enjoy a video
- Identify people and places in the video

Materials
- Class CDs, flashcards, *Ferris Wheel* mat, Mimi puppet

Main vocabulary
- garage, house, yard; cat, dog

Key language
- Is he/she in the (house)? Yes, he/she is. / No, he/she isn't. He's/She's in the (house). He/She isn't in the (garage).

Teacher's tip: Caring for pets Life skills

Ask the children if they have a dog or a cat at home. Use the opportunity to introduce the life skill of caring for pets. Tell children that pets are our friends. Use any toy animals in the classroom to act out stroking and playing with our pets.

Circle time

Hello song & puppet (CD1 Track 2; see TB p 17 & 21)
Opening routines (see TB p 16)
Recycling activity (story song) (CD2 Track 20; see TB p 19)
Lesson aims (see TB p 18)

Name two places in your house.
- Lay out the flashcards face up on the floor or board.
- Children take turns naming two places in their house.

Watch the video.
- Explain that Sam and Anna are visiting Uncle Dan. Uncle Dan helps Sam and Anna look for Anna's cat (Kitty) and Sam's dog (Bruno).
- Ask *Where's Kitty / Bruno?* and encourage children to guess.
- Play the video of Anna and Sam visiting Uncle Dan.
- Ask the questions again and children respond.
- Watch again. Pause and children repeat the questions and answers as they look for Kitty and Bruno.
- Ask *Who's your favorite – Kitty or Bruno?* and listen to children's response.

Table time

Student's Book p 39 Life skills

Watch. Listen and point.
- Children point to Anna, Sam and Uncle Dan in the photo. Play the audio or video. Children point to the places as they hear them in the dialogue.

Check where Kitty and Bruno are.
- Play the audio again. Pause it after each question and answer. Children check the boxes where Kitty and Bruno are. Play the audio again to check children have put the check marks correctly.

CD2 Track 22

Uncle Dan:	Are you OK, Anna?
Anna:	No Uncle Dan. I can't find Kitty!
Uncle Dan:	Oh no! Let's find her. Is Kitty in the garage?
Sam:	No, she isn't.
Uncle Dan:	You're right! She isn't in the garage. Is Kitty in the house?
Uncle Dan:	Oh, Kitty's a toy!
Anna:	Ha, ha. Yes, she is. She's in the house!
Uncle Dan:	Very good!
Sam:	And where's my toy dog, Bruno?
Uncle Dan:	Is Bruno in the house?
Anna:	No, he isn't.
Uncle Dan:	You're right! He isn't in the house. Is Bruno in the yard?
Sam:	No, he isn't!
Uncle Dan:	Wait a minute!
Uncle Dan:	Bruno is in the house, look! Yay!

Draw Kitty and Bruno in your favorite place in your house. Ask and say.
- The children use their imagination to draw Kitty and Bruno in their favorite place in their own house.
- Remind children of the question *Is (Kitty) in the (garage)?* Children ask and answer questions about where Kitty and Bruno are.

Activity Book p 39

Find and circle Bruno the dog and Kitty the cat.
- Children find and circle Bruno and Kitty in the pictures.

Say.
- Children take turns saying where Bruno and Kitty are.

Closing time

Learning review (see TB p 18)
Closing routines (see TB p 16)
Bye bye song & puppet (CD1 Track 3; see TB p 17 & 21)

Use the **Navio App** to watch the video, and encourage children to do the same at home.

Lesson 6

Values Families are different

Home

2:23

hello

Listen, point and sing *Some families are big*. Name the family members in the pictures. Draw a picture of you and your family. Say. Language: family, mommy, daddy, brother, sister, baby, grandma, grandpa; big, small; My family is (small). I have (one brother).

SOCIAL AND EMOTIONAL LEARNING

40

Learning objectives

- Understand that families are different
- Act out the story
- Sing the values song *Some families are big*
- Talk about your family
- Name family members

Materials

- Class CDs, flashcards, *Ferris Wheel* mat, Mimi puppet

Main vocabulary

- family, mommy, daddy, brother, sister, baby, grandma, grandpa; big, small

Key language

- My family is (small). I have (one brother).

Teacher's tip: Making a family photo display

Ask the children to bring in a family photo. Encourage them to point to and name their family members. Make a display with all the photos and stick it in a prominent place. Make the point that all families are different, unique and special.

Circle time

Hello song & puppet (CD1 Track 2; see TB p 17 & 21)
Opening routines (see TB p 16)
Recycling activity *(Is he/she in the …? Yes, he/she is. / No, he/she isn't.)* (see TB p 19)
Lesson aims (see TB p 18)

Watch the *Hide and seek* story video.

- Play the story video.
- Take the part of the narrator yourself. Encourage children to join in acting out the story in three groups (Mimi, Mommy, Daddy).
- Ask e.g. *Does Mimi get fed up in the game?* (Use mime to convey meaning) *(Yes.) Who encourages Mimi to continue the game? (Mommy, Daddy) Is it right (fair) to continue the game?*
- Ask e.g. *Is Mimi's family important? Is your family important? Why?* Listen to the children's response.

***Some families are big* song**

CD2 Track 23

- Elicit or remind children of possible members of the family: *mommy, daddy, brother, sister, baby, grandma, grandpa.*
- Ask *How many family words can you hear in the song?* Play the audio. Children listen. Check the answer and children say the words.
- Play the audio again. Children join in singing the song and doing the actions (see TB p 99).
- Make the point that all families are different, equal and special. It doesn't matter if they are big or small or which family members they have.

Table time

Student's Book p 40

Listen, point and sing *Some families are big.*

CD2 Track 23

- Focus children on the pictures. Play the song. Children listen, point to the family members as they hear them, and sing.

Name the family members in the pictures.

- Point to each family member in each of the pictures. Elicit the word.

Draw a picture of you and your family. Say.

- Children draw a picture of themselves with their family.
- Children show you and each other their pictures and say *My family is (small). I have (one sister).*

Activity Book p 40

Match the pictures with the same family members.

- Children match the pictures that show the same family members.

Name the family members.

- They point and name each family member.

Point and say.

- Children point to each picture and say, e.g. *This family is (big). This family is (small).*

Closing time

Learning review (see TB p 18)
Closing routines (see TB p 16)
Bye bye song and puppet (CD1 Track 3; see TB p 17 & 21)

Use the **Navio App** to listen to the song, and encourage children to do the same at home.

Lesson 7 Content

Home

2:24

hello

Listen and point. Match the things to the places. Circle the things you put away at home. Say. **Language:** box, closet, shelf, recycling bin; books, clothes, paper, toys; I put (paper) in the (recycling bin).

41

Learning objectives

- Identify and name places to put things away at home
- Listen and identify places to put things away
- Talk about things you put away

Materials

- Class CDs, printable content flashcards, *Ferris Wheel* mat, Mimi puppet

Main vocabulary

- box, closet, shelf, recycling bin; books, clothes, paper, toys

Key language

- I put (paper) in the (recycling bin).

Teacher's tip: Putting things away in the classroom

Point out to the children the importance of helping to put things away in the classroom as well as at home. Introduce relevant language and actions e.g. *I put books on the shelf. I put crayons in the box.* Encourage children to say what they do whenever they help put things away in class from now on.

Circle time

Hello song & puppet (CD1 Track 2; see TB p 17 & 21)
Opening routines (see TB p 16)
Recycling activity (see TB p 19)
Lesson aims (see TB p 18)

Introduce content vocabulary.

- Say *Let's learn about where we put things away!*
- Use the puppet and the printable flashcards to introduce the new words *(box, closet, shelf, recycling bin).* Children repeat the words.
- Ask e.g. *Where do you put things away?* and listen to the children's response.

Game: *Go to the closet!*

- Stick the flashcards on different walls around the classroom at the children's height.
- Say e.g. *closet!* Walk towards the closet and mime putting something inside a closet.
- Give similar instructions to pairs or groups of children in turn.

Mime and say.

- Lay out the flashcards.
- Mime opening a closet. Children name the place: *closet.*
- Repeat with the other places. Mime reaching up to a shelf, opening a box, and dropping paper into a recycling bin and children name the places in the same way.
- Reverse the procedure. Point to the places in turn and children say the places and do the mimes.

Table time

Student's Book p 41

Listen and point.

- Say *Sam and Anna are at home. They're putting things away.* Play the audio. Children point to the places as they hear them.

CD2 Track 24

Anna: I put toys in the box.
Sam: I put clothes in the closet.
Anna: I put paper in the recycling bin.
Sam: I put books on the shelf.

Match the things to the places.

- Play the audio again, stopping after the first line. Elicit what things Anna talks about (*toys*) and where she puts them (*in the box*). Demonstrate drawing a line matching the toys to the box.
- Repeat with the other things and places.

Circle the things you put away at home. Say.

- Children circle the things they put at home and say, e.g. *I put toys in the box.*

Activity Book p 41

Draw and color the things in the correct places.

- Children draw and color the items at the top of the page in the correct picture below.

Say.

- They say where they put each item, e.g. *I put the book on the shelf.*

Closing time

Learning review (see TB p 18)
Closing routines (see TB p 16)
Bye bye song and puppet (CD1 Track 3; see TB p 17 & 21)

Use the **Navio App** to play the vocabulary and language games, and encourage children to do the same at home.

Lesson 8

Culture

Watch. Listen, point and say *Round and round the garden*. Trace the numbers. Say the places. Trace and color your favorite teddy bear. **Language:** teddy bear; bedroom, garden, kitchen, living room; Round and round the (garden).

Learning objectives

- Watch, say and act out the traditional rhyme *Round and round the garden*
- Play an action game
- Identify and say places in a home

Materials

- Class CDs, flashcards, *Ferris Wheel* mat, Mimi puppet

Main vocabulary

- teddy bear; bedroom, garden, kitchen, living room, yard

Key language

- Round and round the (garden).

Teacher's tip: Acting out the rhyme as a finger rhyme

Round and round the garden is a traditional finger rhyme. Show the children the finger actions as you say the rhyme by running a finger around your palm, jumping your fingers up your arm, and tickling under your arm. You could also follow the actions suggested on page 99.

Circle time

Hello song & puppet (CD1 Track 2; see TB p 17 & 21)
Opening routines (see TB p 16)
Recycling activity (see TB p 19)
Lesson aims (see TB p 18)

Game: *Round and round the bedroom!*

- Place the home flashcards on the floor or the board, widely spaced apart.
- Say e.g. *Round and round the bedroom! Go to the bedroom flashcard and walk around it in a circle/draw a circle around it.*
- Give similar instructions to groups of children in turn.

***Round and round the garden* rhyme**

CD2 Track 25

- Ask *How many places can you hear in the rhyme? What are they?*
- Play the audio. Children listen and count the places. Check the answers (four: *garden, living room, kitchen, bedroom*).
- Say *Stand up. Let's learn the rhyme "Round and round the garden."*
- Pre-teach actions for the rhyme (see TB p 99).
- Play the audio. Children listen and do the actions for the rhyme with you.
- Repeat. Children join in saying and doing the actions for the rhyme.

Watch the *Round and round the garden* rhyme video.

- Children watch the video and join in saying the rhyme and doing the actions with Anna and Sam.

Table time

Student's Book p 42

Watch. Listen, point and say *Round and round the garden.*

CD2 Track 25

- Play the audio of the rhyme. Children listen, say the rhyme and point to the pictures of the teddy bear.

Trace the numbers. Say the places.

- Children trace the numbers, and point to and name each place.

Trace and color your favorite teddy bear.

- Children trace and color their favorite teddy bear.

Activity Book p 42

Match the teddy bear to the places in the song. Color the places in the song.

- Children match the bear to the four places mentioned in the song and then color the places.

Point and say.

- They point to each place and say the rhyme.

Closing time

Learning review (see TB p 18)
Closing routines (see TB p 16)
Bye bye song and puppet (CD1 Track 3; see TB p 17 & 21)

Use the **Navio App** to watch the video, and encourage children to do the same at home.

I can ...

Vocabulary

Story

Speaking

Content

Color the places you know. Listen, point and say. Ask and say. Complete the faces to show what you can do. **Language:** bathroom, bedroom, dining room, garage, house, kitchen, living room, yard; Where's (Mimi)? He's/She's in the (bedroom). He/She isn't in the (yard).

43

Learning objectives

- Review what you have learned in this unit
- Complete a self-evaluation
- Ask and say where people are

Materials

- Class CDs, flashcards, *Ferris Wheel* mat, Mimi puppet

Main vocabulary

- bathroom, bedroom, dining room, garage, house, kitchen, living room, yard

Key language

- Where's Mimi? He's/She's in the (bedroom). He/She isn't in the (yard).

Teacher's tip: Reflecting on learning

Use the children's self-evaluations to encourage them to reflect on how they learn. Ask questions in the children's shared language e.g. *What activities helped you remember the names of the rooms? How did the video help you understand the story?* Be ready to remind children of activities they have done and encourage them to look back over the unit in their books. Make it clear that there are no correct answers.

Circle time

Hello song & puppet (CD1 Track 2; see TB p 17 & 21)
Opening routines (see TB p 16)
Recycling activity (see TB p 19)
Lesson aims (see TB p 18)

Home flashcard games

- Choose one or two flashcard games with the *Ferris Wheel* mat and/or the puppet to review main vocabulary (see TB p 20 & 21).

Sing *Where's Sam?*

CD2 Track 17

- Hold up the flashcards of Sam and Anna. Lay out the home flashcards. Play the audio. Children sing, point to the flashcards and do the actions (see TB p 99).

Game: *Where's Dylan?*

- Put all the home flashcards on the board and place the flashcards of Anna and Sam nearby.
- Demonstrate secretly choosing a place for Sam or Anna to hide. Choose a volunteer to ask you questions, e.g. *Is he in the bedroom?* Once the child has guessed the correct place, change roles, indicating that the child should secretly choose a new place for Dylan to hide.
- Put the children in pairs and have them take turns asking and answering.

Watch the story video.

- Children watch the story video. Ask e.g. *Is Dylan in the kitchen?*

Table time

Student's Book p 43

Color the places you know.

- Explain and demonstrate the activity.

Listen, point and say.

- Play the audio. Children listen, point to the places and say the words.

CD2 Track 26

Mimi: I'm the teacher! Can you remember the parts of the house, Dylan?
Dylan: Yes, I can. House.
Mimi: House.
Dylan: Living room.
Mimi: Living room.
Dylan: Kitchen.
Mimi: Kitchen.
Dylan: Bedroom.
Mimi: Bedroom.
Dylan: Bathroom.
Mimi: Bathroom.
Dylan: Dining room.
Mimi: Dining room.
Dylan: Yard.
Mimi: Yard.
Dylan: Garage.
Mimi: Garage. Great job, Dylan! Very good!

Ask and say.

- Ask children questions about where Mimi and Dylan are. Have them ask you or the puppet similar questions.

Complete the faces to show what you can do.

- Explain the four pictures: *I can name places in a home; I can understand the story; I can ask and say where people are; I can say where I put things away.*
- Remind them they should complete each face with a smile or frown, depending on how well they think they have done.

Activity Book p 43

Draw Mimi, Dylan, Mommy and Daddy in four different places. Ask and say.

- Children draw the four characters in different places.
- They ask and say where each character is.

Think and circle the number to show your progress.

- Children circle the number.

Closing time

Learning review (see TB p 18)
Closing routines (see TB p 16)
Bye bye song and puppet (CD1 Track 3; see TB p 17 & 21)

Use the **Navio App** to review what children have learned in this unit, and encourage them to do the same at home.

Project

COOPERATIVE LEARNING

1

2

3

Make a house. Put your houses together to make a street. Say. Language: door, house, street, window; carton; colors; numbers; big, small; This is my (house). It's big/small. It's (red). Here's the (window). It's (blue). I have a (red) (house). I like the (yellow) (door). How many (windows)? (Four). Our street is (fantastic)!

44

Learning objectives

- Work together to do a collaborative project
- Talk about places in a home
- Make a house
- Draw and talk about your ideal bedroom

Materials

- Class CDs, Mimi puppet, photocopiable template: house, crayons, glue, drink cartons

Main vocabulary

- door, house, street, window; carton; colors; numbers; big, small

Key language

- This is my (house). It's big/small. It's (red). Here's the (window). It's (blue). I have a (red) (house). I like the (yellow) (door). How many (windows)? (Four). Our street is (fantastic)!

Teacher's tip: Doing activities based on the completed project

Make the most of the children's completed project by playing a variety of games based on their work e.g. *Find the house with the blue door! How many houses are red? Touch the house with the orange window!* Or play *Where's Mimi?* by drawing a small picture of Mimi on a piece of paper, getting children to close or cover their eyes, hiding the picture of Mimi behind one of the houses and encouraging the children to guess where she is.

Circle time

Hello song & puppet (CD1 Track 2; see TB p 17 & 21)
Opening routines (see TB p 16)
Recycling activity (see TB p 19)
Lesson aims (see TB p 18)

Prepare for your project.

- Say *Let's do a project! Let's make a street of houses!* Show children the Student's Book photo to clarify what you mean.
- Show children the example house you have made using the template and drinks carton (see Student's Book). Say e.g. *This is my house! It's (blue). Here are the (windows). They're (yellow). Here is the (door). It's (red).*
- Explain that everyone is going to individually make a house and then you will put all the houses together to make a street.
- Show children the templates. Demonstrate and explain that to make the house children first draw windows and doors on the house. They then color the house, windows and doors. Finally, they glue their house to a drinks carton.

Table time

Student's Book p 44

Make a house.

- Say *We're going to make a street. Look at what we need for our project.* Hold up the objects and elicit the words: *crayons, carton, glue, paper* (the templates).
- Say the words again. Children listen and point to the pictures in their books.
- Make sure children have crayons and glue available. Children color their houses and glue them to the cartons. Be ready to help as necessary.
- Children show and talk about their completed houses, e.g. *This is my house. / It's big. / It's red. / This is the window / door.*

Put your houses together to make a street. Say.

- Children come up individually and place their house in a row to make a "street" of houses. Ask questions and encourage children to talk about the houses as they do this, e.g. *What color is this house? It's blue. / How many houses in our street now? Four.*
- Ask children *Do you like our street of houses?* Make the point that everyone helped make the street and that they couldn't have made such a beautiful street of houses on their own.

Alternative version of project

- Instead of building a 3D street with drink cartons, children could glue their house templates on a large piece of paper to make a mural.

Activity Book p 44

Trace the rectangles. Decorate and paint your ideal bedroom.

- Children trace the rectangles. They paint and decorate the bedroom however they wish.

Say.

- They take turns talking about their ideal bedroom.

Closing time

Learning review (see TB p 18)
Closing routines (see TB p 16)
Bye bye song and puppet (CD1 Track 3; see TB p 17 & 21)

Food
I like ice cream!

Vocabulary and language

- **Main vocabulary:** apples, bananas, bread, carrots, cereal, eggs, ice cream, milk
- **Key language:** I like (carrots). I don't like (cereal). How about you?
- **Content language:** pears, peas, potatoes, tomatoes; I like (potatoes). I don't like (tomatoes). Do you like (carrots)? Yes, I do. / No, I don't.
- **Other language:** brother, cart, cold, daddy, friend, hot, modeling clay, mommy, plate, pudding, teacher; Put the (eggs) in the (cart). I help my (mommy). I have (bananas). How many (apples)? I can see (flour). My (ice cream) is (pink). Our food is (fantastic)!

Unit objectives

- Identify and name food items
- Sing the language song *Yummy, yummy*
- Say food you like and don't like
- Understand and act out the story *I like ice cream!*
- Sing and act out the story song *The shopping song*
- Sing the values song *Little helper*
- Recognize the value of helping
- Identify and name food that grows in the garden
- Sing and act out the traditional song *Peas pudding hot*
- Review your learning and progress
- Participate in a collaborative project

Story

CD2 Track 32

Picture 1

Narrator: Dylan, Mimi and Daddy are in the kitchen.
Daddy: Let's make a shopping list. Eggs, apples, carrots, cereal, bananas, milk.
Dylan: Eggs, apples, carrots, cereal, bananas, milk. Eggs, apples, carrots, cereal, bananas, milk.
Mimi: Oh, Dylan. You are funny!
Daddy: Ssh, Dylan. Come on. Let's go.
Dylan: Oh no. I don't like shopping.

Picture 2

Daddy: Oh no, where's the shopping list?
Dylan: I can help!
Mimi: And I can help too!

Picture 3

Dylan: Eggs!
Daddy: Yes! Very good, Dylan. Put the eggs in the cart.
Mimi: Eggs, apples!
Daddy: Yes! Very good, Mimi. Put the apples in the cart.
Dylan: And ice cream??
Daddy: No, Dylan. Ice cream isn't on the list!
Dylan: Ahhh. I like ice cream!

Picture 4

Dylan: Eggs, apples, carrots!
Daddy: Yes! Very good, Dylan. Put the carrots in the cart.
Mimi: Eggs, apples, carrots, cereal!
Daddy: Yes! Very good, Mimi. Put the cereal in the cart.
Dylan: And ice cream??
Daddy: No, Dylan. Ice cream isn't on the list!
Dylan: Ahhh. I like ice cream!

Picture 5

Dylan: Eggs, apples, carrots, cereal, bananas!
Daddy: Yes! Very good, Dylan. Put the bananas in the cart.
Mimi: Eggs, apples, carrots, cereal, bananas, milk!
Daddy: Yes! Very good, Mimi. Put the milk in the cart.
Dylan: And ice cream??
Daddy: No, Dylan. Ice cream isn't on the list!
Dylan: Ahhh. I like ice cream!

Picture 6

Daddy: Oh look. Here's the shopping list. Silly me! Eggs, apples, carrots, cereal, bananas, milk.
Dylan: Eggs, apples, carrots, cereal, bananas, milk … and ice cream??
Daddy: No, Dylan. Ice cream isn't … er … well, OK, yes! You and Mimi are my little helpers! Let's have a treat! Ice cream is on the shopping list today!
Mimi: Oh, thank you, Daddy. I like ice cream!
Dylan: Thank you, Daddy! I like ice cream too! And I like shopping! Hurray!

Songs

Language song

Yummy, yummy CD2 Track 30

Yummy, yummy! Yucky, yucky! (Rub tummy, then thumbs down)
Yummy, yummy! Yucky, yucky! (Rub tummy, then thumbs down)
I like carrots, (Mime nibbling a carrot)
I like ice cream, (Mime licking an ice cream)
I like apples too. (Mime eating an apple)
I don't like cereal. (Fold arms and shake your head)
How about you? (Arms wide questioningly and point)
(Chorus)
I like bananas, (Mime peeling a banana)
I like eggs, (Mime cracking open an egg)
I like milk too. (Mime drinking milk)
I don't like bread. (Fold arms and shake your head)
How about you? (Arms wide questioningly and point)
(Chorus)

Story song

The shopping song CD2 Track 33

Put the eggs in the cart. Hey, hey. (Mime putting things in the cart)
Put the apples in the cart. (Mime putting things in the cart)
Hurray. (Throw arms up in the air)
And ice cream? Ice cream? (Arms out questioningly)
No ice cream today! (Shake a finger)
Ohhh (Sad face)
Put the carrots in the cart. Hey, hey. (Mime putting things in the cart)
Put the cereal in the cart. (Mime putting things in the cart)
Hurray. (Throw arms up in the air)
And ice cream? Ice cream? (Arms out questioningly)
No ice cream today! (Shake a finger)
Ohhh (Sad face)
Put the bananas in the cart. Hey, hey. (Mime putting things in the cart)
Put the milk in the cart. (Mime putting things in the cart)
Hurray. (Throw arms up in the air)
And ice cream? Ice cream? (Arms out questioningly)
Yes, ice cream today! (Nod)
Yay!! (Throw arms up in the air)

Values song

Little helper CD2 Track 36

I help my mommy (Count off thumb)
I help my daddy (Count off index finger)
I help my brother too (Count off middle finger)
I help my friend (Count off ring finger)
I help my teacher (Count off little finger)
I help you! (Point to partner)

I help my mommy (Count off thumb)
I help my daddy (Count off index finger)
I help my brother too (Count off middle finger)
I help my friend (Count off ring finger)
I help my teacher (Count off little finger)
I help you! (Point to partner)

Culture song

Peas pudding hot CD2 Track 38

Peas pudding hot, (Fan your face)
Peas pudding cold, (Hug yourself and shiver)
Peas pudding on a plate, (Make a plate with your hands)
Hot or cold! (Fan your face and then hug and shiver)

Peas pudding hot, (Fan your face)
Peas pudding cold, (Hug yourself and shiver)
Peas pudding on a plate, (Make a plate with your hands)
Hot or cold! (Fan your face and then hug and shiver)

Peas pudding hot, (Fan your face)
Peas pudding cold, (Hug yourself and shiver)
Peas pudding on a plate, (Make a plate with your hands)
Hot or cold! (Fan your face and then hug and shiver)

Food

I like ice cream!

Vocabulary Lesson 1

2:27 hello 2:28

Listen, point and repeat. Listen and play. Stick the food stickers. Circle the food you like. Say. **Language:** apples, bread, cereal, eggs, ice cream, milk; blue, green, orange, pink, red, yellow

Food

Lesson 1 Vocabulary

Learning objectives

- Identify and name food
- Listen and point to food
- Identify food you like

Materials

- Class CDs, flashcards, *Ferris Wheel* mat, Mimi puppet

Main vocabulary

- apples, bread, cereal, eggs, ice cream, milk; blue, green, orange, pink, red, yellow

Teacher's tip: Associating food and colors

To reinforce the new vocabulary and associate each item with its color, play a guessing game. Place the food flashcards on the floor or the board and describe the color of one, e.g. *They're green.* (*Apples.*) The child that guesses correctly then says the color of one of the other items.

Circle time

Hello song & puppet (CD1 Track 2; see TB p 17 & 21)
Opening routines (see TB p 16)
Lesson aims (see TB p 18)

Introduce food vocabulary

- *Ferris Wheel* mat on the floor or the board with food flashcards face down (one on each color). Use puppet to turn over and name. Children repeat the words.

Game: ***Find the apples!***

- Name the food and one or two children find and touch the correct flashcards as fast as they can.

Game: ***Say the color!***

- Name the food and children name the color. Then do it in reverse.

Table time

Student's Book p 45

Listen, point and repeat.

- Play the audio. The children listen, point to each food as they hear it and repeat the words.

CD2 Track 27

Mimi: Look, Dylan! Cereal … milk … eggs … bread … apples … ice cream. Repeat, Dylan!
Dylan: Yes, Mimi. Cereal … milk … eggs … bread … apples … ice cream.
Mimi: Very good, Dylan. Let's name the food together!
Both: Cereal … milk … eggs … bread … apples … ice cream.

Listen and play.

- Use finger in air to pretend to spin wheel. Children spin their fingers, point to the color when they hear it on the audio and say the word.

CD2 Track 28

Mimi: Spin the wheel
One, two, three
Point and name
The food with me!
Mimi: Orange … eggs!
Dylan: Red … cereal!
Mimi: Pink … apples!
Dylan: Green … ice cream!
Mimi: Blue … milk!
Dylan: Yellow … bread!

- Play the game with you and/or individual children naming colors and others responding with the words.

Stick the food stickers.

- Children stick the food stickers in the correct places.

Circle the food you like.

- Children circle the food they like.

Say.

- Children name the food they like.

Activity Book p 45

Look, find and match.

- Children find and match the food pictures.

Trace and color.

- They trace and color the food in the main picture.

Point and say.

- Children point and name the food.

Closing time

Learning review (see TB p 18)
Closing routines (see TB p 16)
Bye bye song and puppet (CD1 Track 3; see TB p 17 & 21)

Use the **Navio App** to play the vocabulary game, and encourage children to do the same at home.

Lesson 2 Language

2:29 2:30 hello

Listen and find the new food. Listen, point and sing *Yummy, yummy.* Match the food to Sam and Anna. Say what you like and don't like. **Language:** apples, bananas, bread, carrots, cereal, eggs, ice cream, milk; I like (carrots). I don't like (cereal). How about you?

46

Learning objectives

- Talk about food
- Identify and name two new food items
- Sing the language song *Yummy, yummy*
- Ask and say what food you like and don't like

Materials

- Class CDs, flashcards, *Ferris Wheel* mat, Mimi puppet

Main vocabulary

- apples, bananas, bread, carrots, cereal, eggs, ice cream, milk

Key language

- I like (carrots). I don't like (cereal). How about you?

Teacher's tip: Using realia

If possible, bring in real or toy food items to the class. Put them in a shopping bag and take them out one by one, saying *Yummy! I like (carrots)* or *Yucky! I don't like (bananas).* Invite individual children to take turns doing the same.

Circle time

Hello song & puppet (CD1 Track 2; see TB p 17 & 21)

Opening routines (see TB p 16)

Recycling activity (six food words from Lesson 1) (see TB p 19)

Lesson aims (see TB p 18)

Introduce the new food words.

- All eight food flashcards on the floor or the board.
- Children identify the two new words.
- Use the puppet to point to and say the words in turn. Children repeat in chorus.
- Turn the two new flashcards face down. Mix them up. Point to one and ask *Carrots or bananas?* Children guess. Repeat several times.

Introduce *I like … / I don't like …*

- Children name all the food flashcards.
- Have ready the flashcards with smiley and sad faces. Point and say, e.g. *Yummy! I like bananas. / Yucky! I don't like carrots.* Hold up the faces and check the concept is clear.
- Use the puppet to encourage children to say the *Yummy!/Yucky!* sentences about different foods.

Game: ***Yummy or yucky?***

- Stick the yummy and yucky faces on either side of the classroom.
- Say e.g. *Eggs!* Children go to the side of the room that reflects their opinion. They then say *I like / don't like (eggs)* in chorus with their group.

Table time

Student's Book p 46

Listen and find the new food.

- Play the audio. Children listen and find the two new words. Play the audio again. The children listen and say the words.

  CD2 Track 29

  One, two,
  Which words are new?
  Bananas! Bananas!
  Carrots! Carrots!

Listen, point and sing *Yummy, yummy*.

CD2 Track 30

- Play the song. The children listen and point to each food as they hear it.
- Play the song again. Children sing the song and do the actions (see TB p 121).
- Remember that you can use the karaoke version of the song when children are confident.

Match the food to Sam and Anna.

- Play audio of song. Pause after each line. Children listen and practice matching the pictures of food to the pictures of Anna and Sam with their fingers.
- Children now draw lines to match the food to the pictures of Anna and Sam.
- Children sing the song and point to the pictures.

Say what you like and don't like.

- Children now draw lines to say sentences about the food they like and don't like.

Activity Book p 46

Draw and color two foods you like and two foods you don't like.

- Demonstrate that children should draw and color two foods they like under the happy face and two foods they don't like under the sad face. Make sure they realize there are no correct answers.

Say.

- Children say sentences about food they like and don't like.

Closing time

Learning review (see TB p 18)

Closing routines (see TB p 16)

Bye bye song and puppet (CD1 Track 3; see TB p 17 & 21)

Use the **Navio App** to listen to the song, and encourage children to do the same at home.

Lesson 3

Story

2:32

Watch. Listen to the story *I like ice cream!* Circle Dylan's favorite food. Stick the story sticker. Language: apples, bananas, carrots, cereal, eggs, ice cream, milk; Put the (eggs) in the cart. I like (ice cream).

Learning objectives

- Watch, understand and enjoy the story *I like ice cream!*
- Make a prediction about the story
- Say the shopping list chant
- Identify Dylan's favorite food

Materials

- Class CDs, printable story cards, flashcards, *Ferris Wheel* mat, Mimi puppet

Main vocabulary

- apples, bananas, carrots, cereal, eggs, ice cream, milk

Key language

- Put the (eggs) in the cart. I like (ice cream).

Teacher's tip: Acting out the story

Acting out the story focuses attention and encourages children to join in using the language. As they listen to the story, ask children to mime putting the things into the cart. Then, divide the class into two (half play Mimi, half play Dylan). If possible, give them small cards with pictures of the key vocabulary to help them when miming.

Circle time

Hello song & puppet (CD1 Track 2; see TB p 17 & 21)
Opening routines (see TB p 16)
Recycling activity (*I like* … and food) (see TB p 19)
Lesson aims (see TB p 18)

Introduce the story *I like ice cream!*

- Say *It's story time!* Play the *Story rhyme* (CD1 Track 4; see TB p 17).
- Say *Anna and Sam are listening to a story about Mimi and Dylan. Mimi and Dylan go shopping with Daddy. Guess what they buy.* Listen to children's answers and respond.

Watch or listen to the story.

CD2 Track 32

- Watch the video, play the audio, or read the story using the printable story cards. Pause, repeat words, point to the pictures, and ask questions.
- Ask children to name the food they buy. Repeat the story. Encourage children to join in. Ask *Do you like the story?*

Shopping list chant

- Lay out the flashcards in the order of the shopping list in the story.
- Use percussion and get children to say the shopping list with you in a rhythmic chant.

Table time

Student's Book p 47

Watch. Listen to the story *I like ice cream!*

Story questions

Picture 1
Where are Dylan, Mimi and Daddy? *(In the kitchen)*
What food is on the shopping list? *(Eggs/apples/carrots/cereal/bananas/milk)*

Picture 2
Does Daddy have the shopping list? *(No)*
Who can help Daddy? *(Dylan/Mimi)*

Picture 3
What do Dylan and Mimi remember from the list? *(Eggs/apples)*
What does Dylan want? *(Ice cream)*

Picture 4
What do Dylan and Mimi remember from the list? *(Carrots/cereal)*
Does Dylan like ice cream? *(Yes)*

Picture 5
What do Dylan and Mimi remember from the list? *(Bananas/milk)*
Is ice cream on the list? *(No)*

Picture 6
Is ice cream on the list? *(Yes)*
Are Mimi and Dylan happy? *(Yes)*

CD2 Track 32

- Read or play the story again. Children listen and follow.

Circle Dylan's favorite food.

- Children find and circle Dylan's favorite food.

Stick the story sticker.

- Children stick on the story sticker.
- Say sentences from the story in random order. Children listen and point to the correct frames.

Activity Book p 47

Draw lines to show the story sequence.

- Children draw lines to connect the pictures in order.

Color the food Mimi, Dylan and Daddy buy.

- Children color the food the characters buy in the story.

Closing time

Learning review (see TB p 18)
Closing routines (see TB p 16)
Bye bye song and puppet (CD1 Track 3; see TB p 17 & 21)

Use the **Navio App** to watch the video, and encourage children to do the same at home.

Lesson 4 Story Song

Food

Watch. Listen, point and sing *The shopping song*. Color the food they buy. Say.
Language: apples, bananas, carrots, cereal, eggs, ice cream, milk; colors; Put the (apples) in the cart.

48

Learning objectives

- Watch, sing and act out the story song *The shopping song*
- Listen to the story again and identify the food
- Identify the food in the story song
- Identify and name food you buy
- Identify the next food in a sequence

Materials

- Class CDs, printable story cards, flashcards, *Ferris Wheel* mat, Mimi puppet

Main vocabulary

- apples, bananas, carrots, cereal, eggs, ice cream, milk; colors

Key language

- Put the (apples) in the cart.

Teacher's tip: Reinforcing the sequence of the story song

Stick flashcards of the food items from the story song (except ice cream) on the board and play a memory game. Collectively name them in order, e.g. *Put the (eggs) in the cart. Put the (apples) in the cart,* etc. Turn the final card face down and repeat the sequence. Repeat until all the flashcards are face down and the children are saying the whole sequence from memory. Finally, turn all the flashcards face up again to check. This type of game helps children focus and memorize the words and sequence of the song.

Circle time

Hello song & puppet (CD1 Track 2; see TB p 17 & 21)
Opening routines (see TB p 16)
Recycling activity (food) (see TB p 19)
Lesson aims (see TB p 18)

Retell the story *I like ice cream!*

- Play the audio, video or read the story using the printable story cards.
- Demonstrate that children should stomp their feet every time they hear a food word in the story.

The shopping song

CD2 Track 33

- Stick the flashcards of food in the song on different walls around the room.
- Play the audio. Children listen and point to the flashcards.
- Play the audio again. Children listen, sing and act out the song.

Game: *Shopping cart*

- Have ready a box or basket to be the "cart" in the song.
- Say e.g. *Put the eggs in the cart!* Individual children collect the flashcards from the walls in turn and put them in the "cart." Others clap and say *Hurray!* when they do this correctly.

Table time

Student's Book p 48

Watch. Listen, point and sing *The shopping song.*

CD2 Track 33

- Play the audio of the song. Children listen, sing and point to the food in the cart.
- Remember that you can use the karaoke version of the song when children are confident.

Color the food they buy. Say.

- Children color the food that the family buy in the story, using the color dots as a key. They point and say *Put the (eggs) in the cart.*

Activity Book p 48

Draw and color the next food in the sequence.

- Point to each picture on the first row and encourage children to say the words with you, *eggs, apples, eggs, apples, eggs … apples.* Children draw and color apples in the final frame.
- Children draw and color to complete the other sequences.

Trace and color the ice cream. Point and say.

- Children trace and color the ice cream. They point and say the names of all the foods on the page.

Closing time

Learning review (see TB p 18)
Closing routines (see TB p 16)
Bye bye song and puppet (CD1 Track 3; see TB p 17 & 21)

Use the **Navio App** to watch the video, and encourage children to do the same at home.

Watch. Listen and point. Match the food. Circle the food Uncle Dan likes. Color the food you like. Ask and say. Language: apples, bananas, bread, carrots, cereal, eggs, ice cream, milk; I like (milk). I don't like (cereal). Do you like (bananas)? Yes, I do. / No, I don't.

Learning objectives

- Ask and answer questions about what food you like
- Watch, understand and enjoy a video
- Identify food in the video

Materials

- Class CDs, flashcards, *Ferris Wheel* mat, Mimi puppet

Main vocabulary

- apples, bananas, bread, carrots, cereal, eggs, ice cream, milk

Key language

- I like (milk). I don't like (cereal). Do you like (bananas)? Yes, I do. / No, I don't.

Teacher's tip: Life skills
Respecting different opinions

It's important for children to learn to respect their classmates' opinions, which may be different to their own. Encourage them to use the language from the song *Yummy, yummy* (Lesson 2) to show interest in their partner's likes and dislikes.

Circle time

Hello song & puppet (CD1 Track 2; see TB p 17 & 21)
Opening routines (see TB p 16)
Recycling activity (story song) (CD2 Track 33; see TB p 19)
Lesson aims (see TB p 18)

Game: *Stand up if you like (eggs).*

- Lay out the flashcards.
- Point to the eggs flashcard and say *Stand up if you like eggs!* Demonstrate this. Children stand up if they like eggs.
- Say *I like eggs.* Children who are standing repeat the sentence with you. Repeat with other food.
- Say *Fold your arms if you don't like milk!* Demonstrate this. Children fold their arms if they don't like milk. Say *I don't like milk!* Children with arms folded repeat the sentence with you. Repeat with other food.

Game: *What does the puppet say?*

- Use the puppet to hold up food flashcards in turn and say either *Yummy!* or *Yucky!* Children say *I like … / I don't like …* and name the food.

Watch the video.

- Explain that Sam and Anna are talking to Uncle Dan about food. Play the video.
- Ask *What does Uncle Dan say he likes? I like … . What do they all like? (ice cream)*
- Watch again. Pause and children repeat what Uncle Dan says.

Table time

Student's Book p 49 Life skills

Watch. Listen and point.

- Play the audio or video. Children point to the foods as they hear them in the dialogue.

Match the food.

- Children match the food in the photo to the pictures.

Circle the food Uncle Dan likes.

- Play the audio again. Pause it after each question and answer. Children circle the food Uncle Dan likes. Play again to check they have circled correctly.

CD2 Track 35

Uncle Dan:	Come on Sam. Come on Anna. Let's make lunch.
Anna:	What food do you like, Uncle Dan?
Sam:	Oh yes! Tell us, Uncle Dan.
Uncle Dan:	Well, I like milk. And I like eggs.
Sam:	Do you like bread, Uncle Dan?
Uncle Dan:	No, I don't. I don't like bread. And I don't like cereal.
Anna:	Do you like apples?
Uncle Dan:	Yes, I do. I like apples. And I like bananas.
Sam:	Do you like carrots, Uncle Dan?
Uncle Dan:	No, I don't. I don't like carrots. But I like ice cream! It's a treat. How about you? Do you like ice cream?
Sam:	Yes, I do, Uncle Dan!
Anna:	Me too. It's yummy!

Color the food you like. Say.

- Children color the food they like. Children talk about all the foods.

Activity Book p 49

Trace and draw two pictures of you. Circle the food you like blue and color. Circle the food you don't like red.

- Children trace and draw two pictures of themselves. They circle the food they like blue and the food they don't like red. They color the food they like.

Match the food to the correct faces. Ask and say.

- They match the food to the smiley face if they like it, and the sad face if they don't. They ask and answer about the food.

Closing time

Learning review (see TB p 18)
Closing routines (see TB p 16)
Bye bye song and puppet (CD1 Track 3; see TB p 17 & 21)

Use the **Navio App** to watch the video, and encourage children to do the same at home.

Lesson 6 Values Helping others

Listen, point and sing *Little helper*. Color the frames of the people you help. Draw a picture of you helping someone. Say.

Language: mommy, daddy, brother, friend, teacher; I help my (mommy).

2:36

SOCIAL AND EMOTIONAL LEARNING

50

Learning objectives

- Understand the value of helping others
- Act out the story
- Sing the values song *Little helper*
- Say how you help at home

Materials

- Class CDs, flashcards, *Ferris Wheel* mat, Mimi puppet

Main vocabulary

- brother, daddy, friend, mommy, teacher

Key language

- I help my (mommy).

Teacher's tip: Helping with classroom tasks

Encouraging children to help others is an important part of social and emotional learning. If possible, nominate a helper from each table to help you give out or collect books or other classroom equipment. Rotate the helpers on a daily or weekly basis and make sure that everyone is praised for their efforts.

Circle time

Hello song & puppet (CD1 Track 2; see TB p 17 & 21)
Opening routines (see TB p 16)
Recycling activity *(I like … / I don't like …)* (see TB p 19)
Lesson aims (see TB p 18)

Watch the *I like ice cream!* story video.

- Play the story video.
- Take the part of Daddy yourself. Encourage children to join in acting out the story in two groups (Mimi, Dylan).
- Ask e.g. *Who helps Daddy? (Mimi and Dylan). Do you help your mommy and daddy? Is it important to help people?*

***Little helper* song**

CD2 Track 36

- Use the Mimi puppet to say *Listen and find out who I help!*
- Play the audio. Children name the people Mimi helps (*mommy, daddy, brother, friend, teacher*).
- Play the audio again. Have the children pair up to sing the song and do the actions (see TB p 121).

Table time

Student's Book p 50

Listen, point and sing *Little helper.*

CD2 Track 36

- Play the audio of the song. Children sing and point to the pictures in turn.

Color the frames of the people you help.

- Demonstrate that children should color the frames of the pictures that show people they also help.

Draw a picture of you helping someone. Say.

- Ask children to draw and color a picture of them helping someone.
- Children show you and each other their pictures and say who they help.

Activity Book p 50

Circle the pictures of children helping.

- Children circle the pictures that show people helping.

Talk about the people you help.

- Children talk about the people they help.

Closing time

Learning review (see TB p 18)
Closing routines (see TB p 16)
Bye bye song and puppet (CD1 Track 3; see TB p 17 & 21)

Use the **Navio App** to listen to the song, and encourage children to do the same at home.

2:37 hello

Listen and point. Color the circles green to show food that grows in the garden. Ask and say the food you like and don't like. Language: apples, bananas, bread, carrots, eggs, milk, pears, peas, potatoes, tomatoes; I like (potatoes). I don't like (tomatoes). Do you like (carrots)? Yes, I do. / No, I don't.

51

Learning objectives
- Identify and name food that grows in the garden
- Listen and identify food that grows in the garden
- Talk about food you like and don't like

Materials
- Class CDs, printable content flashcards, *Ferris Wheel* mat, Mimi puppet

Main vocabulary
- apples, bananas, bread, carrots, eggs, milk, pears, peas, potatoes, tomatoes

Key language
- I like (potatoes). I don't like (tomatoes). Do you like (carrots)? Yes, I do. / No, I don't.

Teacher's tip: Life skills
Growing your own food

If there is a school garden, take the children outside to see the vegetable patch. If possible, plant some bean seeds using cotton, water and a glass so that children can watch them grow. This will help consolidate the concept of growing our own food.

Circle time

Hello song & puppet (CD1 Track 2; see TB p 17 & 21)
Opening routines (see TB p 16)
Recycling activity (see TB p 19)
Lesson aims (see TB p 18)

Introduce content vocabulary.
- Use the printable flashcards and the puppet to introduce the new words (*pears, peas, potatoes, tomatoes*). Children repeat the words.
- Play one or two flashcard games with the *Ferris Wheel* mat and/or the puppet (see TB p 20 & 21).
- Encourage children to say *I like … / I don't like …* and name the new food.

Introduce the content.
- Have ready an image or drawing of a garden with fruit trees and vegetables growing.
- Show the image to the children. Explain that some food grows in the garden.
- Lay out all the food flashcards in random order. Ask children e.g. *Do eggs grow in the garden? No! / Do potatoes grow in the garden? Yes!*

Sort the flashcards.
- Ask children to help sort the flashcards into two sets: food that grows in the garden and food that doesn't grow in the garden.
- Recap by getting children to name the food that grows in the garden. Ask children to name any other food they know grows in the garden in their shared language.

Game: *Grow in the garden.*
- Ask children to stand up.
- Name food in random order. Children sway and move their bodies like plants if the food grows in the garden and stand still and fold their arms if not.

Table time

Student's Book p 51

Listen and point.
- Say *Sam and Anna are finding out about food that grows in the garden.* Play the audio. Children listen and point to the food that grows in the garden. Use the pause button as necessary.

CD2 Track 37

Woman:	A lot of food grows in the garden. Potatoes grow in the garden.
Sam:	Tomatoes grow in the garden.
Anna:	Peas grow in the garden.
Woman:	Carrots grow in the garden.
Sam:	Pears grow in the garden.
Anna:	Apples grow in the garden.
Sam:	And bananas grow in the garden too.
Woman:	Oh yes!

Color the circles green to show food that grows in the garden.
- Demonstrate that children should color the spots green to show the food that grows in the garden (Answers: apples, bananas, carrots, tomatoes, pears, peas, potatoes).

Ask and say the food you like and don't like.
- Have children ask and answer questions about food that grows in the garden, e.g. *Do you like carrots? Yes, I do. / No, I don't.*

Activity Book p 51

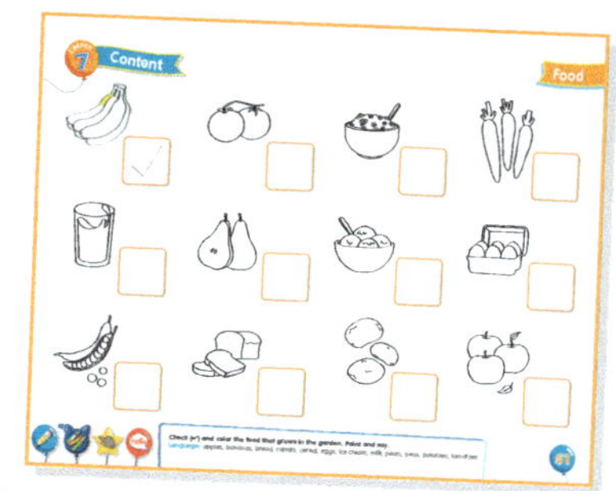

Check (✔) and color the food that grows in the garden.
- Children check and then color the food that grows in the garden (Answers: bananas, tomatoes, carrots, pears, peas, potatoes, apples).

Point and say.
- They point and say the name of the food that grows in the garden.

Closing time

Learning review (see TB p 18)
Closing routines (see TB p 16)
Bye bye song and puppet (CD1 Track 3; see TB p 17 & 21)

Use the **Navio App** to play the vocabulary and language games, and encourage children to do the same at home.

Lesson 8 Culture

Watch. Listen, point and sing *Peas pudding hot*. Match the pictures that are the same. Draw a picture of you eating a vegetable you like. Say. Language: peas, pudding, plate, hot, cold; I like (carrots).

52

Learning objectives

- Watch, sing and act out the traditional song *Peas pudding hot*
- Play a guessing game
- Talk about vegetables you like
- Count the number of peas in a peas pudding

Materials

- Class CDs, flashcards, *Ferris Wheel* mat, Mimi puppet

Main vocabulary

- peas, pudding, plate, hot, cold

Key language

- I like (carrots).

Teacher's tip: Teaching the traditional clapping actions for the song

Peas pudding hot is a traditional clapping game. Teach the children the clapping actions and allow them to play in pairs facing each other (as in the video):

First, clap your hands together, then clap your hands with your partner's hands.

Circle time

Hello song & puppet (CD1 Track 2; see TB p 17 & 21)
Opening routines (see TB p 16)
Recycling activity (see TB p 19)
Lesson aims (see TB p 18)

Game: *Hot or cold*

- Choose a child to close their eyes. Hide one of the food flashcards in the classroom. Ask *Where's the (bread)?* As the child gets near to the flashcard, the class shouts *hot* and as the child moves further away, the class shouts *cold*.

Peas pudding hot song

CD2 Track 38

- Say *Stand up. Let's learn the song "Peas pudding hot."*
- Teach actions for the song (see TB p 121).
- Play the audio. Children listen and do the actions for the song with you.
- Repeat. Children join in singing and doing the actions for the song.

Watch the *Peas pudding hot* video.

- Children watch the video and join in singing the song and doing the actions with Anna and Sam.

Table time

Student's Book p 52

Watch. Listen, point and sing *Peas pudding hot*.

CD2 Track 38

- Play the audio of the song. Children listen, sing and point to the pictures.

Match the pictures that are the same.

- Demonstrate that children should match the pictures that are the same.

Draw a picture of you eating a vegetable you like. Say.

- Children draw a picture of themselves eating a vegetable that they like. Children show you and each other their pictures and say, e.g. *I like (carrots).*

Activity Book p 52

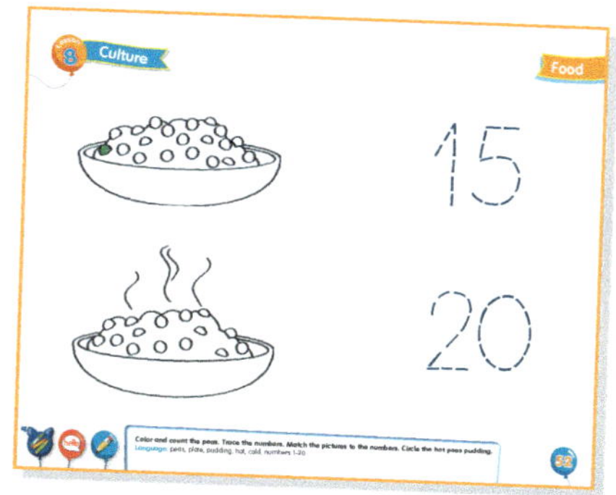

Color and count the peas.

- Children count the peas and then color them.

Trace the numbers. Match the pictures to the numbers.

- They trace the two numbers, then match them to the correct bowl of peas (top 20, bottom 15).

Circle the hot peas pudding.

- They circle the peas pudding that is hot (the bottom one).

Closing time

Learning review (see TB p 18)
Closing routines (see TB p 16)
Bye bye song and puppet (CD1 Track 3; see TB p 17 & 21)

Use the **Navio App** to watch the video, and encourage children to do the same at home.

I can ...

Vocabulary

Story

Speaking

Content

Trace and color the food you know. Listen, point and say. Ask and say. Complete the faces to show what you can do. **Language:** apples, bananas, bread, carrots, cereal, eggs, ice cream, milk; I like (eggs). I don't like (apples). How about you? Do you like (carrots)? Yes, I do. / No, I don't.

Learning objectives

- Review what you have learned in this unit
- Complete a self-evaluation
- Talk about food you like and don't like

Materials

- Class CDs, flashcards, *Ferris Wheel* mat, Mimi puppet

Main vocabulary

- apples, bananas, bread, carrots, cereal, eggs, ice cream, milk

Key language

- I like (eggs). I don't like (apples). How about you? Do you like (carrots)? Yes, I do. / No, I don't.

Teacher's tip: Drawing pictures and reviewing learning in pairs

As an additional way to review learning, give each child a folded piece of paper and ask them to draw items of food that they like on one side and food they don't like on the other. They should pair up and show their drawings to each other and talk about them.

Circle time

Hello song & puppet (CD1 Track 2; see TB p 17 & 21)
Opening routines (see TB p 16)
Recycling activity (see TB p 19)
Lesson aims (see TB p 18)

Food flashcard games

- Choose one or two flashcard games with the *Ferris Wheel* mat and/or the puppet to review main vocabulary (see TB p 20 & 21).

Sing *Yummy, yummy.*

CD2 Track 30

- Listen to the audio or watch the video. Children sing and do the actions.
- Ask children to say food they like and don't like.

Let's go shopping.

- Stick the food flashcards at the children's height on different walls around the classroom. Have the children stand up and mime pushing a cart.
- Say *Put the eggs in the cart.* Children change direction and go to the eggs flashcard.
- Repeat with the other food items.

Game: *I like carrots.*

- Have the children form two lines facing each other. Hold up one of the food flashcards. Children on the right look at the child opposite and say if they like or don't like the food. Their partner then says if they like it or not. Repeat with all the food items.

Watch the story video.

- Children watch the story video. Pause before food words and familiar phrases. Children supply them. Ask *Who helps Daddy? (Dylan, Mimi)*

Table time

Student's Book p 53

Trace and color the food you know.

- Explain and demonstrate the activity.

Listen, point and say.

- Play the audio. Children listen, point to the foods, and say the words.

CD2 Track 39

Mimi: I'm the teacher! Can you remember the food, Dylan?
Dylan: Yes, I can. Cereal.
Mimi: Cereal.
Dylan: Milk.
Mimi: Milk.
Dylan: Eggs.
Mimi: Eggs.
Dylan: Bread.
Mimi: Bread.
Dylan: Apples.
Mimi: Apples.
Dylan: Ice cream.
Mimi: Ice cream.
Dylan: Carrots.
Mimi: Carrots.
Dylan: Bananas.
Mimi: Bananas. Great job, Dylan! Very good!

Ask and say.

- Ask children questions about the food. Have them ask you or the puppet similar questions.

Complete the faces to show what you can do.

- Explain the four pictures: *I can name food; I can understand the story; I can say food I like and don't like; I can recognize food that grows in the garden.*
- Remind them to complete each face with a smiley face or frown depending on how well they think they've done.

Activity Book p 53

Complete the faces to show food you like and food you don't like. Ask and say.

- Children complete the faces with a smile if they like it and a frown if they don't. They ask and answer about the food.

Think and circle the number to show your progress.

- They circle the number.

Closing time

Learning review (see TB p 18)
Closing routines (see TB p 16)
Bye bye song and puppet (CD1 Track 3; see TB p 17 & 21)

Use the **Navio App** to review what children have learned in this unit, and encourage them to do the same at home.

Project

COOPERATIVE LEARNING

1

2

3

Make a plate of food you like. Display your plate of food. Ask and say. Language: apples, bananas, bread, carrots, cereal, eggs, ice cream, milk; modeling clay; I like (eggs). I don't like (apples). Do you like (carrots)? Yes, I do. / No, I don't. I have (bananas). How many (apples)? I can see (four) (eggs). My (ice cream) is (pink). Our food is (fantastic)!

54

Learning objectives

- Work together to do a collaborative project
- Talk about food you like and don't like
- Make a plate of food from modeling clay

Materials

- Class CDs, Mimi puppet, photocopiable templates: plate, modeling clay, crayons
- optional: paper plates

Main vocabulary

- apples, bananas, bread, carrots, cereal, eggs, ice cream, milk; modeling clay

Key language

- I like (eggs). I don't like (apples). Do you like (carrots)? Yes, I do. / No, I don't. I have (bananas). How many (apples)? I can see (four) (eggs). My (ice cream) is (pink). Our food is (fantastic)!

Teacher's tip: Sharing

COOPERATIVE LEARNING

Make sure the children realize the importance of sharing the modeling clay. Show them how to break off chunks and put the remainder back in the box for everyone to use. Praise those who are actively sharing and making sure that the box of clay is within everyone's reach.

Circle time

Hello song & puppet (CD1 Track 2; see TB p 17 & 21)
Opening routines (see TB p 16)
Recycling activity (see TB p 19)
Lesson aims (see TB p 18)

Prepare for your project.

- Say *Let's do a project! Let's make a display of food we like.* Explain that children should work together in groups for this project.
- Show children the modeling clay and paper plates or templates.
- Say e.g. *I like carrots!* Demonstrate making a carrot from the modeling clay.
- Demonstrate decorating the paper plate or template with crayons.

Table time

Student's Book p 54

COOPERATIVE LEARNING

Make a plate of food you like.

- Say *We're going to make a display of food. Look at what we need for our project.* Hold up the objects and elicit the words: *modeling clay, crayons, paper plate.*
- Say the words again. Children listen and point to the pictures in their books.
- Make sure children have a variety of colors of modeling clay, and crayons available. Children make their food and decorate their paper plates or templates. Be ready to help as necessary.

Display your plate of food. Ask and say.

- Children take turns placing their plates on a table to make a class display. Ask questions and encourage children to talk about the food as they do this, e.g. *What's this? Do you like it?*
- Children ask and answer about their completed plate of food, e.g. *Do you like (apples)?*
- Ask children *Do you like our display?* Make the point that everyone helped make the display and that they couldn't have made such a beautiful display of food on their own.

Activity Book p 54

Use finger paints to paint the food.

- Make sure children have a variety of finger paints. They paint the food.

Point and say the colors. Talk about the food you like and don't like.

- They point and say the colors. They talk about the food.

Closing time

Learning review (see TB p 18)
Closing routines (see TB p 16)
Bye bye song and puppet (CD1 Track 3; see TB p 17 & 21)

Farm animals

Aunt Emma's farm

Vocabulary and language

- **Main vocabulary:** cow, dog, duck, goat, hen, horse, rooster, sheep
- **Key language:** There's a (horse) and a (goat). What animals are on the farm? How many (hens)? (Four).
- **Content language:** calf, foal, lamb, puppy. This is a (cow). The baby is a (calf).
- **Other language:** clean, cotton balls, farm, food, home, kind, little, mommy, pond, quack, swimming, tissue paper, water; five little ducks; The sheep goes (baa). I like (dogs). I'm kind to animals. There are (six) (ducks). How many (cows)? I like (goats). My (duck) is (yellow). Our farm animals are (fantastic)!

Unit objectives

- Identify and name farm animals
- Sing the language song *On the farm*
- Say what animals there are on the farm
- Understand and act out the story *Aunt Emma's farm*
- Sing and act out the story song *Don't be silly!*
- Sing the values song *Be kind to animals*
- Recognize the value of being kind to animals
- Identify and name baby farm animals
- Sing and act out the traditional song *Five little ducks*
- Review your learning and progress
- Participate in a collaborative project

Story

CD3 Track 6

Picture 1

Narrator: Mimi and Dylan visit Aunt Emma's farm.
Mimi: Hello, Aunt Emma.
Aunt Emma: Hello, children.
Dylan: Can we see the animals, please?
Aunt Emma: Yes, of course.
Mimi & Dylan: Hurray!

Picture 2

Dylan: Look, Mimi. There's a sheep.
Mimi: And the sheep goes woof, woof, woof.
Aunt Emma: Oh, Mimi. Don't be silly. The sheep goes … (Baa, baa, baa)
Mimi: Oh yes! Ha, ha. The sheep goes baa, baa, baa.

Picture 3

Dylan: And look, Mimi. There's a cow.
Mimi: And the cow goes baa, baa, baa.
Aunt Emma: Oh, Mimi. Don't be silly. The cow goes … (Moo, moo, moo)
Mimi: Oh yes! Ha, ha. The cow goes moo, moo, moo.

Picture 4

Mimi: Look, Dylan. There's a duck.
Dylan: And the duck goes moo, moo, moo.
Aunt Emma: Oh, Dylan. Don't be silly. The duck goes … (Quack, quack, quack)
Dylan: Oh yes! Ha, ha. The duck goes quack, quack, quack.

Picture 5

Dylan: And look up there, Mimi. There's a hen.
Mimi: And the hen goes cluck, cluck, cluck.
Aunt Emma: Very good, Mimi. The hen goes cluck, cluck, cluck. But it isn't a hen. It's a rooster.
Dylan: A rooster? And the rooster goes … ? (Cock-a-doodle-doo)

Picture 6

Mimi & Dylan: Oh … oh … oh … oh … (Splash!)
Aunt Emma: Oh, children!
Mimi & Dylan: And the rooster goes cock-a-doodle-doo.
Aunt Emma: Come on, Mimi and Dylan. Let's get you dry. It's time for a snack.

Songs

Language song

On the farm CD3 Track 4

On the farm there's a horse. (Make a swishy tail with your arm)
On the farm there's a horse and a goat. (Wiggle a hand near your neck like a bell)
On the farm there's a horse and a goat and a rooster. (Wiggle fingers on your head for the rooster's crest)
Wow! We love the farm. (Punch fists in the air three times)

On the farm there's a cow. (Wiggle your fingers like an udder)
On the farm there's a cow and a duck. (Make a beak with your hand for the duck)
On the farm there's a cow and a duck and a hen. (Flap wings for the hen)
Wow! We love the farm. (Punch fists in the air three times)

Story song

Don't be silly! CD3 Track 7

The sheep goes woof. (Put two fingers on head like ears)
Oh no, Mimi. Don't be silly! (Shake head and wag finger)
The sheep goes baa.
The sheep goes baa.
Baa, baa, baa, baa, baa.

The cow goes baa. (Wiggle your fingers like an udder)
Oh no, Mimi. Don't be silly! (Shake head and wag finger)
The cow goes moo.
The cow goes moo.
Moo, moo, moo, moo, moo.

The duck goes moo. (Make a beak with your hand)
Oh no, Dylan. Don't be silly! (Shake head and wag finger)
The duck goes quack.
The duck goes quack.
Quack, quack, quack, quack, quack.

The rooster goes cock-a-doodle-doo. (Wiggle fingers on head)
Oh yes, you're right. Oh, yes, you're right! (nod and thumbs up)
The rooster goes cock-a-doodle-doo.
The rooster goes cock-a-doodle-doo.
Cock-a-doodle-doo, cock-a-doodle-doo, cock-a-doodle-doo.

Values song

Be kind to animals CD3 Track 10

Be kind to animals (Hug yourself)
In every way (Point around you)
Give them food and water (Mime holding out a bowl)
Every day. (Fan your arms out wide)
Give animals a home (Make a roof over your head with your hands)
Keep them clean, too (Mime brushing an animal)
Be kind to animals (Hug yourself)
As people are to you. (Point to self)
Be kind to animals (Hug yourself)
In every way (Point around you)
Give them food and water (Mime holding out a bowl)
Every day. (Fan your arms out wide)

Culture song

Five little ducks CD3 Track 12

Five little ducks go swimming one day (Make swimming motion with your arms)
Over the pond and far away (Shade your eyes with one hand)
Mommy duck says "quack, quack, quack" (Make a beak with one hand)
But only four little ducks come back. (Make swimming motion)
Four little ducks go swimming one day (Make swimming motion)
(etc)
But only three little ducks come back. (Make swimming motion)
Three little ducks go swimming one day (Make swimming motion)
(etc)
But only two little ducks come back. (Make swimming motion)
Two little ducks go swimming one day (Make swimming motion)
(etc)
But only one little duck comes back. (Make swimming motion)
One little duck goes swimming one day (Make swimming motion)
(etc)
And five little ducks come swimming back. (Make swimming motion)

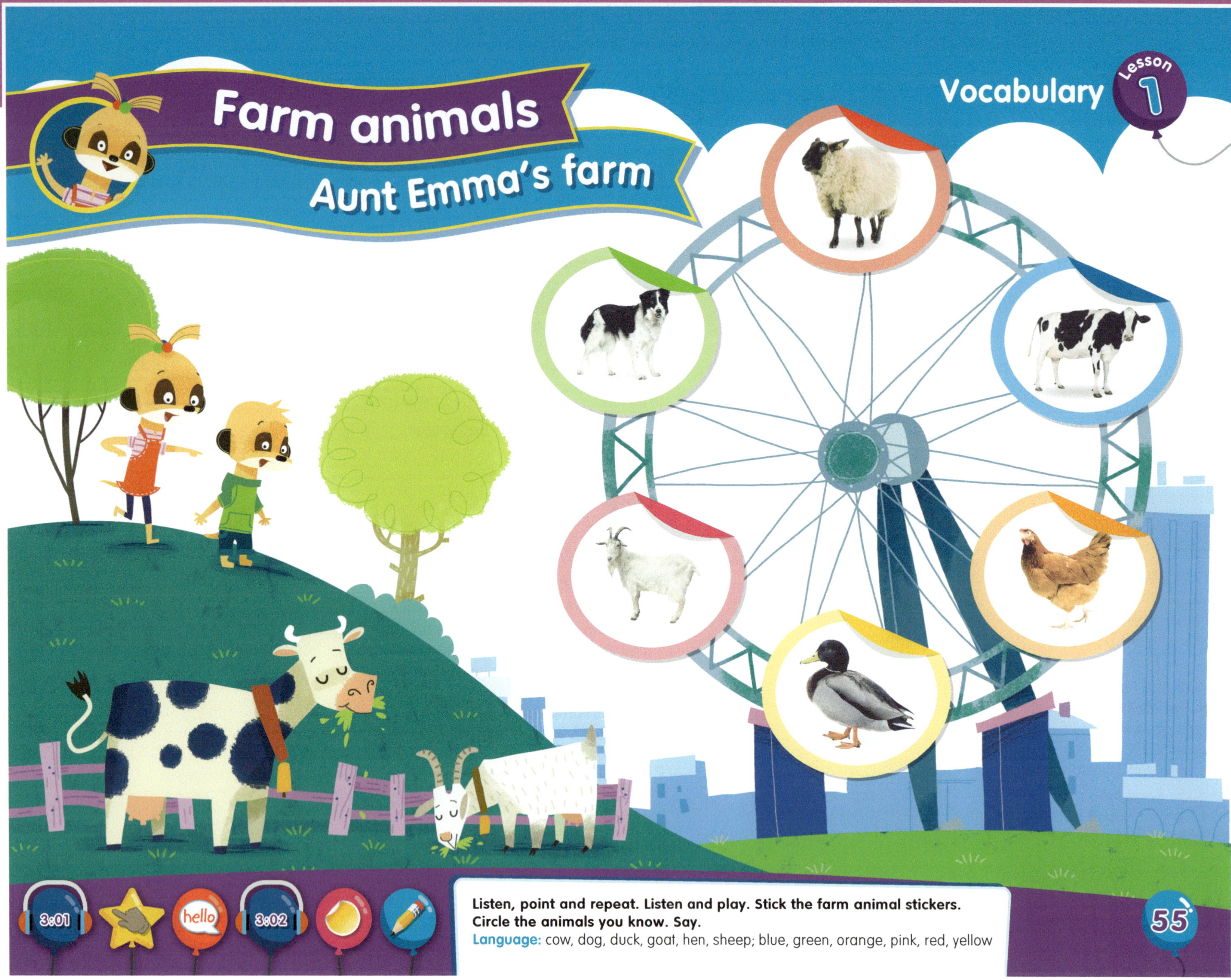
Farm animals
Aunt Emma's farm
Vocabulary
Lesson 1
3:01
hello
3:02
Listen, point and repeat. Listen and play. Stick the farm animal stickers.
Circle the animals you know. Say.
Language: cow, dog, duck, goat, hen, sheep; blue, green, orange, pink, red, yellow
55

Farm animals

Lesson 1 Vocabulary

Learning objectives
- Identify and name farm animals
- Listen and point to farm animals
- Identify the animals you know

Materials
- Class CDs, flashcards, *Ferris Wheel* mat, Mimi puppet

Main vocabulary
- cow, dog, duck, goat, hen, sheep; blue, green, orange, pink, red, yellow

Teacher's tip: Using aural clues before visual

If available, use toy animals from the children's own classroom. Put them in a box or feely bag. Awaken children's interest in the new topic by making the animal noise before you take out each one.

Circle time

Hello song & puppet (CD1 Track 2; see TB p 17 & 21)
Opening routines (see TB p 16)
Lesson aims (see TB p 18)

Introduce farm animals.
- Use the puppet and flashcards to introduce the farm animals. Ask children what animals there are on a farm. As they respond in their shared language, introduce the words in English. Children repeat the words.
- *Ferris Wheel* mat on the floor or board with the farm animal flashcards face down (one on each color). Use puppet to turn over and name. Children repeat the words.

Game: ***Say the color!***
- Name the farm animals on the Ferris Wheel and children name the color. Then do the reverse.

Game: ***Take a photo!***
- Stick the flashcards at the children's height on different walls around the classroom.
- Ask two to four children to stand up. Say e.g. *Take a photo of the duck!* Children respond by walking to the flashcard and pretending to take a photo of it. Repeat with different pairs or groups of children and all the flashcards.

Table time

Student's Book p 55

Listen, point and repeat.
- Play the audio. The children listen, point to each animal as they hear it, and repeat the words.

CD3 Track 1

Mimi: Look, Dylan! Sheep … cow … hen … duck … goat … dog. Repeat, Dylan!
Dylan: Yes, Mimi. Sheep … cow … hen … duck … goat … dog.
Mimi: Very good, Dylan. Let's name the farm animals together!
Both: Sheep … cow … hen … duck … goat … dog.

Listen and play.
- Use finger in air to pretend to spin wheel. Children spin their fingers, point to the color when they hear it on the audio and say the word.

CD3 Track 2

Mimi: Spin the wheel
One, two, three
Point and name
The farm animals with me!
Mimi: Orange … hen!
Dylan: Green … dog!
Mimi: Yellow … duck!
Dylan: Pink … goat!
Mimi: Red … sheep!
Dylan: Blue … cow!

- Play the game with you and/or individual children naming colors and others responding with the words.

Stick the farm animal stickers.
- Children stick the farm animal stickers in the correct places.

Circle the animals you know.
- Children circle the farm animals they know.

Say.
- Children name the farm animals.

Activity Book p 55

Draw and color the next animal in the sequence.
- Focus on the first row of pictures. Point to them one by one, saying the word each time. Point to the empty frame at the end and ask *What's next?* Elicit *duck*, and demonstrate that children should draw a duck in the frame.
- Repeat for the two other sequences (dog and sheep).

Point and say.
- Children point to the pictures and say the words.

Closing time

Learning review (see TB p 18)
Closing routines (see TB p 16)
Bye bye song and puppet (CD1 Track 3; see TB p 17 & 21)

Use the **Navio App** to play the vocabulary game, and encourage children to do the same at home.

Lesson 2 Language

Farm animals

Listen and find the new farm animals. Listen, point and sing *On the farm.* Circle the animals in the song. Point and say.

Language: cow, dog, duck, goat, hen, horse, rooster, sheep; There's a (horse) and a (goat).

56

Farm animals

Lesson 2 Language

Learning objectives
- Talk about farm animals
- Identify and name two new farm animals
- Sing the language song *On the farm*
- Say how many animals there are

Materials
- Class CDs, flashcards, *Ferris Wheel* mat, Mimi puppet, feely bag

Main vocabulary
- cow, dog, duck, goat, hen, horse, rooster, sheep; numbers

Key language
- There's a (horse) and a (goat). How many (hens)? (Four).

Teacher's tip: Sharing ideas with a partner first

When playing *Guess the farm animals*, have children work cooperatively with a partner by sharing their ideas together first. Once they have both suggested an animal that's in the bag, they both raise their hands to tell the class their guess.

Circle time

Hello song & puppet (CD1 Track 2; see TB p 17 & 21)
Opening routines (see TB p 16)
Recycling activity (six farm animals from Lesson 1) (see TB p 19)
Lesson aims (see TB p 18)

Introduce the new farm animals.
- All eight flashcards of farm animals on the floor or the board.
- Children identify the two new farm animals.
- Use the puppet to point to and say the words in turn. Children repeat in chorus.
- Turn the two new flashcards face down. Mix them up. Point to one and ask *Horse or rooster?* Children guess. Repeat several times.

Introduce *There's …*
- Put the flashcards in a feely bag. Use the puppet to take them out of the bag in turn and say, e.g. *There's a (duck). There's a (cow).* Children join in saying the sentences with you.

Game: *Guess the farm animals.*
- Choose three flashcards and put them in the feely bag without children seeing. Invite children to guess the animals in the bag, e.g. *(I think) there's a (duck).*
- At the end, take out the flashcards and children say, e.g. *There's a (horse) and a (dog) and a (cow).* Congratulate the children who guessed correctly.
- Repeat the game once or twice.

Table time

Student's Book p 56

Listen and find the new farm animals.
- Play the audio. Children listen and find the two new words. Play the audio again. The children listen and say the words.

CD3 Track 3

One, two, Which words are new?
Horse! Horse!
Rooster! Rooster!

Listen, point and sing *On the farm*.

CD3 Track 4
- Play the song. The children listen and point to each animal as they hear it.
- Play the song again. Children sing the song and do the actions (see TB p 143).
- Remember that you can use the karaoke version of the song when children are confident.

Circle the animals in the song.
- Play the first verse of the song again. Ask *What animals are on the farm?* Elicit *horse, goat, rooster.* Demonstrate circling those animals with your finger. Repeat with verse 2.
- Play the song again, pausing after each verse. Children listen and circle the animals in the song.

Point and say.
- Remind children of the line from the song: *On the farm, there's a (horse).* Encourage children to point and talk about the animals as in the song.

Activity Book p 56

Find and count the animals in the picture. Trace and circle the correct number for each animal.
- Ask children to find and count the roosters in the main picture (*one*). Draw attention to the rooster at the top and the example *1*.
- Children count the other farm animals and trace and circle the correct number for each one.

Ask and say.
- Encourage children to say with you, e.g. *There's (a rooster). How many (hens)? (Four).*

Closing time

Learning review (see TB p 18)
Closing routines (see TB p 16)
Bye bye song and puppet (CD1 Track 3; see TB p 17 & 21)

Use the **Navio App** to listen to the song, and encourage children to do the same at home.

Story

Farm animals

Watch. Listen to the story *Aunt Emma's farm*. Circle the animal that surprises Mimi and Dylan. Stick the story sticker. **Language:** cow, duck, horse, rooster, sheep; animal noises; There's a (sheep). The (sheep) goes (baa).

Learning objectives

- Watch, understand and enjoy the story *Aunt Emma's farm*
- Make a prediction about the story
- Find and point to the animals in the story
- Identify the animal that surprises Mimi

Materials

- Class CDs, printable story cards, flashcards, *Ferris Wheel* mat, Mimi puppet

Main vocabulary

- cow, duck, horse, rooster, sheep; animal noises

Key language

- There's a (sheep). The (sheep) goes (baa).

Teacher's tip: Checking comprehension

To check comprehension of the animals in the story, name them at random and encourage the children to point to them and say the frame number where they appear.

Circle time

Hello song & puppet (CD1 Track 2; see TB p 17 & 21)

Opening routines (see TB p 16)

Recycling activity (*There's … / There are …* and farm animals) (see TB p 19)

Lesson aims (see TB p 18)

Introduce the story *Aunt Emma's farm*.

- Say *It's story time!* Play the *Story rhyme* (CD1 Track 4; see TB p 17).
- Say *Anna and Sam are listening to a story about Mimi and Dylan. They go to Aunt Emma's farm.* Ask *What animals do they see?* Encourage them to guess and respond.

Watch or listen to the story.

CD3 Track 6

- Watch the video, play the audio, or read the story using the printable story cards. Pause, repeat words, point to the pictures, ask questions.
- Repeat the question and children name the animals in the story. Then ask *Which animal is Dylan scared of? (rooster).*
- Repeat the story. Encourage children to join in with the words and phrases in the story.
- Ask *Do you like the story? Do you like the animals?*

Look and find.

- Say e.g. *Find the horse!* Children look at the story and point to the picture as fast as they can.
- Repeat with other farm animals in the story.

Table time

Student's Book p 57

Watch. Listen to the story *Aunt Emma's farm*.

CD3 Track 6

- Read or play the story again. Children listen and follow the story by pointing to the pictures.

Circle the animal that surprises Mimi and Dylan.

- Children find and circle the animal that surprises Mimi and Dylan (rooster).

Stick the story sticker.

- Children stick on the story sticker.
- Say sentences from the story in random order. Children listen and point to the correct frames.

Activity Book p 57

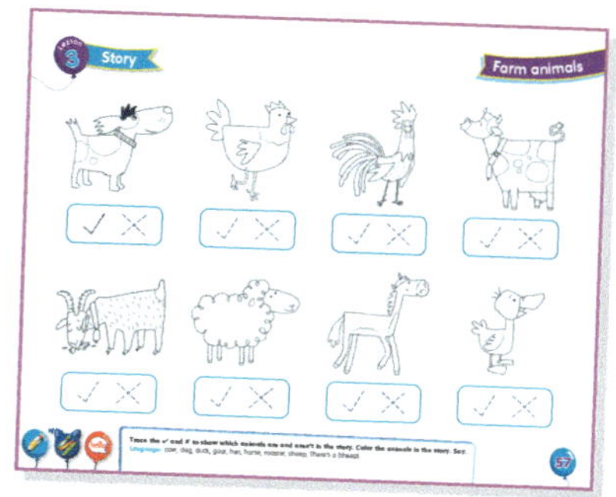

Trace the ✓ and ✗ to show which animals are and aren't in the story.

- Children trace the check mark if the animal is in the story and the cross if not (✓: dog, sheep, cow, duck, rooster; ✗: hen, goat, horse).

Color the animals in the story. Say.

- They color the animals in the story. Then they say, e.g. *There's a dog.*

Closing time

Learning review (see TB p 18)

Closing routines (see TB p 16)

Bye bye song and puppet (CD1 Track 3; see TB p 17 & 21)

Story questions

Picture 1
Where are Mimi and Dylan? *(Aunt Emma's farm)*
What does Dylan want to see? *(The animals)*

Picture 2
What does Dylan see? *(A sheep)*
The sheep goes … *(baa, baa, baa)*

Picture 3
What does Dylan see? *(A cow)*
The cow goes … (moo, moo, moo)

Picture 4
What does Mimi see? *(A duck)*
The duck goes … *(quack, quack, quack)*

Picture 5
The hen goes … *(cluck, cluck, cluck)*
Is it a hen? *(No)*

Picture 6
Where are Mimi and Dylan? *(In the water)*
What animal goes cock-a-doodle-doo? *(A rooster)*

Use the **Navio App** to watch the video, and encourage children to do the same at home.

Lesson 4

Story Song

Farm animals

Watch. Listen, point and sing *Don't be silly!* Follow and draw the path through the maze in the correct order. Point and say. Language: cow, duck, rooster, sheep; animal noises; There's a (sheep). The (sheep) goes (baa).

Learning objectives

- Watch, sing and act out the story song *Don't be silly!*
- Listen to the story again and make animal noises
- Identify the animals in the song
- Talk about the animals in the song
- Identify farm animals and say what noises they make

Materials

- Class CDs, printable story cards, flashcards, *Ferris Wheel* mat, Mimi puppet

Main vocabulary

- cow, duck, rooster, sheep; animal noises

Key language

- There's a (sheep). The (sheep) goes (baa).

Teacher's tip: Lowering your voice as a control measure

If you find it difficult to calm children down after the lively games, lower your voice instead of raising it. Children must then focus in order to hear you. Whisper an instruction, e.g. *Everybody touch your nose.* Children will start to copy and quieten down.

Circle time

Hello song & puppet (CD1 Track 2; see TB p 17 & 21)
Opening routines (see TB p 16)
Recycling activity (farm animals) (see TB p 19)
Lesson aims (see TB p 18)

Retell the story *Aunt Emma's farm*.

- Play the audio, video or read the story using the printable story cards.
- Demonstrate that children should join in saying the correct noises for each farm animal in the story (and stay silent for the incorrect ones).

Game: *There's a duck (in the classroom)!*

- Use the flashcards to elicit or teach the noises made by the animals in the story.
- Demonstrate the game by imitating a farm animal yourself, e.g. *baa, baa.* Children respond by guessing, e.g. *There's a (sheep) (in the classroom)!* The child who guesses correctly has the next turn.
- Repeat several times.

***Don't be silly!* song**

CD3 Track 7

- Play the video or audio of the story song. Children watch/listen and say the animals in the song.
- Play the song again. Children wag their finger for "Don't be silly!" in each verse and join in singing the song.
- Ask e.g. *Do you like the song "Don't be silly!"?* and children respond.

Game: *Don't be silly!*

- Hold up a flashcard, e.g. the dog, and say *The dog goes quack.* Encourage children to respond by waving their fingers and saying *Don't be silly! The dog goes woof!*
- Repeat several times with different flashcards of farm animals from the song.

Table time

Student's Book p 58

Watch. Listen, point and sing *Don't be silly!*

CD3 Track 7

- Play the audio of the song. Children listen, sing and point to the animals in the picture.
- Remember that you can use the karaoke version of the song when children are confident.

Follow and draw the path through the maze in the correct order.

- Children draw a line to show the sequence of the song (sheep, cow, duck, rooster).

Point and say.

- Children point and say, e.g. *There's a (duck). The (duck) goes quack.*

Activity Book p 58

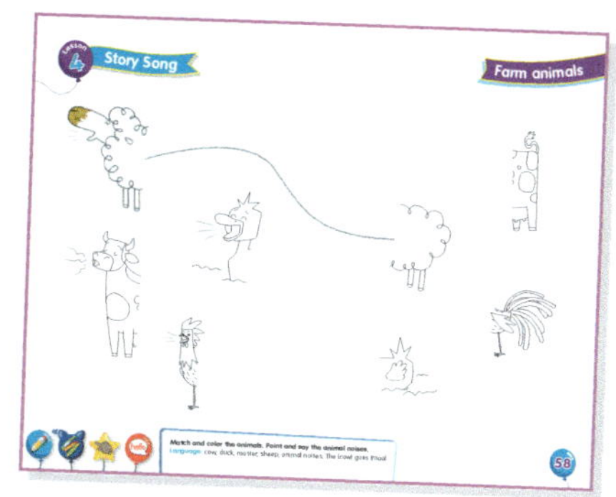

Match and color the animals.

- Children match the front half of the animal to the back half. They color them.

Point and say the animal noises.

- Children point to each animal in turn and say, e.g. *The sheep goes baa.*

Closing time

Learning review (see TB p 18)
Closing routines (see TB p 16)
Bye bye song and puppet (CD1 Track 3; see TB p 17 & 21)

Use the **Navio App** to watch the video, and encourage children to do the same at home.

Speaking

Life skills

Farm animals

3:09

hello

Watch. Listen and point. Match the animals to the photo. Circle your favorite animal. Say. Language: cow, dog, duck, goat, hen, horse, rooster, sheep; There's a (horse). There are (cows).

Farm animals

Lesson 5 Speaking

Learning objectives
- Talk about what animals there are on a farm
- Watch, understand and enjoy a video
- Identify animals in the video

Materials
- Class CDs, flashcards, *Ferris Wheel* mat, Mimi puppet

Main vocabulary
- cow, dog, duck, goat, hen, horse, rooster, sheep

Key language
- There's a (horse). There are (cows).

Teacher's tip: Recognizing that farm animals help us
Life skills

To help children recognize that the animals that live on a farm help us in some way, bring some teacher-made flashcards with pictures of milk, cheese, eggs and a sweater. Talk about how we get these products from farm animals. Ask children if they know other products that come from farm animals.

Circle time

Hello song & puppet (CD1 Track 2; see TB p 17 & 21)
Opening routines (see TB p 16)
Recycling activity (story song) (CD3 Track 7; see TB p 19)
Lesson aims (see TB p 18)

Game: *Guess the flashcard*
- Give out the farm animal flashcards to individual children without others seeing.
- Children take turns making the noise of the animal on their flashcard. Other children listen and guess.

Watch the video.
- Explain that Uncle Dan is showing Sam and Anna a photo of his brother's farm.
- Ask *What animals are on the farm?* and encourage children to guess.
- Play the video of Anna, Sam and Uncle Dan.
- Ask the questions again and children respond.
- Watch again. Pause and children repeat the sentences about all the animals.
- Ask *Do you want to see the animals on the farm?* and listen to children's responses.

CD3 Track 9

Uncle Dan:	Here's a photo of my brother's farm.
Anna:	Oh wow! I love farms.
Sam:	Look at all the animals!
Uncle Dan:	Yes! There's a dog.
Anna:	And look! There's a horse.
Uncle Dan:	Yes, and there are hens.
Anna:	And look! There are goats.
Uncle Dan:	Yes, you're right, Anna. It's a great farm!
Sam:	Can we go with you one day?
Uncle Dan:	Yes, of course! What a good idea!

Anna , Sam and Uncle Dan: Hurray!

Table time

Student's Book p 59 Life skills

Watch. Listen and point.
- Children point to Anna, Sam and Uncle Dan in the photo. Play the audio or video. Children point to the animals as they hear them in the dialogue.

Match the animals to the photo.
- Children match the animals in the photo to the animals around the photo.

Circle your favorite animal.
- Children circle their favorite animal. Play the audio again.

Say.
- Children point to the animals and say sentences as in the dialogue.
- Ask *Do you want to go to the farm with Uncle Dan, Sam and Anna?* and listen to the children's responses.

Activity Book p 59

Find and circle four differences.
- Point to the dog in the first picture. Say *Look. There's a dog.* Point to the rooster in the second picture. Say *Look. There's a rooster.*
- Children find and circle the three other differences (horse/cow, hens/ducks, goats/sheep).

Color the frame of the picture which shows the farm from the video. Say.
- Children color the frame on the left. They talk about the picture.

Closing time

Learning review (see TB p 18)
Closing routines (see TB p 16)
Bye bye song and puppet (CD1 Track 3; see TB p 17 & 21)

Use the **Navio App** to watch the video, and encourage children to do the same at home.

Lesson 6 Values Being kind to animals

3:10

Listen, point and sing *Be kind to animals*. Color the people being kind to animals. Draw a picture of you being kind to an animal. Say. Language: cow, dog, duck, goat, hen, horse, rooster, sheep; clean, food, home, kind, water; I like (dogs). I'm kind to animals.

SOCIAL AND EMOTIONAL LEARNING

60

Farm animals

Lesson 6 Values

Learning objectives

- Understand the value of being kind to animals
- Act out the story
- Sing the values song *Be kind to animals*
- Talk about how you are kind to animals

Materials

- Class CDs, flashcards, *Ferris Wheel* mat, Mimi puppet

Main vocabulary

- cow, dog, duck, goat, hen, horse, rooster, sheep; clean, food, home, kind, water

Key language

- I like (dogs). I'm kind to animals.

Teacher's tip: Taking responsibility for pets

Find out if the children have a pet at home. Establish the importance of taking responsibility for their pet by feeding it, keeping it clean and being kind to it. Have children act out a mini role-play where they pretend to take care of their own pet by doing actions. Say e.g. *Give your animal water. Keep your animal clean,* etc.

Circle time

Hello song & puppet (CD1 Track 2; see TB p 17 & 21)

Opening routines (see TB p 16)

Recycling activity *(There's a … / There are …* and farm animals) (see TB p 19)

Lesson aims (see TB p 18)

Watch the *Aunt Emma's farm* story video.

- Play the story video.
- Take the part of the narrator and Aunt Emma yourself. Encourage children to join in acting out the story in two groups (Mimi, Dylan).
- Ask *Is Aunt Emma kind to the farm animals?* Explain what you mean by "kind." (*Yes*) For example, she gives the animals a home and they are all happy in the story.
- Ask *Is it important to be kind to animals?* and listen to the children's responses.

***Be kind to animals* song**

CD3 Track 10

- Ask *How can we be kind to animals?* Listen to children's ideas and use these to pre-teach or remind children of words in the song, e.g. food, water, home, clean.
- Pre-teach actions for the song (see TB p 143).
- Play the audio. Children listen and do the actions with you.
- Play the audio again. Children do the actions and join in singing the song.
- Make the point that it is important to be kind to all animals, not only farm animals but also pets if you have them and wild animals.

Table time

Student's Book p 60

Listen, point and sing *Be kind to animals.*

CD3 Track 10

- Play the audio of the song. Children sing and point to the pictures of Aunt Emma, Mimi and Dylan being kind to different animals.

Color the people being kind to animals.

- Children color the pictures.

Draw a picture of you being kind to an animal. Say.

- Children draw a picture of themselves being kind to an animal.
- Children show you and each other their pictures and name the animal they have drawn.

Activity Book p 60

Match the objects to the pictures of a child being kind to animals.

- Children match each object to the correct picture (brush/dog, water/horse, hay/cow).

Point and say.

- Children point and talk about being kind to animals.

Closing time

Learning review (see TB p 18)

Closing routines (see TB p 16)

Bye bye song and puppet (CD1 Track 3; see TB p 17 & 21)

Use the **Navio App** to listen to the song, and encourage children to do the same at home.

Lesson 7 Content

Farm animals

Listen and point. Match the animals to their babies. Color the star to show your favorite baby animal. Say. Language: cow, calf, dog, puppy, horse, foal, sheep, lamb; This is a (cow). The baby is a (calf).

Learning objectives

- Identify and name baby farm animals
- Listen and match farm animals to their babies
- Talk about your favorite baby farm animal

Materials

- Class CDs, printable content flashcards, *Ferris Wheel* mat, Mimi puppet

Main vocabulary

- cow, calf, dog, puppy, horse, foal, sheep, lamb

Key language

- This is a (cow). The baby is a (calf).

Teacher's tip: Encouraging the class to help individuals

When playing the memory game, allow children to help the classmates who are turning over the flashcards by recalling where the animals are and saying the animal and baby animal names collectively.

Circle time

Hello song & puppet (CD1 Track 2; see TB p 17 & 21)
Opening routines (see TB p 16)
Recycling activity (see TB p 19)
Lesson aims (see TB p 18)

Introduce content vocabulary.

- Lay out the flashcards of cow, horse, sheep, dog in a row and children say the words.
- Say *Let's learn about the baby animals!*
- Show printable flashcards of the baby animals in turn and say the words (*calf, foal, lamb, puppy*). Children repeat the words.
- Ask individual children to place the flashcard of each baby with the adult animal.
- Point to the flashcards and children say with you, e.g. *Cow – calf / Horse – foal.*

Game: *Memory!*

- Turn all the flashcards face down and mix them up.
- Ask two children to take turns turning over a flashcard and naming the animals, e.g. *Horse! / Puppy!* If the flashcards are a pair (e.g. Horse – foal), remove them from the game. If not, turn the flashcards face down again and two more children have a turn.
- Continue until children have matched all the flashcards.
- Repeat the game once or twice.

Game: *Big or small!*

- Show the flashcards and name adult or baby animals in random order, e.g. *Cow! / Lamb!* Children respond by saying *Big!* or *Small!* depending on whether the animal named is the adult or baby.
- Repeat without showing the flashcards and children respond in the same way.
- Say *Big!* or *Small!* and children respond by naming an adult or baby animal of their choice.

Table time

Student's Book p 61

Listen and point.

- Say *Sam and Anna are finding out about baby animals.* Play the audio. Children point to the animals as they hear them.

CD3 Track 11

Woman: Animals have babies.
This is a cow. And the cow's baby is a calf.
This is a horse. And the horse's baby is a foal.
This is a sheep. And the sheep's baby is a lamb.
This is a dog. And the dog's baby is a puppy.

Match the animals to their babies.

- Play the audio again. Children listen and draw lines to match the animals to their babies. Use the pause button as necessary.

Color the star to show your favorite baby animal. Say.

- Children color a star to show their favorite baby animal. Children say their favorite baby animal and/or stand next to their favorite baby animal flashcard on the classroom wall.

Activity Book p 61

Draw the babies next to the animals.

- Children draw the baby animal next to its parent.

Say.

- They talk about the animals and their babies.

Closing time

Learning review (see TB p 18)
Closing routines (see TB p 16)
Bye bye song and puppet (CD1 Track 3; see TB p 17 & 21)

Use the **Navio App** to play the vocabulary and language games, and encourage children to do the same at home.

Lesson 8 Culture

1 2 3 4 5

Watch. Listen, point and sing *Five little ducks.* Color the little ducks. Trace the numbers. Count the little ducks and circle the correct number. Say.
Language: duck, little, mommy, pond, quack, swimming; numbers; five little ducks

62

Learning objectives

- Watch, sing and act out the traditional song *Five little ducks*
- Play an action game
- Identify and say the numbers 1–5
- Count the number of ducks and say how many

Materials

- Class CDs, flashcards, *Ferris Wheel* mat, Mimi puppet

Main vocabulary

- duck, little, mommy, pond, quack, swimming; numbers

Key language

- five little ducks

Teacher's tip: Acting out the song in groups

Once the children are familiar with the song *Five little ducks*, have them act it out in groups of five. Number the children 1–5. They should stand and walk around a small circle as if swimming. When only four ducks come back, the number 5s sit down and so on until all the children stand up again at the end. Encourage the children to prompt the other members of their group to help build a team spirit.

Circle time

Hello song & puppet (CD1 Track 2; see TB p 17 & 21)
Opening routines (see TB p 16)
Recycling activity (see TB p 19)
Lesson aims (see TB p 18)

Mime being little ducks.

- Ask children to stand up. Say *Let's be little ducks!*
- Mime holding your hands by your side and moving them as wings. Pretend to swim like a little duck. Children copy what you do.
- Say *I'm Mommy (or Daddy) Duck. Let's go swimming in the pond!*
- Move around the classroom and mime swimming like a duck. Children do the same and follow you.
- At the end, say e.g. *Stop swimming now, little ducks! Very good!*

Make little duck groups.

- Children stay standing up. Give instructions, e.g. *Three little ducks!* Explain and demonstrate that children should make groups of three and mime swimming like little ducks.
- Repeat by saying in turn *Two/Four/Five little ducks!* and children adjust their groups accordingly. Be ready to help children count and get into groups.

***Five little ducks* song**

CD3 Track 12

- Say *Let's sing the song "Five little ducks."*
- Pre-teach actions for the song (see TB p 143).
- Play the audio. Children listen and do the actions with you.
- Play the audio again. Children do the actions and join in singing the song.

Watch the *Five little ducks* video.

- Children watch the video and join in singing the song and doing the actions with Anna and Sam.

Table time

Student's Book p 62

Watch. Listen, point and sing *Five little ducks*.

CD3 Track 12

- Play the audio of the song. Children listen, sing and point to the ducks.

Color the little ducks. Trace the numbers.

- Children color the little ducks and trace the numbers.

Count the little ducks and circle the correct number. Say.

- Children count the little ducks and circle the correct number. They point and say *Five little ducks.*

Activity Book p 62

Color the little ducks yellow. Count the little ducks and trace the correct number.

- Children color the ducks yellow. They count the ducks and trace the correct number.

Say.

- They point and say *Twenty little ducks.*

Closing time

Learning review (see TB p 18)
Closing routines (see TB p 16)
Bye bye song and puppet (CD1 Track 3; see TB p 17 & 21)

Use the **Navio App** to watch the video, and encourage children to do the same at home.

Review

Farm animals

I can ...

Vocabulary

Story

Speaking

Content

Trace and color the farm animals you know. Listen, point and say. Ask and say how many animals there are. Complete the faces to show what you can do. Language: cow, dog, duck, goat, hen, horse, rooster, sheep; numbers; There's a (horse). There are (ducks). The sheep goes (baa). How many (hens)? (Three).

Farm animals

Learning objectives

- Review what you have learned in this unit
- Complete a self-evaluation
- Ask and answer about what farm animals there are

Materials

- Class CDs, flashcards, *Ferris Wheel* mat, Mimi puppet

Main vocabulary

- cow, dog, duck, goat, hen, horse, rooster, sheep

Key language

- There's a (horse). There are (ducks). The (sheep) goes (baa). How many (hens)? (Three).

Teacher's tip: Using positive language with a partner

Put the children into pairs and have them point to the animals in the review. They should say *There's a sheep. / There are ducks* as appropriate. Encourage them to use positive language with their partner. If the answer is incorrect, encourage them to say *Try again*. If it's correct, say *Very good*, etc.

Circle time

Hello song & puppet (CD1 Track 2; see TB p 17 & 21)
Opening routines (see TB p 16)
Recycling activity (see TB p 19)
Lesson aims (see TB p 18)

Farm animal flashcard games

- Choose one or two flashcard games with the *Ferris Wheel* mat and/or the puppet to review main vocabulary (see TB p 20 & 21).

Sing *On the farm*.

CD3 Track 4

- Lay out the farm animal flashcards.
- Play the audio. Children sing, point to the flashcards and wave their arms at the end of each verse.

Game: ***Guess the animal.***

- Hide a farm animal flashcard behind a book. Children guess by saying *I think there's a (horse)*. Slowly reveal the flashcard.

Game: ***There's a cow in the classroom!***

- Give out the farm animal flashcards to individual children without others seeing.
- Children take turns making the noise of the animal on their flashcard. Other children listen and say, e.g. *There's a cow in the classroom!*

Watch the story video.

- Children watch the story video. Ask children to say the animals, e.g. *There's a dog. / There are ducks.*

Table time

Student's Book p 63

Trace and color the farm animals you know.

- Explain and demonstrate the activity.

Listen, point and say.

- Play the audio. Children listen, point to the animals, and say the words.

CD3 Track 13

Mimi: I'm the teacher! Can you remember the farm animals, Dylan?
Dylan: Yes, I can. Sheep.
Mimi: Sheep.
Dylan: Cow.
Mimi: Cow.
Dylan: Hen.
Mimi: Hen.
Dylan: Duck.
Mimi: Duck.
Dylan: Goat.
Mimi: Goat.
Dylan: Dog.
Mimi: Dog.
Dylan: Rooster.
Mimi: Rooster.
Dylan: Horse.
Mimi: Horse. Great job, Dylan! Very good!

Ask and say how many animals there are.

- Ask children to say the animals in the pictures e.g. *There's a horse. / There are hens.* Then ask *How many? (Two).*

Complete the faces to show what you can do.

- Explain the four pictures: *I can name farm animals; I can understand the story; I can say animals there are on the farm; I can name baby animals.*
- Remind children to complete each face with a smile or a frown depending on how well they think they have done.

Activity Book p 63

Choose and color the farm animals you want to play with. Ask and say.

- Children color the animals they want to play with. They ask and say about the animals.

Think and circle the number to show your progress.

- Children circle the number.

Closing time

Learning review (see TB p 18)
Closing routines (see TB p 16)
Bye bye song and puppet (CD1 Track 3; see TB p 17 & 21)

Use the **Navio App** to review what children have learned in this unit, and encourage them to do the same at home.

Project

COOPERATIVE LEARNING

Farm animals

1

2

3

Make your favorite farm animal. Make a poster of the class's favorite farm animals. Ask and say.
Language: cow, duck, goat, sheep; cotton balls, tissue paper; numbers; colors; There's a (sheep).
There are (six) (ducks). How many (cows)? I like (goats). My (duck) is (yellow). Our farm animals are (fantastic)!

64

Farm animals

Learning objectives

- Work together to do a collaborative project
- Follow instructions
- Make a favorite farm animal
- Choose and draw animals for a farm

Materials

- Class CDs, Mimi puppet, photocopiable templates: duck, sheep, cow, goat, cotton balls, crayons, glue, tissue paper
- optional: photocopiable template: duck

Main vocabulary

- cow, duck, goat, sheep; cotton balls, tissue paper; numbers; colors

Key language

- There's a (sheep). There are (six) (ducks). How many (cows)? I like (goats). My (duck) is (yellow). Our farm animals are (fantastic)!

Teacher's tip: Helping one another

COOPERATIVE LEARNING

Children's fine motor skills develop at different rates. Encourage those who finish their animal quickly to go around and help their classmates rolling the tissue paper balls, gluing them or the cotton balls on, or helping clean up. Encourage them to say *Can I help you?*

Circle time

Hello song & puppet (CD1 Track 2; see TB p 17 & 21)
Opening routines (see TB p 16)
Recycling activity (see TB p 19)
Lesson aims (see TB p 18)

Prepare for your project.

- Say *Let's do a project! Let's make a poster of our favorite farm animals.* Explain that children should work together in groups for this project.
- Show children the animal templates, tissue paper and cotton balls.
- Demonstrate coloring the duck's beak and feet with crayons.
- Demonstrate making small balls of tissue paper and gluing them on the duck template for feathers.
- Demonstrate coloring the sheep's head and legs with crayons.
- Demonstrate gluing cotton balls to the sheep template for wool.

Table time

Student's Book p 64

COOPERATIVE LEARNING

Make your favorite farm animal.

- Say *We're going to make a poster of our favorite farm animals. Look at what we need for our project.* Hold up the objects and elicit the words: *cotton balls, crayons, glue, tissue paper, paper* (the templates).
- Say the words again. Children listen and point to the pictures in their books.
- Make sure children have crayons, pieces of tissue paper, cotton balls and glue available. Children choose the template of their favorite animal. They color the head and legs of the animal, and glue either tissue paper or cotton balls on the rest of the animal. Be ready to help as necessary.

Make a poster of the class's favorite farm animals. Ask and say.

- Children take turns gluing their animals on a poster to make a class display. Praise the children's work as they come up.
- Ask children *Do you like our farm poster?* Make the point that everyone helped make the poster and that they couldn't have made such a beautiful poster on their own.

Alternative version of project

- Children could use the large duck template on TB p 239 to make a poster of a duck pond. Children color the duck's beak and feet, and glue pieces of yellow tissue paper on the body. They then glue their ducks on a blue background to make a duck pond.

Activity Book p 64

Draw a picture of you. Choose and draw animals for your farm. Color or paint the farm.

- Children draw a picture of themselves in the space provided.
- They choose animals from the top to draw in the farm.
- Children color or paint the farm.

Say.

- Children take turns asking and answering about their farm.

Closing time

Learning review (see TB p 18)
Closing routines (see TB p 16)
Bye bye song and puppet (CD1 Track 3; see TB p 17 & 21)

Transportation

Let's go by bike!

Vocabulary and language

- **Main vocabulary:** bike, boat, bus, car, plane, train, truck
- **Key language:** Let's go by (bus)! Yes. / No. I want to go by (bike). Do you want to go by (bus)? Yes, I do. / No, I don't.
- **Content language:** air, road, track, water; A (bus) goes on the (road). A (plane) goes (in the air).
- **Other language:** card, dream, friend, paper shapes, row, scissors, stream, teacher; I think of my (daddy). I say please/sorry/thank you. Row, row, row your boat. This is my (truck). It's (red). How many (planes)? (Two).

Unit objectives

- Identify and name forms of transportation
- Sing the language song *Let's go by boat!*
- Suggest and say how you want to travel
- Understand and act out the story *Let's go by bike!*
- Sing and act out the story song *I want to go by bike*
- Sing the values song *I think of my mommy*
- Recognize the value of being polite and considerate
- Identify and name where different forms of transportation go
- Sing and act out the traditional song *Row, row, row your boat*
- Review your learning and progress
- Participate in a collaborative project

Story

CD3 Track 19

Picture 1

Narrator: Mommy, Daddy, Mimi and Dylan are going to Grandma and Grandpa's house.
Mimi: Oh great! I love Grandma and Grandpa. Let's go by bike.
Dylan: Oh yes, please. I want to go by bike too!
Mommy: Come on then. Let's go by bike!
Mimi: Hurray! Thank you.

Picture 2

Daddy: Oh no. It's raining.
Mommy: We can't go by bike.
Mimi: Hmmm. I have an idea. Let's go by car!
Dylan: Oh yes, please. I want to go by car too.
Daddy: Come on then. Let's go by car.
Dylan: Hurray! Thank you.

Picture 3

Mommy: Oh no. Look at the wheel.
Daddy: We can't go by car.
Mimi: Hmmm. I have an idea. Let's go by train!
Dylan: Oh yes, please. I want to go by train too.
Mommy: Come on then. Let's go by train.
Mimi: Hurray! Thank you.

Picture 4

Daddy: Oh no. The train is full.
Mommy: We can't go by train.
Daddy: Come on then. Let's go home!
Mimi: But I want to go to Grandma and Grandpa's house.
Dylan: Me too! Please, Mommy. Please, Daddy.
Mommy: No, sorry. We can't go to Grandma and Grandpa's house today. Let's go home.
Mimi & Dylan: Ohhh.

Picture 5

Dylan: Oh look! Here's Mrs. Cat and the school bus.
Mimi: I have an idea. Let's go by bus! Hello, Mrs. Cat.
Mrs. Cat: Hello, Mimi. Hello, Dylan. Hello, Mr. and Mrs. Meerkat. Hop on!
Mimi: Oh thank you, Mrs. Cat. We want to go to Grandma and Grandpa's house.
Mrs. Cat: No problem!
Mommy & Daddy: Oh, thank you, Mrs. Cat.

Picture 6

Mimi: Hello, Grandma.
Dylan: Hello, Grandpa.
Grandpa: Hello, Mimi.
Grandma: Hello, Dylan. Come in. And bring your friends.
Grandpa: It's time for a snack!
Mimi: Oh thank you, Grandma. Thank you, Grandpa. Come on, everyone! Hurray!

Songs

Language song

Let's go by boat! CD3 Track 17

Let's go by boat! Let's go by boat! (Mime rowing a boat)
No, no, no! No, no, no! (Wag a finger)
Let's go by plane! Let's go by plane! (Spread your arms wide for the wings)
Yes, yes, yes! Off we go! (Thumbs up and beckon)
Let's go by truck! Let's go by truck! (Mime turning a big steering wheel)
No, no, no! No, no, no! (Wag a finger)
Let's go by train! Let's go by train! (Make circular motions with your arms)
Yes, yes, yes! Off we go! (Thumbs up and beckon)
Let's go by motorcycle! Let's go by motorcycle! (Mime holding onto the handlebars and sway from side to side)
No, no, no! No, no, no! (Wag a finger)
Let's go by bus! Let's go by bus! (Mime holding the strap and swaying)
Yes, yes, yes! Off we go! (Thumbs up and beckon)

Story song

I want to go by bike CD3 Track 20

I want to go by bike, by bike (Mime pedalling)
Oh yes, please. Me too! (Put a hand up enthusiastically)
Come on then. Let's go by bike. (Beckon)
I want to go with you. (Point to someone)

I want to go by car, by car (Mime turning a steering wheel)
Oh yes, please. Me too! (Put a hand up enthusiastically)
Come on then. Let's go by car. (Beckon)
I want to go with you. (Point to someone)

I want to go by train, by train (Move arms in circular motion)
Oh yes, please! Me too! (Put a hand up enthusiastically)
Come on then. Let's go by train. (Beckon)
I want to go with you. (Point to someone)

I want to go by bus, by bus (Mime holding the strap and swaying)
Oh yes, please! Me too! (Put a hand up enthusiastically)
Come on then. Let's go by bus. (Beckon)
I want to go with you. (Point to someone)

Values song

I think of my mommy CD3 Track 23

I think of my mommy,
And my daddy too.
I say "please."
I say "sorry."
I say "thank you."
I think of my teacher,
And my friends too.
I say "please."
I say "sorry."
I say "thank you."
I think of my grandma,
And my grandpa too.
I say "please."
I say "sorry."
I say "thank you."
I think of my brother,
And my sister too.
I say "please."
I say "sorry."
I say "thank you."

Culture song

Row, row, row your boat CD3 Track 25

Row, row, row your boat, (Mime rowing a boat)
Gently down the stream,
Merrily, merrily, merrily, merrily, (Wave arms over head back and forth)
Life is but a dream. (Turn around slowly)
Row, row, row your boat, (Mime rowing a boat)
Gently down the stream,
Merrily, merrily, merrily, merrily, (Wave arms over head back and forth)
Life is but a dream. (Turn around slowly)
Row, row, row your boat, (Mime rowing a boat)
Gently down the stream,
Merrily, merrily, merrily, merrily, (Wave arms over head back and forth)
Life is but a dream. (Turn around slowly)

Transportation

Let's go by bike!

Vocabulary Lesson 1

Listen, point and repeat. Listen and play. Stick the transportation stickers. Circle the forms of transportation you use. Say. Language: bike, boat, bus, car, plane, train; blue, green, orange, pink, red, yellow

65

Learning objectives

- Identify and name transportation
- Listen and point to transportation
- Identify the transportation you use

Materials

- Class CDs, flashcards, *Ferris Wheel* mat, Mimi puppet

Main vocabulary

- bike, boat, bus, car, plane, train; blue, green, orange, pink, red, yellow

Teacher's tip: Using mime and prediction to present vocabulary

As an alternative to using the flashcards to introduce the transportation, use mime and make the noise of each one, bringing in an element of prediction. As children respond in their shared language, say the word in English and then show them the flashcard to confirm.

Circle time

Hello song & puppet (CD1 Track 2; see TB p 17 & 21)
Opening routines (see TB p 16)
Lesson aims (see TB p 18)

Introduce transportation.

- Use the puppet and flashcards to introduce transportation. Ask children what transportation they know. As they respond in their shared language, introduce the words in English. Children repeat the words.
- *Ferris Wheel* mat on floor or board with the transportation flashcards face down (one on each color). Use puppet to turn over and name. Children repeat the words.

Game: *Say the color!*

- Name the forms of transportation on the Ferris Wheel and children name the color. Then the reverse.

Game: *Mime the transportation!*

- Teach the children mimes for the transportation as follows: bus (hold on to strap and sway your body), boat (pretend to row), plane (move your arms as wings), bike (lean forward and mime hands on handlebars), car (pretend to hold steering wheel and drive), train (bend knees and arms at elbows and make circular chugging movements).
- Say the words and children do the mimes.
- Mime one form of transportation and children guess what it is.
- Invite individual children to do mimes and others guess the transportation in the same way.

Table time

Student's Book p 65

Listen, point and repeat.

- Play the audio. The children listen, point to each object as they hear it, and repeat the words.

CD3 Track 14

Mimi: Look, Dylan! Bus … boat … plane … bike … car … train. Repeat, Dylan!
Dylan: Yes, Mimi. Bus … boat … plane … bike … car … train.
Mimi: Very good, Dylan. Let's name the transportation together!
Both: Bus … boat … plane … bike … car … train.

Listen and play.

- Use finger in air to pretend to spin wheel. Children spin their fingers, point to the color when they hear it on the audio and say the word.

CD3 Track 15

Mimi: Spin the wheel
One, tw3o, three
Point and name
The transportation with me!
Mimi: Red … bus!
Dylan: Pink … car!
Mimi: Blue … boat!
Dylan: Green … train!
Mimi: Yellow … bike!
Dylan: Orange … plane!

- Play the game with you and/or individual children naming colors and others responding with the words.

Stick the transportation stickers.

- Children stick the transportation stickers.

Circle the forms of transportation you use. Say.

- Children circle the transportation they use in real life and say the words.

Activity Book p 65

Look, find and match.

- Children identify the toy transportation Mimi and Dylan are playing with. Children find and match the pictures.

Color.

- They then color the toys to match the ones Mimi and Dylan are playing with.

Point and say.

- Children point and name the toys.

Closing time

Learning review (see TB p 18)
Closing routines (see TB p 16)
Bye bye song and puppet (CD1 Track 3; see TB p 17 & 21)

Use the **Navio App** to play the vocabulary game, and encourage children to do the same at home.

Language

3:16 3:17 hello

Listen and find the new transportation. Listen, point and sing *Let's go by boat!* Color the circles green for *yes* and red for *no*. Point and say.
Language: boat, bus, motorcycle, plane, train, truck; Let's go by (bus)! Yes. / No.

Learning objectives
- Talk about what transportation you want to use
- Identify and name two new items of transportation
- Sing the language song *Let's go by boat!*
- Say the transportation you want to use

Materials
- Class CDs, flashcards, *Ferris Wheel* mat, Mimi puppet

Main vocabulary
- boat, bus, motorcycle, plane, train, truck

Key language
- Let's go by (bus)! Yes. / No.

Teacher's tip: Cooperating in pairs

Play *Let's go by ...!* (see below) but this time, ask children to play with a partner. One of the children says the sentence and the other one gives the answer. When they say the correct transportation, have them do the correct mime. Then have them switch.

Circle time

Hello song & puppet (CD1 Track 2; see TB p 17 & 21)

Opening routines (see TB p 16)

Recycling activity (six transportation words from Lesson 1) (see TB p 19)

Lesson aims (see TB p 18)

Introduce the new transportation.
- All eight transportation flashcards on the floor or board. Children identify the two new forms of transportation. Use the puppet to point to and say the words in turn. Children repeat in chorus.
- Turn the two new flashcards face down. Mix them up. Point to one and ask *Motorcycle or truck?* Children guess. Repeat several times.

Introduce *Let's go by ... !*
- Ask the children to imagine that they're going on vacation and need to decide how to go.
- Lay the flashcards out, point to one and suggest, e.g. *Let's go by train!* Use the puppet to say *no*.
- Repeat with other flashcards. Encourage children to say the sentences with you. Use the puppet to respond *no* until the last flashcard, which is *yes*.

Game: *Guess the transportation.*
- Choose two flashcards, e.g. *bus* and *train*. Turn them face down and mix them up.
- Point to one flashcard and say, e.g. *Let's go by bus!* Children respond *yes* if they think the flashcard is the bus and *no* if they don't.
- Turn the flashcard over and children say *Hurray!* if they guessed the flashcard correctly.
- Repeat the game with different flashcards.

Table time

Student's Book p 66

Listen and find the new transportation.
- Play the audio. Children listen and find the two new words. Play the audio again. The children listen and say the words.

CD3 Track 16

One, two, Which words are new?
Motorcycle! Motorcycle!
Truck! Truck!

Listen, point and sing *Let's go by boat!*

CD3 Track 17
- Play the song. The children listen and point to each form of transportation as they hear it.
- Play the song again. Children sing the song and do the actions (see TB p 165).
- Remember that you can use the karaoke version of the song when children are confident.

Color the circles green for *yes* and red for *no*.
- Play the first verse of the song again. Ask *Do they go by boat?* Elicit *No*. Demonstrate coloring the spot by the boat red. Ask *Do they go by plane?* Elicit *Yes*. Demonstrate coloring the spot by the plane green.
- Play the audio again. Use the pause button. Children color the spots under the photos red or green.

Point and say.
- Children point and say with you, e.g. *Let's go by (train)!* and respond *Yes* or *No* following the colors of the spots.

Activity Book p 66

Choose and color the transportation you want to use.
- Explain that children should choose four forms of transportation they want to use and color them green.
- They color the other forms of transportation red.
- Say e.g. *Let's go by bus!* Children respond *yes* or *no* depending on how they have colored the pictures.

Point and say.
- Invite individual children to take turns making suggestions and the rest of the class respond.

Closing time

Learning review (see TB p 18)

Closing routines (see TB p 16)

Bye bye song and puppet (CD1 Track 3; see TB p 17 & 21)

Use the **Navio App** to listen to the song, and encourage children to do the same at home.

3:19

Watch. Listen to the story *Let's go by bike!* Circle the form of transportation Mimi and Dylan use. Stick the story sticker.

Language: bike, bus, car, train; Let's go by (bike)! I want to go by (car).

Learning objectives

- Watch, understand and enjoy the story *Let's go by bike!*
- Make a prediction about the story
- Imitate transportation
- Identify and order the transportation Mimi and Dylan use

Materials

- Class CDs, printable story cards, flashcards, *Ferris Wheel* mat, Mimi puppet

Main vocabulary

- bike, bus, car, train

Key language

- Let's go by (bike)! I want to go by (car).

Teacher's tip: Personalizing the story

Personalize the story by asking the children if they have family members who live far away. How do they go to see them? Encourage the children to talk about how they feel when they get there.

Circle time

Hello song & puppet (CD1 Track 2; see TB p 17 & 21)
Opening routines (see TB p 16)
Recycling activity (*Let's go by …* and transportation vocabulary) (see TB p 19)
Lesson aims (see TB p 18)

Introduce the story *Let's go by bike!*

- Say *It's story time!* Play the *Story rhyme* (CD1 Track 4; see TB p 17).
- Say *Anna and Sam are listening to a story about Mimi, Dylan, Mommy and Daddy.* Ask *Where do they go? How do they go?* Encourage children to guess.

Watch or listen to the story.

CD3 Track 19

- Watch the video, play the audio, or read using the printable story cards. Pause, repeat words, point and ask questions.
- Ask the questions again and check the answers.
- Repeat the story.
- Ask: *Do you like the story? Do you like going to visit your family?*

Make the sounds, mime and say.

- Name the transportation in the story. Children respond by making the sounds and miming the transportation (see Lesson 1).

Table time

Student's Book p 67

Watch. Listen to the story *Let's go by bike!*

- Read or play the story again. Children listen and follow the story by pointing to the pictures.

Story questions

Picture 1
Where are Mommy, Daddy, Mimi and Dylan going? *(Grandma and Grandpa's house)*
Do they want to go by car? *(No)*

Picture 2
Is it raining? *(Yes)* Can they go by bike? *(No)*

Picture 3
Can they go by car? *(No)*
How does Mimi want to go? *(By train)*

Picture 4
Can they go by train? *(No)*
Do Mimi and Dylan want to go home? *(No)*

Picture 5
Who does Dylan see on the bus? *(Mrs. Cat)*
Can they go to Grandma and Grandpa's house by bus? *(Yes)*

Picture 6
Do Mimi and Dylan's friends go to Grandma and Grandpa's house too? *(Yes)*
What is it time for? *(A snack)*

Circle the form of transportation Mimi and Dylan use.

- Children find the transportation Mimi and Dylan use (bus) and circle it.

Stick the story sticker.

- Children stick on the story sticker.
- Ask *Are Mommy, Daddy, Mimi and Dylan happy at the end of the story?* and children respond.

Activity Book p 67

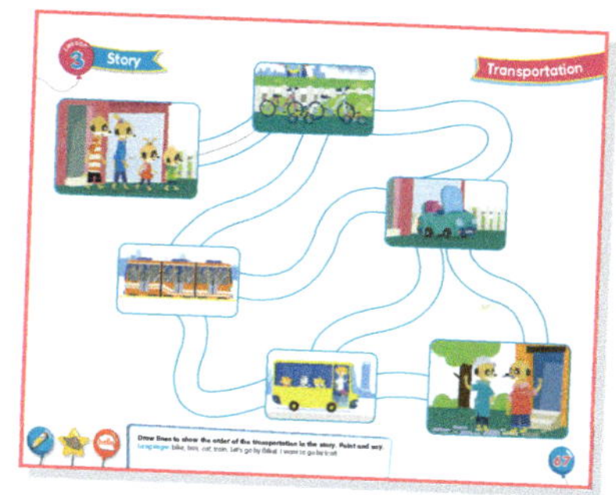

Draw lines to show the order of the transportation in the story.

- Children draw lines to connect the pictures in the correct order.

Point and say.

- They point and talk about each picture.

Closing time

Learning review (see TB p 18)
Closing routines (see TB p 16)
Bye bye song and puppet (CD1 Track 3; see TB p 17 & 21)

Use the **Navio App** to watch the video, and encourage children to do the same at home.

Story Song

1 2 3 4

Watch. Listen, point and sing *I want to go by bike*. Trace the numbers. Match to order the pictures. Point and say.

Language: bike, bus, car, train; numbers 1–4; I want to go by (bike). Let's go by (car)!

Learning objectives

- Watch, sing and act out the story song *I want to go by bike*
- Listen to the story again and do the sounds and actions
- Identify the order of transportation in the song
- Identify and name transportation you want to use

Materials

- Class CDs, printable story cards, flashcards, *Ferris Wheel* mat, Mimi puppet

Main vocabulary

- bike, bus, car, train; numbers 1–4

Key language

- I want to go by (bike). Let's go by (car)!

Teacher's tip: Building listening skills

Play a listening game. Children sit in rows of four. Whisper a form of transportation to the first child in the first row. The child whispers it to the next child and so on. The last child says the name. If it is correct, their team gets a point. Repeat with other teams. The team with most points wins.

Circle time

Hello song & puppet (CD1 Track 2; see TB p 17 & 21)
Opening routines (see TB p 16)
Recycling activity (transportation vocabulary) (see TB p 19)
Lesson aims (see TB p 18)

Retell the story *Let's go by bike!*

- Play the audio, video or read the story using the printable story cards.
- Demonstrate that children should join in saying the sounds and doing the actions for the different forms of transportation.

Game: *I want to go by boat!*

- Choose any four transportation flashcards and stick them on different walls in the classroom at the children's height.
- Tell children they are going to visit a family member. They stand by the transportation they want to go by.
- When children are standing in groups by each flashcard, get them to repeat their sentence, e.g. *I want to go by boat* with you several times.

***I want to go by bike* song**

CD3 Track 20

- Ask children if they can remember the transportation Mimi and Dylan want to go by in the story (*bike, car, train, bus*).
- Play the video or audio of the story song. Children watch/listen and say the transportation words when they hear them.
- Play the song again. Children mime and join in.

Table time

Student's Book p 68

Watch. Listen, point and sing *I want to go by bike.*

CD3 Track 20

- Play the audio of the song. Children listen, sing and point to the transportation in their book.
- Remember that you can use the karaoke version of the song when children are confident.

Trace the numbers. Match to order the pictures.

- Children trace the numbers 1–4. Play the audio of the song again, pausing after each verse. Children listen and match the numbers to the transportation to show the order Mimi and Dylan sing them in the song (1 = bike, 2 = car, 3 = train, 4 = bus).

Point and say.

- Children point to the pictures and say *I want to go by (bus). / Let's go by (car)!*

Activity Book p 68

Match the puzzle pieces.

- Children match the puzzle pieces.

Circle the two puzzle pieces with the transportation the meerkats use in the story.

- They circle the two puzzle pieces that show the transportation the meerkats use in the story (the bus).

Point and say.

- They talk about the transportation they want to use.

Closing time

Learning review (see TB p 18)
Closing routines (see TB p 16)
Bye bye song and puppet (CD1 Track 3; see TB p 17 & 21)

Use the **Navio App** to watch the video, and encourage children to do the same at home.

Lesson 5 Speaking

Life skills

Watch. Listen and point. Circle the form of transportation that Uncle Dan, Sam and Anna use to go to town. Draw a picture of your favorite form of transportation. Ask and say. Language: bike, bus, car; Let's go by (car)! I want to go by (bike). Do you want to go by (bus)? Yes, I do. / No, I don't.

Learning objectives

- Talk about your favorite transportation to use
- Watch, understand and enjoy a video
- Identify the transportation in the video
- Match the transportation and say what transportation you want to use

Materials

- Class CDs, flashcards, *Ferris Wheel* mat, Mimi puppet

Main vocabulary

- bike, bus, car

Key language

- Let's go by (car)! I want to go by (bike). Do you want to go by (bus)? Yes, I do. / No, I don't.

Teacher's tip: Using transportation safely

Life skills

Use the opportunity to make sure the children know how to use transportation safely. Say *Let's go by bus*. Mime getting on the bus and sitting down. Say *Let's go by bike* and mime putting on a helmet and holding on to the handlebars. Repeat for the other forms of transportation.

Circle time

Hello song & puppet (CD1 Track 2; see TB p 17 & 21)
Opening routines (see TB p 16)
Recycling activity (story song) (CD3 Track 20; see TB p 19)
Lesson aims (see TB p 18)

Game: *Guess the flashcard.*

- Give out the transportation flashcards to individual children without others seeing.
- Children take turns miming and making the sound of the transportation on their flashcard. Other children listen and guess the transportation.

Watch the video.

- Explain that Uncle Dan wants to go to town.
- Ask *Can Sam and Anna go with Uncle Dan? How do they go?* and encourage children to guess.
- Play the video.
- Ask the questions again and children respond.

CD3 Track 22

Uncle Dan:	I want to go to town.
Anna:	Can we come, Uncle Dan?
Uncle Dan:	Yes, of course.
Sam:	Thank you, Uncle Dan. Let's go by car!
Anna:	Oh, yes. I want to go by car.
Uncle Dan:	No, sorry. I don't have my car today.
Anna:	Let's go by bike!
Uncle Dan:	No, sorry. I don't have my bike today. I know. Let's go by bus! Do you want to go by bus?
Sam & Anna:	Yes, please.
Uncle Dan:	Hurry up then! The bus leaves now!

Table time

Student's Book p 69

Life skills

Watch. Listen and point.

- Children point to Anna, Sam and Uncle Dan in the photo. Play the audio or video. Children point to the transportation as they hear them in the dialogue.

Circle the form of transportation that Uncle Dan, Sam and Anna use to go to town.

- Play the audio again. Children circle the transportation Uncle Dan, Sam and Anna use to go to town (the bus).

Draw a picture of you on your favorite form of transportation. Ask and say.

- Children draw a picture of themselves using a favorite form of transportation. Children show you and each other their pictures and ask and say *Do you want to go by (bus)? Yes, I do. / No, I don't. I want to go by (bike).*

Activity Book p 69

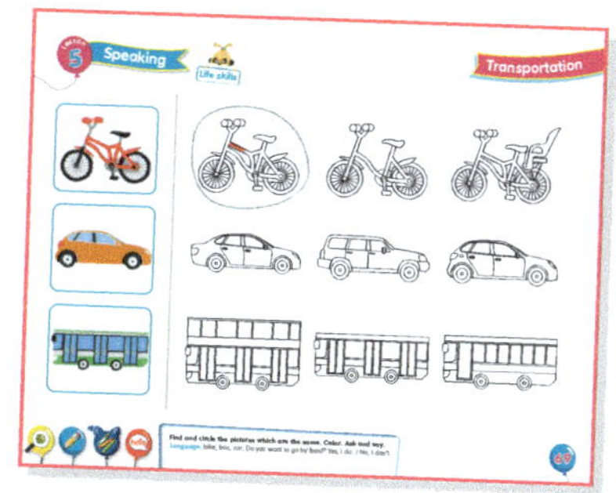

Find and circle the pictures which are the same.

- Children circle the picture that matches the transportation on the left.

Color.

- They color the picture they circled the same color as the transportation on the left.

Ask and say.

- They ask and answer about the transportation they want to use.

Closing time

Learning review (see TB p 18)
Closing routines (see TB p 16)
Bye bye song and puppet (CD1 Track 3; see TB p 17 & 21)

Use the **Navio App** to watch the video, and encourage children to do the same at home.

Lesson 6 Values Thinking of others

3:23

hello

Listen, point and sing *I think of my mommy*. Color the frames of the people you think of. Say. **Language:** mommy, daddy, brother, sister, grandma, grandpa, friend, teacher; I think of my (daddy). I say please/sorry/thank you.

SOCIAL AND EMOTIONAL LEARNING

70

Learning objectives

- Understand the value of thinking of others
- Act out the story
- Sing the values song *I think of my mommy*
- Talk about people you think of
- Identify people thinking of others and show how you think of others

Materials

- Class CDs, flashcards, *Ferris Wheel* mat, Mimi puppet

Main vocabulary

- mommy, daddy, brother, sister, grandma, grandpa, friend, teacher

Key language

- I think of my (daddy). I say please/sorry/thank you.

Teacher's tip: Being polite

An important part of social and emotional learning is beginning to think of others. Incorporate the ideas and language from the song into the daily routines in your classroom. Make sure children always say *please* and *thank you* when asking for or being given classroom items. Encourage them to say *sorry* to their friends when something goes wrong.

Circle time

Hello song & puppet (CD1 Track 2; see TB p 17 & 21)

Opening routines (see TB p 16)

Recycling activity (*I want to go by …* and transportation) (see TB p 19)

Lesson aims (see TB p 18)

Watch the *Let's go by bike!* story video.

- Play the story video.
- Take the parts of the narrator, Mommy, Daddy, Mrs. Cat, Grandma and Grandpa yourself. Encourage children to join in acting out the story in two groups (Mimi, Dylan).
- Ask *Who helps Mimi and Dylan?* Listen to the children's answers in their shared language e.g. *Mrs. Cat – she takes them to their grandparents' house on the school bus. Are Mimi and Dylan polite? Yes, they say "please" and "thank you". Is Grandma considerate? Yes, she gives them all a snack at the end of the story.*
- Ask *Is it important to think of other people?* and listen to the children's responses.

***I think of my mommy* song**

CD3 Track 23

- Ask *Who do you think of?* Give an example, e.g. *I think of my grandma.* Listen to children's ideas and use these to pre-teach or remind them of people named in the song, e.g. grandpa, teacher, friend, brother, sister.
- Ask *Who do Mimi and Dylan think of in the song?* Play the audio. Check the answers (mommy, daddy, teacher, friends, grandma, grandpa, brother, sister).
- Ask *What words do they say? (please, sorry, thank you).*
- Play the audio again. Children join in singing the song and doing the actions (see TB p 165).
- Make the point that it is important to think of others and not only of yourself.

Table time

Student's Book p 70

Listen, point and sing *I think of my mommy*.

CD3 Track 23

- Children sing and point to the pictures of Mimi and Dylan thinking of others.

Color the frames of the people you think of. Say.

- Children color the frames of the pictures of people they think of.
- Children say e.g. *I think of my (daddy). / I say "thank you".*

Activity Book p 70

Check (✔) the pictures which show children thinking of others.

- Children check the pictures that show children thinking of others.

Choose and color one picture to show how you think of others. Say.

- Children choose one of the pictures they checked and color it.
- They use the picture to say how they think of others.

Closing time

Learning review (see TB p 18)

Closing routines (see TB p 16)

Bye bye song and puppet (CD1 Track 3; see TB p 17 & 21)

Use the **Navio App** to listen to the song, and encourage children to do the same at home.

Lesson 7

Content

Transportation

Listen and point. Match the forms of transportation to the places. Say. Language: air, road, track, water; bike, boat, bus, car, motorcycle, plane, train, truck; A (bus) goes (on the road). A (plane) goes (in the air).

Learning objectives

- Identify and name places where different transportation goes, and understand which transportation goes in which place
- Listen and identify where transportation goes
- Talk about transportation

Materials

- Class CDs, printable content flashcards, *Ferris Wheel* mat, Mimi puppet

Main vocabulary

- air, road, track, water; bike, boat, bus, car, motorcycle, plane, train, truck

Key language

- A (bus) goes on the (road). A (plane) goes (in the air).

Teacher's tip: Using mime to reinforce concepts and help memory

Using mime for the different places where transportation goes can help the children recall the concept and language more easily. Wiggle one hand up and down for water, raise your hands up for air, push your hands out in front of you to make parallel lines for tracks, and run one hand from right to left for the road.

Circle time

Hello song & puppet (CD1 Track 2; see TB p 17 & 21)
Opening routines (see TB p 16)
Recycling activity (see TB p 19)
Lesson aims (see TB p 18)

Introduce content vocabulary.

- Say *Let's learn about transportation!*
- Show the printable flashcards of *road, track, air* and *water* in turn and say, e.g. *This is a road. A car goes on the road.* Children repeat the new words.
- Hold up the transportation flashcards in turn. Children identify the transportation and where it goes e.g. *Boat – water / Train – track.*

Sort the flashcards.

- Lay out the flashcards of *road, track, air* and *water.*
- Hold up the transportation flashcards in turn. Invite individual children to name the transportation and place it under the correct flashcard. Say e.g. *Yes, very good. A motorcycle goes on the road.* as they do this.
- Continue until children have placed all the flashcards.
- Ask e.g. *How many go on the water / road / track / in the air?* Children count and name the flashcards in each group.
- Ask if children can think of other transportation in any of the groups and listen to their response (in their shared language) e.g. *tractor, rocket, ship.*

Table time

Student's Book p 71

Listen and point.

- Say *Sam and Anna are finding out about transportation.* Play the audio. Children and point to the transportation and places as they hear them.

CD3 Track 24

Transportation is different.
A boat goes on the water.
A plane goes in the air.
A car goes on the road.
A train goes on the track.

Match the forms of transportation to the places.

- Play the audio again. Children listen and draw lines to match the transportation to where it goes. Use the pause button as necessary. They then match the other items that don't appear in the audio, e.g. bike to road.

Say.

- Children point to their pictures and say e.g. *A (bike) goes (on the road).*

Activity Book p 71

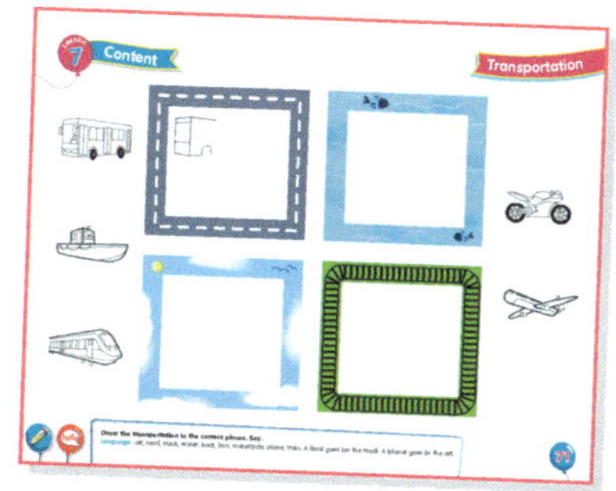

Draw the transportation in the correct places.

- Point out the frames showing a road, water, air and a track.
- Children draw each form of transportation inside the correct frame. (Note both bus and motorcycle go in the first frame.)

Say.

- Point to each frame. Children say the transportation and where it goes.

Closing time

Learning review (see TB p 18)
Closing routines (see TB p 16)
Bye bye song and puppet (CD1 Track 3; see TB p 17 & 21)

Use the **Navio App** to play the vocabulary and language games, and encourage children to do the same at home.

Lesson 8 Culture

Transportation

Watch. Listen, point and sing *Row, row, row your boat*. Draw a line to follow the stream. Draw a picture of you in the boat. Say.
Language: boat, dream, row, stream; Row, row, row your boat.

72

Learning objectives

- Watch, sing and act out the traditional song *Row, row, row your boat*
- Play an action game
- Draw a picture of yourself
- Trace a boat path and identify your favorite boat

Materials

- Class CDs, flashcards, *Ferris Wheel* mat, Mimi puppet

Main vocabulary

- boat, dream, row, stream

Key language

- Row, row, row your boat.

Teacher's tip: Raising physical self-awareness

Physical self-awareness is a skill that we can begin to develop in the classroom. Seat the children in a line of pairs facing each other and holding hands. They should bend their knees as if in a rowing boat. As they sing the song, they should move back and forth in time with the music. This creates the need to concentrate and work with their partner moderating their own body movements as they do so.

Circle time

Hello song & puppet (CD1 Track 2; see TB p 17 & 21)
Opening routines (see TB p 16)
Recycling activity (see TB p 19)
Lesson aims (see TB p 18)

Game: *Freeze!*

- Explain and demonstrate that children should mime the transportation you say (see Lesson 1) and move around the classroom without bumping into anyone else.
- Give instructions, e.g. *Car! Stop!*, and children freeze in position to show the transportation. Say e.g. *What a great plane! / That's a fantastic car!* as they do this.
- Make *Boat! Stop!* the last instruction and use this to lead into the next activity.

***Row, row, row your boat* song**

CD3 Track 25

- Say *Let's sing the song "Row, row, row your boat."*
- Play the audio. Children listen and do the actions with you (see TB p 165).
- Play the audio again. Children do the actions and join in singing the song.

Watch the *Row, row, row your boat* video.

- Children watch the video and join in singing the song and doing the actions with Anna and Sam.

Table time

Student's Book p 72

Watch. Listen, point and sing *Row, row, row your boat.*

CD3 Track 25

- Play the audio of the song. Children listen, sing and point to the boat and the stream in the picture when they are mentioned.

Draw a line to follow the stream.

- Children draw a line following the path of the stream.

Draw a picture of you in the boat. Say.

- Children draw a picture of themselves in the boat and say *Row, row, row your boat.*

Activity Book p 72

Trace the paths. Color your favorite rowing boat.

- Children trace each path. They choose and color their favorite boat.

Say.

- Children say *Row, row, row your boat.*

Closing time

Learning review (see TB p 18)
Closing routines (see TB p 16)
Bye bye song and puppet (CD1 Track 3; see TB p 17 & 21)

Use the **Navio App** to watch the video, and encourage children to do the same at home.

Review

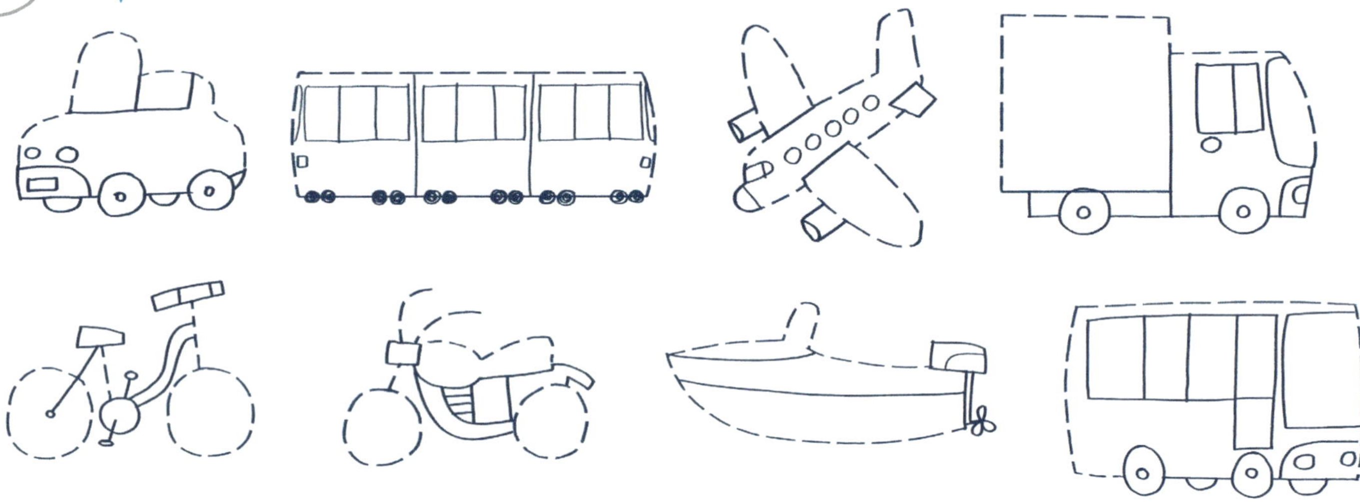

I can ...

Vocabulary

Story

Speaking

Content

Trace and color the forms of transportation you know. Listen, point and say. Ask and say which forms of transportation you want to use. Complete the faces to show what you can do. **Language:** bike, boat, bus, car, motorcycle, plane, train, truck; Let's go by (car)! I want to go by (bike). Do you want to go by (train)? Yes. / No.

Learning objectives

- Review what you have learned in this unit
- Complete a self-evaluation
- Talk about transportation you want to use

Materials

- Class CDs, flashcards, *Ferris Wheel* mat, Mimi puppet

Main vocabulary

- bike, boat, bus, car, motorcycle, plane, train, truck

Key language

- Let's go by (car)! I want to go by (bike). Do you want to go by (train)? Yes. / No.

Teacher's tip: Reviewing vocabulary cooperatively

Encourage the children to review the transportation cooperatively by miming and guessing with a partner. The first child makes the transportation noise and does the mime. Their partner names the transportation.

Circle time

Hello song & puppet (CD1 Track 2; see TB p 17 & 21)
Opening routines (see TB p 16)
Recycling activity (see TB p 19)
Lesson aims (see TB p 18)

Transportation flashcard games

- Choose one or two flashcard games with the *Ferris Wheel* mat and/or the puppet to review main vocabulary (see TB p 20 & 21).

Sing *Let's go by boat!*

CD3 Track 17

- Lay out the transportation flashcards.
- Play the audio. Children sing and do the actions.

Game: *Let's go by bus.*

- Stick the flashcards at the children's height on different walls around the classroom.
- Say *Let's go by plane*. Children go to the plane flashcard and mime being a plane. When they get to the flashcard, they all say *Let's go by plane!*
- Repeat with all the transportation.

Watch the story video.

- Children watch the story video. Ask children to say the transportation Mimi and Dylan want to go by in the story, e.g. *Let's go by (car). I want to go by train.*

Table time

Student's Book p 73

Trace and color the forms of transportation you know.

- Explain and demonstrate the activity.

Listen, point and say.

- Play the audio. Children listen, point to the transportation, and say the words.

CD3 Track 26

Mimi: I'm the teacher! Can you remember the transportation, Dylan?
Dylan: Yes, I can. Bus.
Mimi: Bus.
Dylan: Boat.
Mimi: Boat.
Dylan: Plane.
Mimi: Plane.
Dylan: Bike.
Mimi: Bike.
Dylan: Car.
Mimi: Car.
Dylan: Train.
Mimi: Train.
Dylan: Truck.
Mimi: Truck.
Dylan: Motorcycle.
Mimi: Motorcycle. Great job, Dylan! Very good!

Ask and say which forms of transportation you want to use.

- Ask children to point to the pictures and suggest or say how to go on vacation (or to town), e.g. *Let's go by bus. / I want to go by train.*

Complete the faces to show what you can do.

- Explain the four pictures: I *can name transportation; I can understand the story; I can talk about transportation I want to use; I can say where transportation goes.*
- Remind children to complete each face with a smile or frown depending on how well they think they have done.

Activity Book p 73

Draw yourself on your favorite forms of transportation. Ask and say.

- Children draw themselves on their favorite forms of transportation.
- They ask and say about the transportation.

Think and circle the number to show your progress.

- Children circle the number.

Closing time

Learning review (see TB p 18)
Closing routines (see TB p 16)
Bye bye song and puppet (CD1 Track 3; see TB p 17 & 21)

Use the **Navio App** to review what children have learned in this unit, and encourage them to do the same at home.

Project

COOPERATIVE LEARNING

Transportation

Make different forms of transportation from paper shapes. Make a poster to show the transportation that goes on land, water and in the air. Say. Language: bike, boat, bus, car, motorcycle, plane, train, truck; air, road, track, water; card, paper shapes, scissors; colors; numbers; A (car) goes (on the road). This is my (truck). It's (red). How many (planes)? (Two).

74

Transportation

Learning objectives

- Work together to do a collaborative project
- Talk about transportation
- Make different forms of transportation from paper shapes
- Identify transportation with wheels

Materials

- Class CDs, Mimi puppet, photocopiable templates: shapes, colored card, crayons, scissors, glue

Main vocabulary

- bike, boat, bus, car, motorcycle, plane, train, truck; air, road, track, water; card, paper shapes, scissors; colors; numbers

Key language

- A (car) goes (on the road). This is my (truck). It's (red). How many (planes)? (Two.)

Teacher's tip: Encouraging pairs to support each other

COOPERATIVE LEARNING

When children come up to glue their transportation in the correct place, encourage them to do so in pairs so that stronger students can support weaker ones.

Circle time

Hello song & puppet (CD1 Track 2; see TB p 17 & 21)
Opening routines (see TB p 16)
Recycling activity (see TB p 19)
Lesson aims (see TB p 18)

Prepare for your project.

- Say *Let's do a project and make a poster to show transportation that goes on land, water and in the air!* Show children the poster in the Student's Book to clarify what you mean. Explain the meaning of "land" and that both cars and trains go on land.
- Show children an example of a car you have made from gluing different colored paper shapes (or gummed paper) on to card (i.e. a semi-circle and two small circles as in the Student's Book). Say *This is my car! It's (green).*
- Explain that everyone is going to individually make transportation of their choice and then put them all together on a poster to show transportation that goes on land, water and in the air.
- Demonstrate and explain that to make the transportation children glue colored paper shapes on card.
- Create each form of transportation on the board by drawing or sticking templates of shapes. Elicit the names of each form of transportation as you do this. Leave these on the board for children to refer to.

Table time

Student's Book p 74

COOPERATIVE LEARNING

Make different forms of transportation from paper shapes.

- Say e.g. *We're going to make a poster to show transportation that goes on land, water and in the air like this. Look at what we need for our project: card, crayons, scissors, glue, paper* (templates of shapes). Children listen and point to the pictures.
- Give a piece of card to each child and put a selection of different colored paper shapes on each table. Make sure children have glue (or water if using gummed paper) available.
- Children glue the colored shapes to make transportation of their choice. Remind them to follow the examples on the board. Be ready to help as necessary.
- Children show and talk about their completed transportation, e.g. *This is my (train). It's (yellow).*

Make a poster to show transportation that goes on land, water and in the air. Say.

- Stick the poster you prepared at children's height on the board. Draw attention to the three sections. Children take turns gluing their transportation in the corresponding section on the poster. Talk about the transportation as they do this, e.g. *What a great (plane)! A (boat) goes in the (water). What color is the (car)? It's (blue). How many (planes) can you see? (Four).*
- Ask children *Do you like our poster of transportation?* Make the point that everyone helped make the poster and that they couldn't have made such a beautiful poster of transportation on their own.

Activity Book p 74

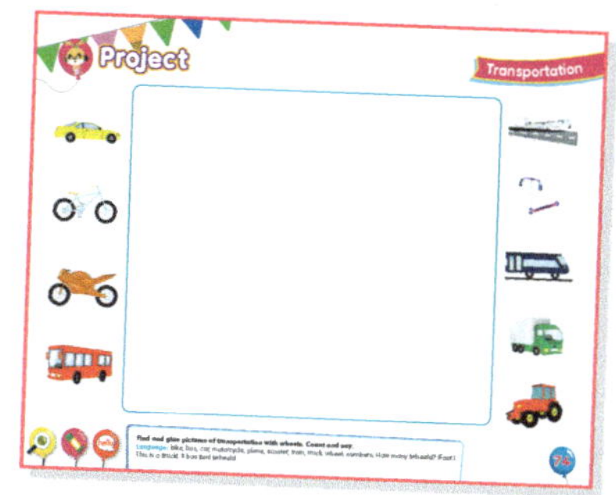

Find and glue pictures of transportation with wheels.

- Children find pictures of transportation with wheels and glue them in the space provided.

Count and say.

- They count and say the number of wheels on each form of transportation.

Closing time

Learning review (see TB p 18)
Closing routines (see TB p 16)
Bye bye song and puppet (CD1 Track 3; see TB p 17 & 21)

Space
Mimi's dream

Vocabulary and language

- **Main vocabulary:** astronaut, Earth, moon, planet, rocket, sky, star, sun
- **Key language:** What's this? It's the (sun). It's (a planet). Can you see the (moon)? Yes, I can. / No, I can't. How many stars can you see?
- **Content language:** clouds, day, night, rainbow; In the day, I can see (clouds). At night, I can see (stars).
- **Other language:** angry, calm, happy, sad, scared, sleepy; cat, cow, dish, dog, dream, good night, spoon; stickers, toilet roll; Sometimes I'm (sleepy). My favorite character is the (cow). My rocket is (blue). What's this? It's (a rocket). What can you see? I can see (a planet). I like (the stars).

Unit objectives

- Identify and name things in space
- Sing the language song *What's this?*
- Ask and say what you can see
- Understand and act out the story *Mimi's dream*
- Sing and act out the story song *Rocket to the moon*
- Sing the values song *Sometimes I'm happy*
- Recognize and respect that we have different feelings
- Understand and name differences between day and night
- Say and act out the traditional rhyme *Hey diddle, diddle*
- Review your learning and progress
- Participate in a collaborative project

Story

CD3 Track 32

Picture 1

Narrator: It's time for bed.
Dylan: Look at the stars.
Mimi: And look at the moon. Can we go on vacation to the moon, Daddy?
Daddy: No, Mimi. We can't. Good night, Mimi. Good night, Dylan.
Dylan: Good night, Daddy.
Mimi: Good night, Daddy.
Daddy: Sweet dreams!
Dylan: Thank you. Good night, stars!
Mimi: Good night, moon!

Picture 2

Narrator: Mimi and Dylan go to sleep. Mimi has a dream.
Teddy: Hello, Mimi. It's Teddy. I'm on the moon. I'm on vacation. Come and visit me!

Picture 3

Mimi: Come on, Dylan. Let's visit Teddy on the moon.
Dylan: Great idea, Mimi! What's this?
Mimi: It's a rocket. And I'm an astronaut.
Dylan: Oh wow! Look. I'm an astronaut too.
Mimi: Great! Jump in my rocket, Dylan! Are you ready? Five … , four … , three … , two … , one. Blast off!
Mimi & Dylan: Wo-ow!

Picture 4

Dylan: Wow! What's this, Mimi?
Mimi: It's a star!
Dylan: Can you see the Earth?
Mimi: No, I can't. It's very far!
Dylan: What's this, Mimi?
Mimi: It's a planet!
Dylan: Can you see the moon?
Mimi: Yes, I can. We're nearly there!
Dylan: Can you see Teddy?
Mimi: Yes, I can. Listen!
Teddy: Hello, Mimi. Hello, Dylan. Welcome to the moon!

Picture 5

Dylan: Hurray! We're on the moon!
Mimi: We're with Teddy! We're on vacation!
Teddy: Let's jump and play! Look at me! Jump … wee ... jump … wee ... jump … wee.
Dylan: Oh, great! Jump … wee ... jump … wee ... jump … wee.
Mimi: Oh Teddy, this is great! I love the moon! Jump … wee ... jump … wee ... JUMP …

Picture 6

Mimi: Oh no! Where's Teddy? He's on the moon!
Dylan: Don't be silly, Mimi. Teddy's here!
Mimi: Oh good. I'm happy. It's only a dream!
Dylan: You are funny, Mimi! Oh, let's go to sleep now. Good night, Mimi.
Mimi: Good night, Dylan! Good night, Teddy! Good night, moon!

Songs

Language song

What's this? CD3 Track 30

What's this? What's this? (Hold arms out questioningly)
It's the sun. It's yellow and bright. It's the sun. (Slowly move one hand from side to side)

What's this? What's this? (Hold arms out questioningly)
It's the moon. It's shiny at night. It's the moon. (Make a crescent moon with your hand)

What's this? What's this? (Hold arms out questioningly)
It's a star. It's up high. It's a star. (Open and close one hand)

What's this? What's this? (Hold arms out questioningly)
It's a planet. It's in the sky. It's a planet. (Mime looking through a telescope)

What's this? What's this? (Hold arms out questioningly)
It's an astronaut. Ready to go! It's an astronaut. (Mime striding slowly as if on the moon)

What's this? What's this? (Hold arms out questioningly)
It's a rocket. Zoom! Zoom! It's a rocket. (Zoom both hands upwards quickly)

Story song

Rocket to the moon CD3 Track 33

Rocket to the moon. (Zoom both hands upwards quickly)
Zoom, zoom, zoom. (Zoom around in a circle)

Teddy's on the moon. Let's visit Teddy. (Make a crescent moon with a hand, then beckon)
Jump in my rocket. Are you ready? (Zoom both hands upwards quickly, then beckon)
(Chorus)

Can you see a planet? Can you see a star? (Mime looking through a telescope, then open and close one hand)
Can you see the Earth? (Make a ball shape with your hands)
It's very far. (Shade eyes with one hand)

(Chorus)

Can you see the moon? Can you see Teddy? (Make a crescent moon with a hand, then shade eyes as if looking)
We're nearly there. Are you ready? (Punch fists in the air, then beckon)
(Chorus)

We're on the moon. Let's jump and play. (Punch fists in the air, then jump around)
We're with Teddy. (Mime cradling teddy)
We're on vacation. (Punch fists in the air)

(Chorus)

Values song

Sometimes I'm happy CD3 Track 36

Sometimes I'm happy, (Smile)
I'm happy. Are you? (Point to a child)
Sometimes I'm sad, (Turn your mouth down)
I'm sad. Are you? (Point to a child)

Sometimes I'm calm (Put your palms downwards)
I'm calm. Are you? (Point to a child)
Sometimes I'm scared (Open your mouth wide)
I'm scared. Are you? (Point to a child)

Sometimes I'm angry (Fold your arms and frown)
I'm angry. Are you? (Point to a child)
Sometimes I'm sleepy (Mime yawning)
I'm sleepy. Are you? (Point to a child)

We all have feelings (Gesture all around)
Can you see? (Point to your eyes)
I'm glad you're YOU! (Point to a child)
I'm glad I'm ME! (Point to yourself)

Culture rhyme

Hey diddle, diddle CD3 Track 38

Hey diddle, diddle, (Wave arms in the air)
The cat and the fiddle, (Mime playing a fiddle)
The cow jumps over the moon. (Make cow horns with two fingers and jump)
The little dog laughs (Cup your mouth with both hands)
To see such fun,
And the dish runs away (Run in place)
With the spoon. (Mime holding a spoon)

Space
Mimi's dream

Vocabulary Lesson 1

3:27 hello 3:28

Listen, point and repeat. Listen and play. Stick the space stickers. Circle where we live. Say. Language: Earth, moon, planet, sky, star, sun; blue, green, orange, pink, red, yellow

75

Space

Learning objectives

- Identify and name things in space
- Listen and point to things in space
- Identify where we live

Materials

- Class CDs, flashcards, *Ferris Wheel* mat, Mimi puppet

Main vocabulary

- Earth, moon, planet, sky, star, sun; blue, green, orange, pink, red, yellow

Teacher's tip: Practicing the pronunciation of *S*

Three of the key words begin with the letter *s*. Take the opportunity to practice pronunciation of this initial sound. Emphasize the sound by elongating it and making sure all the children are starting with the correct mouth formation (teeth together, lips slightly open).

Circle time

Hello song & puppet (CD1 Track 2; see TB p 17 & 21)
Opening routines (see TB p 16)
Lesson aims (see TB p 18)

Introduce space.

- Walk to the window and introduce the words *sky* and *sun* (if you can see it; if not, use the flashcard).
- Use the puppet and flashcards to introduce the remaining space vocabulary. Ask *What's in the sky? Sun and …* show the flashcards of moon, star and planet as they respond. Show the flashcard of Earth and say *This is our planet, Earth. We live on Earth.*
- *Ferris Wheel* mat on floor or board with the space flashcards face down (one on each color). Use puppet to turn over and name. Children repeat the words.

Game: *Say the color!*

- Name the space vocabulary on the Ferris Wheel and children name the color. Then the reverse.

Game: *Telescope!*

- Stick the flashcards on walls around the room.
- Use your hands to mime looking through a telescope.
- Say the words in random order and children respond by turning towards the flashcard you name and mime looking at it through their "telescope."
- Invite individual children to take turns giving instructions. The others turn towards the flashcards and mime in the same way.

Table time

Student's Book p 75

Listen, point and repeat.

- Play the audio. The children listen, point to each object as they hear it, and repeat the words.

CD3 Track 27

Mimi: Look, Dylan! Planet … sun … moon … sky … star … Earth. Repeat, Dylan!
Dylan: Yes, Mimi. Planet … sun … moon … sky … star … Earth.
Mimi: Very good, Dylan. Let's name the things in space together!
Both: Planet … sun … moon … sky … star … Earth.

Listen and play.

- Use finger in air to pretend to spin wheel. Children spin their fingers, point to the color when they hear it on the audio and say the word.

CD3 Track 28

Mimi: Spin the wheel
One, two, three
Point and name
The things in space with me!
Mimi: Blue … sun!
Dylan: Red … planet!
Mimi: Yellow … sky!
Dylan: Green … Earth!
Mimi: Pink … star!
Dylan: Orange … moon!

- Play the game with you and/or individual children naming colors and others saying the words.

Stick the space stickers.

- Children stick the space stickers in the correct places.

Circle where we live.

- Children circle where we live (Earth).

Say.

- Children name the things in space.

Activity Book p 75

Follow and draw the path through the maze.

- Demonstrate that children should first follow the maze with their fingers and then draw the path.

Point and say.

- Children point to the pictures and name the objects.

Closing time

Learning review (see TB p 18)
Closing routines (see TB p 16)
Bye bye song and puppet (CD1 Track 3; see TB p 17 & 21)

Use the **Navio App** to play the vocabulary game, and encourage children to do the same at home.

Lesson 2 Language

3:29 3:30

Listen and find the new things in space. Listen, point and sing *What's this?* Match the pictures. Color. Ask and say.

Language: astronaut, moon, planet, rocket, star, sun; What's this? It's (the sun).

Learning objectives

- Talk about things in space
- Identify and name two new things in space
- Sing the language song *What's this?*
- Ask and say what you can see

Materials

- Class CDs, flashcards, *Ferris Wheel* mat, Mimi puppet

Main vocabulary

- astronaut, moon, planet, rocket, star, sun

Key language

- What's this? It's the (sun). It's (a planet).

Teacher's tip: Doing actions from the song in groups

Divide the class into groups of six. Give each child a role: the sun, the moon, a star, a planet, an astronaut and a rocket. Ask all the suns to come forward and practice the action. Repeat with the other space items. Play the song and have the children do their action in turn every time they hear their word.

Circle time

Hello song & puppet (CD1 Track 2; see TB p 17 & 21)
Opening routines (see TB p 16)
Recycling activity (six space words from Lesson 1) (see TB p 19)
Lesson aims (see TB p 18)

Introduce the new space vocabulary.

- All eight space flashcards on the floor or the board.
- Children identify the two new items.
- Use the puppet to point to and say the words in turn. Children repeat in chorus.
- Turn the two new flashcards face down. Mix them up. Point to one and ask *Astronaut or rocket?* Children guess. Repeat several times.

Introduce (or review) *What's this? It's the …*

- Cover one of the flashcards with another flashcard or a piece of paper.
- Gradually reveal the flashcard, asking *What's this?* Encourage children to respond, e.g. *It's the sun* as soon as they can see or guess the flashcard.
- Repeat with different flashcards.

Game: *Guess the flashcard*

- Choose three flashcards, e.g. *sun, moon, star*. Children name the flashcards.
- Turn the three flashcards face down and mix them up. Point to one of the flashcards and ask *What's this?* Children guess, e.g. *It's the moon!*
- Turn the flashcard over and children say *Hurray!* if they guessed the flashcard correctly.
- Repeat the game using different flashcards.

Table time

Student's Book p 76

Listen and find the new things in space.

- Play the audio. Children listen and find the two new words.
- Play the audio again. The children listen and say the words.

CD3 Track 29

One, two,
Which words are new?
Astronaut! Astronaut!
Rocket! Rocket!

Listen, point and sing *What's this?*

CD3 Track 30

- Play the song. The children listen and point to each object as they hear it.
- Play the audio again. Children sing the song and do the actions (see TB p 187).
- Remember that you can use the karaoke version of the song when children are confident.

Match the pictures. Color.

- Children identify the objects in the drawings and match them to the photos. They then color them.
- Play the song again, pausing after each question and answer.

Ask and say.

- Ask *What do Anna and Sam ask?* Encourage children to point and ask and answer the questions as in the song.

Activity Book p 76

Match the pictures to the puzzle pieces.

- Children match pictures to the puzzle pieces.

Color the pictures that are in the puzzle.

- Children color the pictures that are in the puzzle.

Ask and say.

- Children point to the puzzle pieces, ask and say, e.g. *What's this? It's a (star).*

Closing time

Learning review (see TB p 18)
Closing routines (see TB p 16)
Bye bye song and puppet (CD1 Track 3; see TB p 17 & 21)

Use the **Navio App** to listen to the song, and encourage children to do the same at home.

Lesson 3 **Story**

Watch. Listen to the story *Mimi's dream*. Circle where Mimi, Dylan and Teddy go. Stick the story sticker. Language: astronaut, Earth, moon, planet, rocket, star, sun; What's this? It's (a planet). Can you see (the moon)? Yes, I can. / No, I can't.

Learning objectives

- Watch, understand and enjoy the story *Mimi's dream*
- Make a prediction about the story
- Find and point to space objects
- Identify where Mimi, Dylan and Teddy go

Materials

- Class CDs, printable story cards, flashcards, *Ferris Wheel* mat, Mimi puppet

Main vocabulary

- astronaut, Earth, moon, planet, rocket, star, sun

Key language

- What's this? It's (a planet). Can you see (the moon)? Yes, I can. / No, I can't.

Teacher's tip: Asking questions about the story in pairs

After working with the story, allow the children to ask and answer questions about the main vocabulary in pairs. Encourage them to point to the different frames and ask *What's this? It's a (rocket)*, etc.

Circle time

Hello song & puppet (CD1 Track 2; see TB p 17 & 21)
Opening routines (see TB p 16)
Recycling activity (*What's this?* and space vocabulary) (see TB p 19)
Lesson aims (see TB p 18)

Introduce the story *Mimi's dream*.

- Say *It's story time!* Play the *Story rhyme* (CD1 Track 4; see TB p 17).
- Say *Anna and Sam are listening to a story about Mimi's dream.* Use mime to explain "dream." Ask *Where does Mimi go in her dream?* Encourage children to guess.

Watch or listen to the story.

CD3 Track 32

- Watch the video, play the audio, or read the story using the printable story cards. Pause, repeat words, point to the pictures, ask questions.
- Ask the question again and check the answer.
- Repeat the story. Encourage children to join in.
- Ask *Do you like the story? Do you have dreams?*

Can you see the moon?

- Ask *Can you see the moon (in the story)?* Children point to the moon and say *Yes, I can!* Repeat with other story items.

Table time

Student's Book p 77

Watch. Listen to the story *Mimi's dream*.

- Read or play the story again. Children listen and follow the story by pointing to the pictures.

Story questions

Picture 1
Where are Mimi and Dylan? *(In the bedroom)*
What can Mimi and Dylan see? *(Stars/moon)*

Picture 2
Is Mimi asleep? *(Yes)*
Where is Teddy? *(On the moon)*

Picture 3
Where is Mimi now? *(In a rocket)*
What are Mimi and Dylan? *(Astronauts)*

Picture 4
What can Mimi and Dylan see? *(A star/a planet/ the moon)*
Can Mimi see the Earth? *(No)*

Picture 5
Where are Mimi and Dylan now? *(On the moon)*
What do Mimi and Dylan do on the moon? *(Jump/ play)*

Picture 6
Where is Teddy now? *(In the bedroom)*
Is Mimi happy? *(Yes)*

Circle where Mimi, Dylan and Teddy go.

- Children find where Mimi, Dylan and Teddy go, and circle it (the moon).

Stick the story sticker.

- Children stick on the story sticker.
- Ask *Is Mimi happy it's only a dream?*

Activity Book p 77

Find and circle four differences. Point and say.

- Children find and circle the four differences. They point, ask and say.

Color the spot under the picture from the story.

- They color the spot under the story picture on the left.

Closing time

Learning review (see TB p 18)
Closing routines (see TB p 16)
Bye bye song and puppet (CD1 Track 3; see TB p 17 & 21)

Use the **Navio App** to watch the video, and encourage children to do the same at home.

Lesson 4

Story Song

Space

1 2 3 4

Watch. Listen, point and sing *Rocket to the moon.* Trace the numbers. Match to order the pictures. Ask and say. Language: Earth, moon, planet, star, teddy; I can/ can't see (the moon). Can you see (a star)? Yes, I can. / No, I can't.

Learning objectives

- Watch, sing and act out the story song *Rocket to the moon*
- Listen to the story again and identify things in space
- Identify the order of space objects in the song
- Ask and answer about space objects
- Draw and color a space scene and count to ten

Materials

- Class CDs, printable story cards, flashcards, *Ferris Wheel* mat, Mimi puppet

Main vocabulary

- Earth, moon, planet, star, teddy

Key language

- I can/can't see (the moon). Can you see (a star)? Yes, I can. / No, I can't.

Teacher's tip: Playing a game cooperatively in pairs

COOPERATIVE LEARNING

To encourage the children to work cooperatively, have them play the game *Can you see a star?* in pairs. The first child to locate the named flashcard should help their partner, by making sure they are pointing to the correct place and gently guiding them if they aren't.

Circle time

Hello song & puppet (CD1 Track 2; see TB p 17 & 21)
Opening routines (see TB p 16)
Recycling activity (space vocabulary) (see TB p 19)
Lesson aims (see TB p 18)

Retell the story *Mimi's dream*.

- Play the audio, video or read the story using the printable story cards.
- Demonstrate that children should wave their arms in the air every time they hear a space word in the story.

Mime the story.

- Say *Let's be Mimi!* Mime the story, following the sequence in the story song, except the chorus (see TB page 187). Say sentences from the song as you do this.
- Repeat the story mime and sentences and encourage children to join in doing these with you.

***Rocket to the moon* song**

CD3 Track 33

- Play the audio. Children listen and act out the song (see TB p 187).
- Play the audio again. Children mime and join in singing the song.
- Ask *Do you like the song?* and children respond.

Game: *Can you see the star?*

- "Hide" the flashcards in different places around the classroom (so they are visible but children need to look carefully to see them).
- Ask questions e.g. *Can you see the rocket?* Children look, point to the flashcard and respond *Yes, I can.*
- Repeat for all the flashcards.

Table time

Student's Book p 78

Watch. Listen, point and sing *Rocket to the moon*.

CD3 Track 33

- Play the audio of the song. Children listen, sing and point to the pictures.
- Remember that you can use the karaoke version of the song when children are confident.

Trace the numbers. Match to order the pictures.

- Children trace the numbers 1–4. Play the audio of the song again, pausing after each verse. Children listen and match the numbers to the pictures to show the order of the story song.

Ask and say.

- Children ask and say, e.g. *I can see (the moon). Can you see a (planet)? Yes, I can.*

Activity Book p 78

Count and connect the dots to complete the picture.

- Children connect the numbered dots in order to complete the picture of the rocket. Encourage them to count to 10 as they do this.

Count and color the stars. Ask and say.

- Point to each star in turn and encourage children to count them with you. They color the stars. They then take turns asking and answering about the number of stars.

Closing time

Learning review (see TB p 18)
Closing routines (see TB p 16)
Bye bye song and puppet (CD1 Track 3; see TB p 17 & 21)

Use the **Navio App** to watch the video, and encourage children to do the same at home.

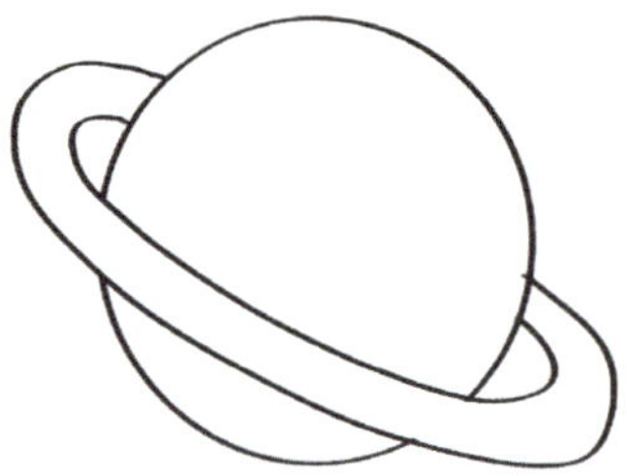

Watch. Listen and point. Match and color the things in space. Count. Ask and say.
Language: Earth, moon, planet, star, sun; numbers; What's this? It's (a planet). Can you see (planets)? Yes, I can. / No, I can't. What can you see? I can see (the stars). How many (stars) can you see?

79

Learning objectives

- Talk about what you can see in space
- Watch, understand and enjoy a video
- Identify and count the things in space in the video
- Draw a space picture and talk about it

Materials

- Class CDs, flashcards, *Ferris Wheel* mat, Mimi puppet

Main vocabulary

- Earth, moon, planet, star, sun; numbers

Key language

- What's this? It's (a planet). Can you see the (moon)? Yes, I can. / No, I can't. What can you see? I can see (the stars). How many stars can you see?

Teacher's tip: Using props to encourage individual participation in speaking activities

Life skills

To encourage participation in speaking activities, pass a plastic or teacher-made microphone around the circle. If a child isn't ready to give an answer, she passes the microphone to the next child. Using a prop in this way makes children feel safe (they hide behind the microphone), and often motivates them to participate more.

Circle time

Hello song & puppet (CD1 Track 2; see TB p 17 & 21)
Opening routines (see TB p 16)
Recycling activity (story song) (CD3 Track 33; see TB p 19)
Lesson aims (see TB p 18)

Game: *Guess what I can see!*

- Hold one flashcard without children seeing. Say *Guess what I can see!*
- Children ask you, e.g. *Can you see a star? No, I can't. / Yes, I can!* and guess the flashcard.
- The child who guesses the flashcard correctly has the next turn. Repeat with different children.

Watch the video.

- Explain that Uncle Dan, Sam and Anna are in a planetarium (a museum where you can see things in space). Ask *What can Uncle Dan, Sam and Anna see?* and encourage children to guess.
- Play the video.
- Ask the question again and children respond.
- Ask *How many stars / planets can they see?*
- Watch again. Pause and children repeat Uncle Dan's questions with *Can … ?*
- Ask *Do you want to go to a planetarium?*

Table time

Student's Book p 79 Life skills

Watch. Listen and point.

- Children point to Anna, Sam and Uncle Dan in the photo. Play the audio or video. Children point to the things in space as they hear them in the dialogue.

CD3 Track 35

Uncle Dan: What can you see, Anna?
Anna: I can see the Earth.
Uncle Dan: Can you see the Earth, Sam?
Sam: No, I can't.
Uncle Dan: Look over there! We live on the Earth.
Sam & Anna: Oh!
Uncle Dan: Can you see the moon?
Anna: No, I can't.
Uncle Dan: Look over there!
Anna: Oh, yes, I can. It's yellow.
Uncle Dan: It's beautiful. Can you see the stars?
Anna: Yes, I can.
Uncle Dan: How many stars?
Sam: One, two, three, four, five, six stars!
Uncle Dan: And look over there. What can you see, Sam?
Sam: I can see the planets.
Uncle Dan: How many planets?
Anna: I can see one … two planets.
Sam: Wow! This is great!
Anna: It's amazing!
Sam & Anna: Thank you, Uncle Dan.

Match and color the things in space.

- Play the audio again. Pause it after each question and answer. Children color the things according to what they hear or see in the photo.

Count. Ask and say.

- Children count the stars and planets.
- Children ask and say, e.g. *What's this? It's a (star). Can you see the (moon)? Yes, I can.*

Activity Book p 79

Draw three more stars and one more planet. Color the picture.

- Children draw three more stars and a planet, and color the picture.

Count, ask and say.

- Children count the objects in their picture and talk about it.

Closing time

Learning review (see TB p 18)
Closing routines (see TB p 16)
Bye bye song and puppet (CD1 Track 3; see TB p 17 & 21)

Use the **Navio App** to watch the video, and encourage children to do the same at home.

Listen, point and sing *Sometimes I'm happy*. Color the circles to show the feelings you sometimes have. Draw and color a face to show how you feel now. Say.
Language: angry, calm, happy, sad, scared, sleepy; colors; Sometimes I'm (sleepy).

SOCIAL AND EMOTIONAL LEARNING

80

Learning objectives

- Understand and recognize feelings
- Act out the story
- Sing the values song *Sometimes I'm happy*
- Talk about own feelings

Materials

- Class CDs, flashcards, *Ferris Wheel* mat, Mimi puppet

Main vocabulary

- angry, calm, happy, sad, scared, sleepy; colors

Key language

- Sometimes I'm (sleepy).

Teacher's tip: Building personal connections by asking about feelings

Once the children are familiar with the new feelings vocabulary, use it to form a personal connection with the children at the start of following lessons. Sing a verse from the song or simply say, *I'm (happy). Are you?* and encourage children to talk about how they feel.

Circle time

Hello song & puppet (CD1 Track 2; see TB p 17 & 21)
Opening routines (see TB p 16)
Recycling activity *(Can you see the (moon)?)* (see TB p 19)
Lesson aims (see TB p 18)

Watch the *Mimi's dream* story video.

- Play the story video.
- Take the part of the narrator, Daddy and Teddy yourself. Encourage children to join in acting out the story in two groups (Mimi, Dylan).
- Ask *How does Mimi feel at the beginning / end of the story? (sleepy / happy). How does Teddy feel in the story? (happy).*
- Explain that we all have different feelings and that it's important to be aware of and to respect other people's feelings.
- Ask *What kind of feelings do you have?* and listen to the children's response. Use this to introduce or remind children of vocabulary in the song.

***Sometimes I'm happy* song**

CD3 Track 36

- Ask *What feelings can you hear in the song?* Play the audio. Check the answers. Be ready to prompt and use mime, gesture and your voice as necessary to convey the meaning of the feelings.
- Play the audio again. Children join in doing actions with you to convey each feeling and singing the song.
- Make the point that we're all different and we all have different feelings and that it's important to respect and value our own and other people's feelings.

Table time

Student's Book p 80

Listen, point and sing *Sometimes I'm happy*.

CD3 Track 36

- Play the audio of the song. Children sing and point to the emojis.

Color the circles to show the feelings you sometimes have.

- Children color the spots to show the feelings they sometimes have (i.e. probably all of them).

Draw and color a face to show how you feel now. Say.

- Children draw and color the blank face to show how they feel now.
- Children say how they feel, e.g. *I'm happy.* Encourage children to explain why they feel that way using their shared language.

Activity Book p 80

Match the feelings to the pictures.

- Children match the emojis to the correct pictures.

Say.

- They talk about how they sometimes feel.

Closing time

Learning review (see TB p 18)
Closing routines (see TB p 16)
Bye bye song and puppet (CD1 Track 3; see TB p 17 & 21)

Use the **Navio App** to listen to the song, and encourage children to do the same at home.

Lesson 7 Content

Space

Listen and point. Circle the things you can see in the day blue. Circle the things you can see at night black. Say. **Language:** day, night; clouds, moon, rainbow, sky, stars, sun; In the day, I can see (clouds). At night, I can see (stars).

Learning objectives

- Identify and name things you can see in the sky in the day and at night
- Listen and identify things you can see in the day and at night
- Talk about things you can see in the day or at night.
- Draw things you can see in the day and at night

Materials

- Class CDs, printable content flashcards, *Ferris Wheel* mat, Mimi puppet

Main vocabulary

- day, night; clouds, moon, rainbow, sky, stars, sun

Key language

- In the day, I can see (clouds). At night, I can see (stars).

Teacher's tip: Categorizing

Learning to sort and classify is an essential thinking skill, which helps children establish links between groups of items. This in turn facilitates the memory process. Once you have classified all the items collectively, give out some paper and have the children draw the sun on one side and the moon on the other. They should then draw the items in the correct place according to when they see them.

Circle time

Hello song & puppet (CD1 Track 2; see TB p 17 & 21)
Opening routines (see TB p 16)
Recycling activity (see TB p 19)
Lesson aims (see TB p 18)

Introduce content vocabulary.

- Hold up the printable flashcards of day and night and say *Let's learn about differences between day and night!* Children repeat the words.
- Show the flashcards of clouds and rainbow in turn. Say e.g. *In the day, I can (sometimes) see clouds. I can (sometimes) see a rainbow.* Children repeat the new words.

Sort the flashcards.

- Place the flashcards of day and night on either side of the circle.
- Hold up the flashcards of *sun, moon, sky, clouds, stars, rainbow* in turn. Invite individual children to say *Day!* or *Night!* and place the flashcards on the correct side of the circle. Say e.g. *Yes, very good. I can see the sun in the day* as they do this.

Table time

Student's Book p 81

Listen and point.

- Say *Sam and Anna are talking about what they can see in the day and at night.* Play the audio. Children listen and point to the photos of day and night as they hear them.
- Play the audio again. Use the pause button. Children point to the pictures of the things and repeat the sentences.

CD3 Track 37

Anna: In the day, I can see the sky.
I can see the sun.
I can see clouds.
I can see a rainbow.
Sam: At night, I can see the moon.
I can see stars.

Circle the things you can see in the day blue.
Circle the things you can see at night black.

- Draw children's attention to the circled examples. Then they circle in blue what they can see in the day, and circle in black what they can see at night.

Say.

- Children point to their pictures and say, e.g. *In the day, I can see (the sun). At night, I can see (stars).*

Activity Book p 81

Draw the things you can see in the day and at night.

- Children draw things they can see in the day in the first picture. They draw things they can see at night in the second picture.

Ask and say.

- They ask and answer about the things in each picture.

Closing time

Learning review (see TB p 18)
Closing routines (see TB p 16)
Bye bye song and puppet (CD1 Track 3; see TB p 17 & 21)

Use the **Navio App** to play the vocabulary and language games, and encourage children to do the same at home.

Lesson 8 Culture

Watch. Listen, point and say *Hey diddle, diddle*. Color the characters in the rhyme. Circle your favorite character. Say.

Language: cat, cow, dish, dog, moon, spoon; My favorite character is the (cow).

Learning objectives

- Watch, say and act out the traditional rhyme *Hey diddle, diddle*
- Name things you can see in the sky in the day and at night
- Talk about your favorite character in the rhyme
- Identify and talk about the characters in the rhyme

Materials

- Class CDs, flashcards, *Ferris Wheel* mat, Mimi puppet

Main vocabulary

- cat, cow, dish, dog, moon, spoon

Key language

- My favorite character is the (cow).

Teacher's tip: Building confidence through performance

Providing children with the opportunity to give a performance helps build confidence in their ability to speak English. Allow them to perform songs and rhymes for other teachers, their parents or carers, or record them and allow them to watch their own performance.

Circle time

Hello song & puppet (CD1 Track 2; see TB p 17 & 21)
Opening routines (see TB p 16)
Recycling activity (see TB p 19)
Lesson aims (see TB p 18)

Game: *Day or night!*

- Stick the flashcards of day and night on either side of the classroom.
- Hold up flashcards and say the words in turn, e.g. *Sun! / Stars!* Children respond by moving to the correct side of the classroom and saying, e.g. *I can see clouds in the day.*
- Make *Moon!* the last instruction and use this to lead into the next activity.

***Hey diddle, diddle* rhyme**

CD3 Track 38

- Say *Let's say the rhyme "Hey diddle, diddle."*
- Ask *What space word can you hear in the rhyme?* Play the audio. Check the answer (*moon*).
- Ask *What animals are in the rhyme?* Play the audio again. Check the answer (*cat, cow, dog*).
- Hold up page 82 of the Student's Book. Play the audio again. Point to the pictures and encourage children to join in saying the rhyme with you.
- Ask *Do you think the rhyme is funny?* and listen to their response.

Watch the *Hey diddle, diddle* video.

- Children watch the video and join in saying the rhyme and doing the actions with Anna and Sam.

Table time

Student's Book p 82

Watch. Listen, point and say *Hey diddle, diddle.*

CD3 Track 38

- Play the audio of the rhyme. Children listen, say the rhyme, and point to the characters in the picture.

Color the characters in the rhyme.

- Children color the characters in the rhyme.

Circle your favorite character. Say.

- They then circle their favorite character.
- Ask individual children in turn *What's your favorite character?* and children respond.

Activity Book p 82

Match the pictures. Trace and color.

- Children match the characters at the top to the correct picture below. They trace and color the bottom pictures.

Point, ask and say.

- They take turns asking and answering about the pictures.

Closing time

Learning review (see TB p 18)
Closing routines (see TB p 16)
Bye bye song and puppet (CD1 Track 3; see TB p 17 & 21)

Use the **Navio App** to watch the video, and encourage children to do the same at home.

Space

I can …

Vocabulary

Story

Speaking

Content

Color the things in space you know. Listen, point and say. Ask and say. Complete the faces to show what you can do. **Language:** astronaut, Earth, moon, planet, rocket, sky, star, sun; What's this? It's (a star). Can you see (the moon)? Yes, I can. / No, I can't. What can you see? I can see (the moon).

Learning objectives

- Review what you have learned in this unit
- Complete a self-evaluation
- Ask and answer about things in space

Materials

- Class CDs, flashcards, *Ferris Wheel* mat, Mimi puppet

Main vocabulary

- astronaut, Earth, moon, planet, rocket, sky, star, sun

Key language

- What's this? It's (a star). Can you see (the moon)? Yes, I can. / No, I can't. What can you see? I can see (the moon).

Teacher's tip: Checking vocabulary in pairs

As an alternative to children completing the first part of the review alone, children work in pairs and check that their partner knows the vocabulary before they begin to color. Children take turns pointing and asking *What's this?* about each item. Children should only color the items they remember.

Circle time

Hello song & puppet (CD1 Track 2; see TB p 17 & 21)
Opening routines (see TB p 16)
Recycling activity (see TB p 19)
Lesson aims (see TB p 18)

Space flashcard games

- Choose one or two flashcard games with the *Ferris Wheel* mat and/or the puppet to review main vocabulary (see TB p 20 & 21).

Sing *What's this?*

CD3 Track 30

- Lay out the space flashcards face up on the floor or the board.
- Play the audio. Children listen and point to the flashcards with you as they hear them in the song.

Game: *Space trip*

- Tell the children you are going on a trip to space. Climb aboard the rocket by having them forming a line behind you. As you zoom around the classroom, show the flashcards and ask, e.g. *Can you see a star?* Children answer, *Yes, I can / No, I can't.* Repeat with all the space flashcards.

Mimi's trip

- Tell the children Mimi is going on a space trip and they can speak to her on the space telephone. Have Mimi hold one of the flashcards so that the children can't see it. They ask e.g. *Can you see an astronaut?* Answer in Mimi's voice until they guess the item. The child who guesses the flashcard correctly has the next turn. Repeat with different children.

Watch the story video.

- Children watch the story video.
- Children ask and say what they can see in the story, e.g. *Can you see a (planet)? Yes, I can / No, I can't.*

Table time

Student's Book p 83

Color the things in space you know.

- Explain and demonstrate the activity.

Listen, point and say.

- Play the audio. Children listen, point to the things in space, and say the words.

CD3 Track 39

Mimi: I'm the teacher! Can you remember the things in space, Dylan?
Dylan: Yes, I can. Planet.
Mimi: Planet.
Dylan: Sun.
Mimi: Sun.
Dylan: Moon.
Mimi: Moon.
Dylan: Sky.
Mimi: Sky.
Dylan: Star.
Mimi: Star.
Dylan: Earth.
Mimi: Earth.
Dylan: Rocket.
Mimi: Rocket.
Dylan: Astronaut.
Mimi: Astronaut. Great job, Dylan! Very good!

Ask and say.

- Children point to the pictures and ask and say, e.g. *What's this? It's a planet. / Can you see a rocket? Yes, I can. / No, I can't.*

Complete the faces to show what you can do.

- Explain the four pictures: *I can name things in space; I can understand the story; I can ask questions to identify things and to say what I can see; I understand differences between day and night.*
- Remind children they should complete each face with a smile or frown depending on how well they think they have done.

Activity Book p 83

Trace the paths. Color the pictures. Ask and say.

- Children trace the paths, then color the pictures. They take turns talking about what they can see.

Think and circle the number to show your progress.

- Children circle the number.

Closing time

Learning review (see TB p 18)
Closing routines (see TB p 16)
Bye bye song and puppet (CD1 Track 3; see TB p 17 & 21)

Use the **Navio App** to review what children have learned in this unit, and encourage them to do the same at home.

Project

COOPERATIVE LEARNING

Space

Make a space rocket. Act out a journey to space. Make a class display. Ask and say. **Language:** astronaut, Earth, moon, planet, rocket, sky, star, sun; toilet roll, stickers; colors; numbers; My rocket is (blue). What's this? It's (a rocket). Can you see (the sun)? Yes, I can. / No, I can't. What can you see? I can see (a planet). I like (the stars).

84

Space

Learning objectives

- Work together to do a collaborative project
- Ask and answer questions about space
- Make a space rocket and act out a journey to space
- Draw a picture of you on the moon and talk about it

Materials

- Class CDs, Mimi puppet, glue, paints, stickers, tissue paper, toilet roll
- optional: photocopiable template: rocket, crayons

Main vocabulary

- astronaut, Earth, moon, planet, rocket, sky, star, sun; stickers, toilet roll; colors; numbers

Key language

- My rocket is (blue). What's this? It's a (rocket). I can see (stars). Can you see (the sun)? Yes, I can. / No, I can't. I like (the stars).

Teacher's tip: Being careful with scissors

Life skills

When you ask the children to cut out triangles of paper to make the nose of their rocket, draw the triangle onto a bigger piece of paper to show them where to cut. Monitor carefully to make sure that they are holding the scissors correctly. When they get up to put any scraps of paper in the bin, make sure they leave the scissors on the table and don't walk around the class with them.

Circle time

Hello song & puppet (CD1 Track 2; see TB p 17 & 21)
Opening routines (see TB p 16)
Recycling activity (see TB p 19)
Lesson aims (see TB p 18)

Prepare for your project.

- Say *Let's make our own space rocket and act out a journey to space!*
- Show children the example rocket you have made from the toilet roll and paper. Say e.g. *This is my rocket! It's (red).*
- Explain that everyone is going to individually make a rocket and then act out a journey to space.
- Demonstrate and explain that to make the rocket children paint a toilet roll. They cut out a triangle of paper, paint it and glue it to the toilet roll to make the nose of the rocket. They then glue tissue paper strips on the bottom of the rocket and decorate it with stickers.
- Explain that when everyone has made their rocket, you are going to act out a journey to space together.

Table time

COOPERATIVE LEARNING

Student's Book p 84

Make a space rocket.

- Say e.g. *We're going to make a rocket like this. Look at what we need for our project: toilet roll, paints, stickers, tissue paper and glue.* Children listen and point to the pictures.
- Give a toilet roll and some paper to each child and put a selection of paints, different colored (tissue) paper and stickers on each table. Make sure children have scissors and glue available.
- Children make their rocket. Be ready to help as necessary.
- Children show and talk about their completed rocket, e.g. *This is my (rocket). It's (red).*

Act out a journey to space.

- When everyone is ready, say *Let's go to space in our rockets!* Walk around the class holding your rocket horizontally as if flying through space and get the children to follow you and do the same. Point out different imaginary landmarks as you do this, e.g. *Look! I can see stars. Can you see stars? How many stars? And look! What's this? It's a planet. Where's the moon? Oh, look. I can see the moon. Can you see the moon?* Once children get the idea of pretending to fly their rockets, encourage them to also ask questions and invent what they can see in space.

Make a class display. Ask and say.

- Help the children glue their rockets to a poster to make a class display. Make the point that everyone has worked hard to make the display and to use their imaginations to go to space together.

Alternative version of project

- Children could use the rocket template on TB p 241 to make a space rocket mobile. Children color the template and decorate it with star stickers. They then glue tissue paper strips on the bottom of the rocket. Help the children hang their rockets from a coat hanger to make a mobile.

Activity Book p 84

Draw a picture of you on the moon. Color the sun yellow, the Earth blue and the other planet red.

- Children draw their face inside the astronaut's helmet. They color the sun, Earth and other planet.

Ask and say.

- Children take turns talking about their picture.

Closing time

Learning review (see TB p 18)
Closing routines (see TB p 16)
Bye bye song and puppet (CD1 Track 3; see TB p 17 & 21)

Colors

Listen, point and say. Match and color the balloons.
Color the star to show your favorite color. Say.
Language: blue, brown, orange, pink, purple

Colors

Pink, orange, purple, blue, brown

Learning objectives

- Identify and name colors
- Say what colors you like

Materials

- Class CDs, flashcards, *Ferris Wheel* mat, Mimi puppet, feely bag

Main vocabulary

- blue, brown, orange, pink, purple

Teacher's tip: Reinforcing the concept

In addition to the flashcards, use familiar items of different colors to reinforce the concept, e.g. an orange for orange, a blue crayon for blue, etc. Pass the items around and encourage the children to name the color each time.

Circle time

Hello song & puppet (CD1 Track 2; see TB p 17 & 21)
Opening routines (see TB p 16)
Lesson aims (see TB p 18)

Introduce the colors

- Use the flashcards, puppet and feely bag to introduce or remind children of the colors. Say the words and encourage children to repeat them with you. Repeat for all the words.
- Play one or two flashcard games with the Ferris Wheel mat and/or the puppet (see TB p 20 & 21).
- Encourage children to say *I like …* and name the colors they like.

Table time

Student's Book p 85

Listen, point and say.

- Hold up your book. Play the audio and point to the colored balloons in turn.
- Play the audio again. Children listen, point to the balloons in their books, and say the colors.

CD3 Track 40

Pink … orange … purple … blue … brown
Pink … orange … purple … blue … brown
Pink … orange … purple … blue … brown

Match and color the balloons.

- Children match and color the balloons.

Color the star to show your favorite color.

- Children color the star to show which of the colors on the page is their favorite.

Say.

- Children say which of the colors on the page is their favorite.

Activity Book p 85

Color the balloons following the key.

- Point out the key. Children color the balloons the correct color.

Point and say.

- Children point and say the colors.

Closing time

Learning review (see TB p 18)
Closing routines (see TB p 16)
Bye bye song and puppet (CD1 Track 3; see TB p 17 & 21)

Cross-curricular activities

- See also the activities in the other Colors lesson (see TB p 211).

Drama

Explain that children are going to do a drama activity in which they show how different colors make them feel. Make sure children understand that there are no correct answers.

Demonstrate the activity. Say e.g. *Blue!* and mime that this makes you feel calm and relaxed. Follow this by e.g. *Orange!* that makes you feel in a lively and sunny mood.

Name colors and children respond by acting out different moods the colors make them feel.

Math

Give tables or groups of children objects, e.g. crayons, blocks, pieces of card in several different colors.

Children sort the objects into sets of different colors and name the colors.

If you wish to focus on numbers as well, children count the number of objects in each color set.

Colors

3:41

Listen, point and say. Color the picture following the key. Say your favorite color.
Language: black, green, red, white, yellow

86

Colors

Red, green, yellow, black, white

Learning objectives

- Identify and name colors
- Say what color you like
- Say numbers 1–5

Materials

- Class CDs, flashcards, *Ferris Wheel* mat, Mimi puppet, feely bag

Main vocabulary

- black, green, red, white, yellow

Teacher's tip: Reinforcing the concept

In addition to the flashcards, use familiar items of different colors to reinforce the concept, e.g. a banana for yellow, a pear or a leaf for green, etc. Pass the items around and encourage the children to name the color each time.

Circle time

Hello song & puppet (CD1 Track 2; see TB p 17 & 21)
Opening routines (see TB p 16)
Lesson aims (see TB p 18)

Introduce the colors

- Use the flashcards, puppet and feely bag to introduce or remind children of the colors. Say the words and encourage children to repeat them with you. Repeat for all the words.
- Play one or two flashcard games with the *Ferris Wheel* mat and/or the puppet (see TB p 20 & 21).
- Encourage children to say *I like* … and name the colors they like.

Table time

Student's Book p 86

Listen, point and say.

- Hold up your book. Play the audio and point to the colors in the key at the top of the page in turn.
- Play the audio again. Children listen, point to the colors in the key, and say the name of the color.

CD3 Track 41

Red … green … yellow … black … white
Red … green … yellow … black … white
Red … green … yellow … black … white

Color the picture following the key.

- Children look at the key and color the picture. Encourage them to tell you which colors they are using as they work.

Say your favorite color.

- Children say which of the colors on the page is their favorite.

Activity Book p 86

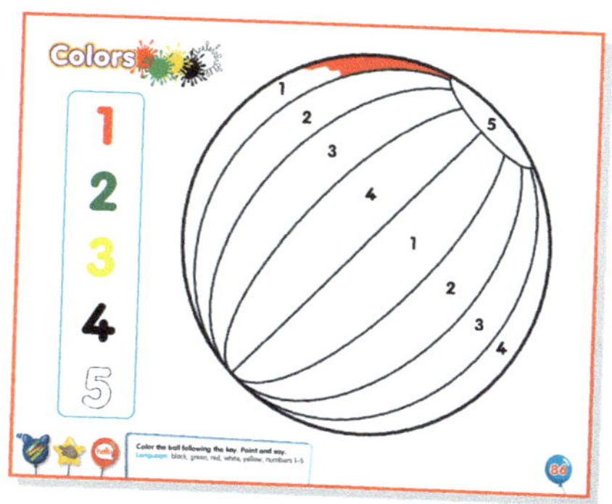

Color the ball following the key.

- Children color the ball following the number key.

Point and say.

- They point and say the number and the color.

Closing time

Learning review (see TB p 18)
Closing routines (see TB p 16)
Bye bye song and puppet (CD1 Track 3; see TB p 17 & 21)

Cross-curricular activities

- See also the activities in the other Colors lesson (see TB p 209).

Art and craft

Prepare a half sheet of construction paper with six arcs in the shape of a rainbow (one rainbow for each group or table of children).

Children work at their tables or in groups and either color, paint or glue colored tissue paper on each section of the rainbow (red, orange, yellow, green, blue, purple).

Display the rainbows. Children point and name the colors.

Science

Children use finger paints and experiment with mixing different colors on paper, e.g. red and yellow to make orange.

Numbers 123

One to twenty

Listen, point and say. Draw a line to join the numbers in sequence. Say.
Language: numbers 1–20

Learning objectives

- Learn, reinforce, consolidate or review numbers

Materials

- Class CDs, flashcards, *Ferris Wheel* mat, Mimi puppet, feely bag

Main vocabulary

- numbers 1–20

Teacher's tip: Recognizing numbers by touch

Use wooden or foam numbers to accustom the children to the number formation. Place them in a feely bag and encourage the children to guess which number they are touching before they remove it from the bag.

Circle time

Hello song & puppet (CD1 Track 2; see TB p 17 & 21)
Opening routines (see TB p 16)
Lesson aims (see TB p 18)

Introduce the numbers.

- Use the flashcards, puppet and feely bag to introduce or remind children of the numbers. Say the words and encourage children to repeat them with you.
- Play one or two flashcard games with the *Ferris Wheel* mat and/or the puppet (see TB p 20 & 21).
- Get children to count different classroom objects with you.

Table time

Student's Book p 87

Listen, point and say.

- Hold up your book. Play the audio and point to the numbers in turn.
- Play the audio again. Children listen, point to the numbers in their books, and say the words.

CD3 Track 42

One … two … three … four … five … six
seven … eight … nine … ten … eleven … twelve …
thirteen … fourteen … fifteen … sixteen …
seventeen … eighteen … nineteen … twenty

Draw a line to join the numbers in sequence.

- Children draw lines to join the numbers from 1 to 20. Encourage them to say the numbers as they join them.

Say.

- Hold up your book and point to a block. Children say the number on the block.

Activity Book p 87

Count and match each picture to the correct number.

- Children count the items in each picture and match to the correct number.

Point and say.

- The children point to each picture and say the number.

Closing time

Learning review (see TB p 18)
Closing routines (see TB p 16)
Bye bye song and puppet (CD1 Track 3; see TB p 17 & 21)

Cross-curricular activities

- See also the activities in the other Numbers lesson (see TB p 215).

Physical movement

Explain that children are going to do a movement activity in which they make groups of different numbers.

Children stand up. Play lively dance music and encourage children to dance and move to the rhythm of the music.

Pause the music and call a number, e.g. *Three!* Demonstrate that children should get into groups of the number you call as fast as they can. Anyone left out and not in a group makes a special group with you.

Repeat with different numbers.

Math

Get 20 plastic cups and write the numbers 1–20 on them. Give each table or group of children a few of the cups, and sets of small objects, e.g. dried beans or pasta shapes.

Children work together and count out the correct number of objects to put in each cup.

Children check they have put the correct number of objects in each cup by taking them out again and counting out loud. Take back the cups and give out different cups to each group.

Numbers 123

One to twenty

1 2 3 4 5 6 7 8 9 10

11 12 13 14 15 16 17 18 19 20

Listen, point and say. Trace the numbers. Count the balls and circle the correct number.
Language: numbers 1–20

Numbers

One to twenty

Learning objectives

- Learn, reinforce, consolidate or review numbers

Materials

- Class CDs, flashcards, *Ferris Wheel* mat, Mimi puppet, feely bag

Main vocabulary

- numbers 1–20

Teacher's tip: Recognizing numbers by touch

Use wooden or foam numbers to accustom the children to the shape and form of each number. Place them in a feely bag and encourage children to guess which number they are touching before they remove it from the bag.

Circle time

Hello song & puppet (CD1 Track 2; see TB p 17 & 21)
Opening routines (see TB p 16)
Lesson aims (see TB p 18)

Introduce the numbers.

- Use the flashcards, puppet and feely bag to remind children of the numbers. Say the words and encourage children to repeat them with you.
- Play one or two flashcard games with the *Ferris Wheel* mat and/or the puppet (see TB p 20 & 21).
- Get children to count different classroom objects with you.

Table time

Student's Book p 88

Listen, point and say.

CD3 Track 42

- Hold up your book. Play the audio (see TB p 213) and point to the numbers in turn.
- Play the audio again. Children listen, point to the numbers in their books, and say the words.

Trace the numbers.

- Children trace the numbers.

Count the balls and circle the correct number.

- Children count the balls and circle the correct number (20).

Activity Book p 88

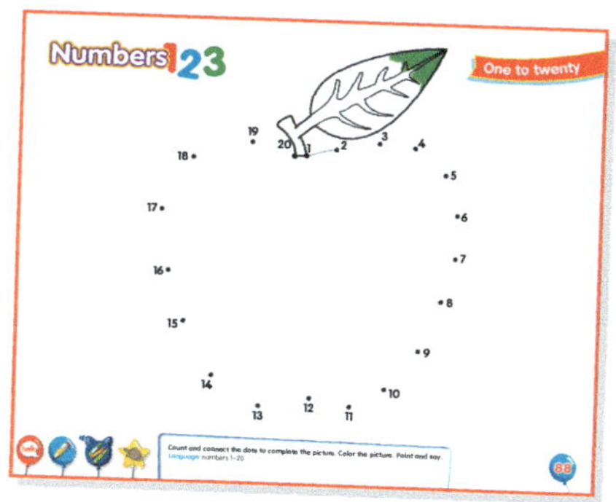

Count and connect the dots to complete the picture. Color the picture.

- Encourage children to count as they connect the numbered dots in order. They color the picture of the apple.

Point and say.

- Children point to each number in turn and say it.

Closing time

Learning review (see TB p 18)
Closing routines (see TB p 16)
Bye bye song and puppet (CD1 Track 3; see TB p 17 & 21)

Cross-curricular activities

- See also the activities in the other Numbers lesson (see TB p 213).

Art and craft

Give a number flashcard and some modeling clay to each group or table of children.

Give each child a sheet of paper with the same number as on the flashcard lightly drawn on it.

Check children know the number on their paper and flashcard.

Children use the modeling clay to make a model of their number and place it on their sheet of paper.

When they are ready, get children to arrange the papers with different modeling clay numbers in sequence.

Children point to and say the numbers with you.

Social science

Point to furniture and objects in the classroom, e.g. door, windows, shelves. Children observe, count and say how many of each thing there are.

Shapes

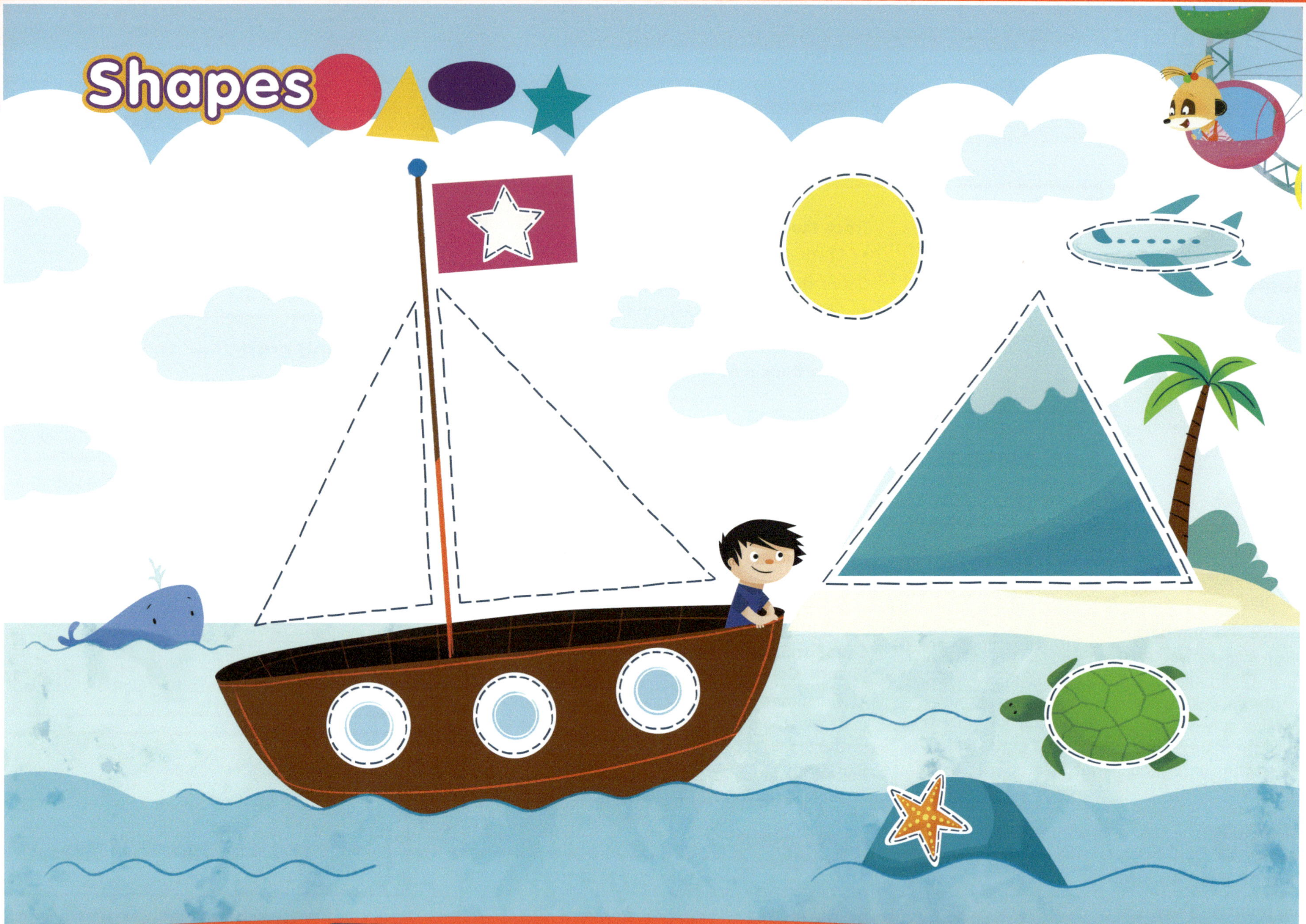

Listen, point and say. Trace the shapes in the picture. Say.
Language: circle, oval, star, triangle

Learning objectives

- Learn, reinforce, consolidate or review shapes

Materials

- Class CDs, flashcards, *Ferris Wheel* mat, Mimi puppet , feely bag

Main vocabulary

- circle, oval, star, triangle; colors

Teacher's tip: Associating shapes with familiar objects

Encourage the children to associate objects with their shapes. Name one of the shapes and have children point to or touch anything in the classroom of that shape. Alternatively, take the children for a short walk outside their classroom. Put them in pairs and encourage them to point out and name different shapes to their partner.

Circle time

Hello song & puppet (CD1 Track 2; see TB p 17 & 21)
Opening routines (see TB p 16)
Lesson aims (see TB p 18)

Introduce the shapes.

- Use the flashcards, puppet and feely bag to introduce or remind children of the shapes. Say the words and encourage children to repeat them with you.
- Play one or two flashcard games with the *Ferris Wheel* mat and/or the puppet (see TB p 20 & 21).
- Get children to identify shapes in the classroom with you, e.g. the clock = circle.

Table time

Student's Book p 89

Listen, point and say.

- Hold up your book. Play the audio and point to the shapes in turn.
- Play the audio again. Children listen, point to the shapes in their books, and say the words.

CD3 Track 43

Circle … triangle … oval … star
Circle … triangle … oval … star
Circle … triangle … oval … star

Trace the shapes in the picture.

- Children trace the circles, triangles, ovals and stars in the picture.

Say.

- Children point to the pictures and name the shapes.

Activity Book p 89

Match and trace the shapes. Color the shapes so they are the same.

- Children match the shapes, then trace them. They color the similar shapes the same color.

Point and say.

- Children point to each shape and say its name and color.

Closing time

Learning review (see TB p 18)
Closing routines (see TB p 16)
Bye bye song and puppet (CD1 Track 3; see TB p 17 & 21)

Cross-curricular activities

- See also the activities in the other Shapes lesson (see TB p 219).

Drama

Stand with your back to the children and draw a shape in the air, e.g. circle. Children guess and name the shape.

Repeat several times with different shapes.

Ask a child to come to the front and stand with their back to you and the class. Use your finger to draw a shape on the child's back and encourage the child to guess the shape. Get the rest of the class to say if the guess is correct or not.

Repeat several times with different children.

Physical movement

Use adhesive tape to make large shapes on the classroom floor or walls.

Children stand up and walk around the classroom. When you call the name of a shape, e.g. *Square!*, they jump inside the correct shape on the floor, or they run and touch the correct shape on the wall.

Shapes

Listen, point and say. Match the presents which are the same. Say.
Language: diamond, rectangle, square

90

Learning objectives

- Learn, reinforce, consolidate or review shapes

Materials

- Class CDs, flashcards, *Ferris Wheel* mat, Mimi puppet, feely bag

Main vocabulary

- diamond, rectangle, square; colors

Teacher's tip: Associating shapes with familiar objects

Encourage the children to associate objects with their shapes. Name one of the shapes and have children point to or touch anything in the classroom of that shape. Alternatively, take the children for a short walk outside their classroom. Put them in pairs and encourage them to point out and name different shapes to their partner.

Circle time

Hello song & puppet (CD1 Track 2; see TB p 17 & 21)
Opening routines (see TB p 16)
Lesson aims (see TB p 18)

Introduce the shapes.

- Use the flashcards, puppet and feely bag to introduce or remind children of the shapes. Say the words and encourage children to repeat them with you.
- Play one or two flashcard games with the *Ferris Wheel* mat and/or the puppet (see TB p 20 & 21).
- Get children to identify shapes in the classroom with you, e.g. the board = rectangle.

Table time

Student's Book p 90

Listen, point and say.

- Hold up your book. Play the audio and point to the shapes in turn.
- Play the audio again. Children listen, point to the shapes in their books, and say the words.

CD3 Track 44

Square … rectangle … diamond
Square … rectangle … diamond
Square … rectangle … diamond

Match the presents which are the same.

- Children match the presents that are the same shape.

Say.

- Children point to the presents and name the shapes.

Activity Book p 90

Find and color the shapes which are the same.

- Point out the shapes on the left of the page. Children find and color the shape that is the same in each row.

Point and say.

- Children point to each shape and say its name and color.

Closing time

Learning review (see TB p 18)
Closing routines (see TB p 16)
Bye bye song and puppet (CD1 Track 3; see TB p 17 & 21)

Cross-curricular activities

- See also the activities in the other Shapes lesson (see TB p 217).

Math

Give each table or group of children a set of colored pipe cleaners or straws (some full length and others cut in half).

Children use the pipe cleaners or straws to make different shapes (square, diamond, rectangle and triangle with straws, and including circle if you are using pipe cleaners that bend flexibly).

Children look at and name the shapes that they and other children have made. If you like, children can then glue their shapes onto colored card and these can be displayed.

Social science

Point to furniture and objects in the classroom, e.g. door, window, clock. Children observe and name the shapes.

Concepts

Listen, point and say. Find and circle four differences in the pictures to show hot and cold. Say.
Language: hot, cold

Learning objectives

- Learn, reinforce, consolidate or review concepts

Materials

- Class CDs, flashcards, *Ferris Wheel* mat, Mimi puppet, feely bag

Main vocabulary

- hot, cold

Circle time

Hello song & puppet (CD1 Track 2; see TB p 17 & 21)
Opening routines (see TB p 16)
Lesson aims (see TB p 18)

Introduce the concepts *hot* and *cold*.

- Use the flashcards, puppet and feely bag to introduce or remind children of the concepts. Say the words and encourage children to repeat them with you.
- Play one or two flashcard games with the *Ferris Wheel* mat and/or the puppet (see TB p 20 & 21).
- Check that children clearly recognize and understand each concept.

Table time

Student's Book p 91

Listen, point and say.

- Hold up your book. Play the audio and point to the pictures in turn.
- Play the audio again. Children listen, point to the pictures in their books, and say the words.

CD3 Track 45

Hot … cold … hot … cold
Hot … cold … hot … cold
Hot … cold … hot … cold

Find and circle four differences in the pictures to show hot and cold.

- Children find and circle four differences in the pictures (Answers: boy in summer/winter clothes; tree with/without leaves; sky with sun/clouds; dog with/without coat).

Say.

- Children point to the differences in the pictures and say *hot* or *cold*.

Activity Book p 91

Draw things for hot and cold weather.

- Point out the items for hot and cold weather. Children draw each item under the sun if it is for hot weather and under the clouds if it is for cold weather.

Point and say.

- Children point to each item and say *hot* or *cold*.

Closing time

Learning review (see TB p 18)
Closing routines (see TB p 16)
Bye bye song and puppet (CD1 Track 3; see TB p 17 & 21)

Cross-curricular activities

- See also the activities in the other Concepts lessons (see TB p 223 & 225).

Drama

Children stand up. Explain and demonstrate that you're going to say a concept word e.g. *Hot!* or *Cold!* Children respond by doing to mime to show they understand, e.g. wiping their brow to show they're hot or shivering to show they're cold.

Alternate giving instructions for the two concepts in the pair you're working on, and children respond.

Concepts

3:46

hello

Listen, point and say. Circle the noisy children red. Circle the quiet children blue. Say.
Language: noisy, quiet

92

Learning objectives

- Learn, reinforce, consolidate or review concepts

Materials

- Class CDs, flashcards, *Ferris Wheel* mat, Mimi puppet, feely bag

Main vocabulary

- noisy, quiet

Teacher's tip: Reinforcing positive behavior in the classroom

Use the concepts *noisy* and *quiet* to reinforce positive behavior in the classroom. Remind children to use inside voices in the classroom and outside voices in the playground.

Circle time

Hello song & puppet (CD1 Track 2; see TB p 17 & 21)
Opening routines (see TB p 16)
Lesson aims (see TB p 18)

Introduce the concepts *noisy* and *quiet*.

- Use the flashcards, puppet and feely bag to introduce or remind children of the concepts. Say the words and encourage children to repeat them with you.
- Play one or two flashcard games with the Ferris Wheel mat and/or the puppet (see TB p 20 & 21).
- Check that children clearly recognize and understand each concept.

Table time

Student's Book p 92

Listen, point and say.

- Hold up your book. Play the audio and point to the noisy and quiet children in turn.
- Play the audio again. Children listen, point to the children in their books, and say the words.

CD3 Track 46

Noisy … quiet … noisy … quiet
Noisy … quiet … noisy … quiet
Noisy … quiet … noisy … quiet

Circle the noisy children red. Circle the quiet children blue.

- Children circle the noisy children red and the quiet children blue.

Say.

- Children point to the pictures of children being noisy and quiet, and say the words.

Activity Book p 92

Color the frames of the pictures of noisy children red. Color the frames of the pictures of quiet children blue.

- Children color the frames of the pictures of noisy children red and of quiet children blue.

Point and say.

- Children point to each picture and say *noisy* or *quiet*.

Closing time

Learning review (see TB p 18)
Closing routines (see TB p 16)
Bye bye song and puppet (CD1 Track 3; see TB p 17 & 21)

Cross-curricular activities

- See also the activities in the other Concepts lessons (see TB p 221 & 225).

Social science

Ask questions and give prompts to encourage children to think about and say how the concept applies to them, e.g. *Are you quiet in the playground / classroom?*

Talk about any values related to the concepts, e.g. *Is it helpful to be quiet at home / school? When? Why?*

Concepts

Listen, point and say. Color the frames of the clean rooms. Say.
Language: clean, messy

Learning objectives

- Learn, reinforce, consolidate or review concepts

Materials

- Class CDs, flashcards, *Ferris Wheel* mat, Mimi puppet, feely bag

Main vocabulary

- clean, messy

Teacher's tip: Reinforcing positive behavior in the classroom

Use the concepts *clean* and *messy* to reinforce positive behavior in the classroom. Remind children to keep their classroom clean as it belongs to all of them.

Circle time

Hello song & puppet (CD1 Track 2; see TB p 17 & 21)
Opening routines (see TB p 16)
Lesson aims (see TB p 18)

Introduce the concepts *clean* and *messy*.

- Use the flashcards, puppet and feely bag to introduce or remind children of the concepts. Say the words and encourage children to repeat them with you.
- Play one or two flashcard games with the *Ferris Wheel* mat and/or the puppet (see TB p 20 & 21).
- Check that children clearly recognize and understand each concept.

Table time

Student's Book p 93

Listen, point and say.

- Hold up your book. Play the audio and point to the pictures of clean and messy rooms in turn.
- Play the audio again. Children listen, point to the pictures in their books, and say the words.

CD3 Track 47

Clean … messy … clean … messy
Clean … messy … clean … messy
Clean … messy … clean … messy

Color the frames of the clean rooms.

- Children color the frames of the clean rooms (pictures 1 and 4).

Say.

- Children point to the pictures of clean and messy rooms and say the words.

Activity Book p 93

Match the objects to the correct places to clean up the classroom.

- Children match the objects to the correct places.

Point and say.

- Children point to each item in its old position and say *messy*. They point to the item in its new position and say *clean*.

Closing time

Learning review (see TB p 18)
Closing routines (see TB p 16)
Bye bye song and puppet (CD1 Track 3; see TB p 17 & 21)

Cross-curricular activities

- See also the activities in the other Concepts lessons (see TB p 221 & 223).

Art and craft

Children choose one pair of concepts and draw and color or paint a picture of themselves being, e.g. clean or messy.

Children show each other their pictures and say, e.g. *(You're) clean!*

Festivals

Peace Day

Listen and point. Listen and sing *We love the world.* Trace and color the bird of peace. Say.
Language: animals, bird, children, fly, happy, peace, world

94

Learning objectives

- Identify and name Peace Day vocabulary
- Sing and act out the song *We love the world*
- Trace and color the bird of peace
- Participate in celebrating a festival
- Color and talk about things you love

Materials

- Class CDs, printable Peace Day flashcards, *Ferris Wheel* mat, Mimi puppet

Main vocabulary

- animals, bird, children, fly, happy, peace, world

Key language

- I love the (bird).

Teacher's Tip: Peace Day

Peace Day may not be something children are familiar with in the country they live, but you can take the opportunity to promote values like respect, tolerance, etc. now that they are starting this new school year. It may also help you set rules in the classroom for good behavior since this day is celebrated on September 21.

Circle time

Hello song & puppet (CD1 Track 2; see TB p 17 & 21)
Opening routines (see TB p 16)
Lesson aims (see TB p 18)

Introduce Peace Day.

- Explain the meaning of *peace*. Ask children if they want to celebrate Peace Day in English.
- Use the puppet to show the flashcards and introduce the new words (*world, bird of peace, children, animals*). Say each word and children repeat.
- Ferris Wheel mat on floor or board with flashcards face down (on different colored pods). Use the puppet to turn over and name. Children repeat the words.

Game: *Say the color!*

- Name the peace words and children say the color of the wheel. Then the reverse.

Game: *Guess and say!*

- Turn the flashcards face down and mix them up.
- Use the puppet to point to one of the flashcards and children guess what it is. Turn the flashcard over and see if they're correct. Repeat several times.

Table time

Student's Book p 94

Listen and point.

- Hold up your book. Play the audio and point to the pictures in turn.

CD3 Track 48

It's Peace Day.
Look! The world … children … animals … and the bird of peace!

- Play the audio again. Children listen, point to the pictures in their books, and say the words.

Listen and sing *We love the world.*

- Hold up the flashcard of the world and say *Let's listen to the song "We love the world."*
- Play the audio. Children listen and point to the pictures in their books in turn. In the chorus they mime flying like a bird.
- Children stand up. Stick the flashcards of *world, children* and *animals* on different walls in the classroom.
- Play the audio again. Children listen, sing and point to the flashcards in each verse and mime flying towards them in the chorus. Repeat once or twice.

CD3 Track 49

We love the world
We want peace
And peace begins
With you and me
Bird of peace, fly, fly, fly
Fly all over the world

We love children
We want peace
And peace begins
With you and me
(Chorus)

We love animals
We want peace
And peace begins
With you and me
(Chorus)

Trace and color the bird of peace.

- Children trace and color the bird of peace.
- Play the song again. Children point to the pictures and join in singing the song.

Say.

- Using L1, ask e.g. *Is peace important? How does peace begin with you and me?* and children respond.
- Say *Happy Peace Day!* and encourage children to say this to each other and to you.

Activity Book p 94

Match. Color the things you love.

- Children match each silhouette to the correct picture. They choose and color the picture or pictures of things they love.

Point and say.

- Children point and talk about the things they love.

Closing time

Learning review (see TB p 18)
Closing routines (see TB p 16)
Bye bye song and puppet (CD1 Track 3; see TB p 17 & 21)

Festivals

Carnival

Listen and point. Listen and sing *It's Carnival today*. Match and color the pictures. Color the circle to show your Carnival costume. Say.
Language: Carnival, clown, crown, king, pirate, queen; happy; I'm a (pirate).

Festivals

Carnival

Learning objectives
- Identify and name Carnival vocabulary
- Sing and act out the song *It's Carnival today*
- Match pictures, choose and talk about your Carnival costume
- Participate in celebrating a festival

Materials
- Class CDs, printable Carnival flashcards, *Ferris Wheel* mat, Mimi puppet

Main vocabulary
- Carnival, clown, crown, king, pirate, queen; happy

Key language
- I'm a (pirate).

Teacher's Tip: Carnival

Carnivals may not be something children from your city are familiar with. Talk to children about Carnival and plan a costume parade in the classroom or even outside in the yard, inviting parents to come. Allow children to choose their costume and provide props and face paints to add to the fun.

Circle time

Hello song & puppet (CD1 Track 2; see TB p 17 & 21)
Opening routines (see TB p 16)
Lesson aims (see TB p 18)

Introduce Carnival.
- Ask children if they want to celebrate Carnival in English. Ask children what people dress up as at Carnival. As they answer, use the puppet to introduce the new words (*pirate*, *clown*, *king*, *queen*). Say each word and children repeat.
- Ferris Wheel mat on floor or board with flashcards face down (on different colored pods). Use puppet to turn over and name. Children repeat the words.

Game: *Guess and say!*
- Turn the flashcards face down and mix them up.
- Use the puppet to point to one of the flashcards and children guess what it is. Turn the flashcard over and see if they're correct. Repeat several times.

Game: *Mime and guess!*
- Mime being one of the Carnival characters and children guess.
- Repeat with different characters. When you mime being a king or queen, mime putting a crown on your head and introduce the word.
- Invite children to mime being different characters and the rest of the class guesses.

Table time

Student's Book p 95

Listen and point.
- Hold up your book. Play the audio and point to the pictures in turn.

CD3 Track 50

It's Carnival.
Look! A pirate … a clown … a king … a queen!

- Play the audio again. Children listen, point to the pictures in their books, and say the words.

Listen and sing *It's Carnival today.*
- Play the song. Children listen and point to the pictures as they hear the words in each verse.
- Play the song again. Children sing, mime the characters and do the actions for the chorus.

CD3 Track 51

Clap your hands, turn around
Wave your arms, touch the ground
It's Carnival today!

I'm a pirate
I'm a clown
I'm a king
I have boots
It's Carnival today
(Chorus)

I'm a pirate
I'm a clown
I'm a queen
I have a crown
It's Carnival today
(Chorus)

Match and color the pictures. Color the circle to show your Carnival costume.
- Children match and color the pictures.
- Children color the spot under one of the pictures to show the Carnival costume they like best.

Say.
- Children take turns saying the costume they chose, e.g. *I'm a pirate.*
- Ask e.g. *Do you like Carnival?* and children respond.
- Say *Happy Carnival!* and children do the same.

Activity Book p 95

Choose, draw and color your Carnival costume.
- Point out the hats for each Carnival costume. Children draw themselves wearing one of the hats.

Point and say.
- Children point and say the costume they chose.

Closing time

Learning review (see TB p 18)
Closing routines (see TB p 16)
Bye bye song and puppet (CD1 Track 3; see TB p 17 & 21)

Festivals

Children's Day

Listen and point. Listen and sing *It's Children's Day*. Color the frames of the things you love to do. Draw a picture of you doing something you love. Say.
Language: children; hug, play, run, talk; I love to (play).

Learning objectives

- Identify and name Children's Day vocabulary
- Sing and act out the song *It's Children's Day*
- Identify things you love to do and draw a picture
- Participate in celebrating a festival
- Identify activities children are doing

Materials

- Class CDs, printable Children's Day flashcards, *Ferris Wheel* mat, Mimi puppet

Main vocabulary

- children; hug, play, run, talk

Key language

- I love to (play).

Teacher's tip: Making a mural

Encourage the children to draw and color a picture of themselves for a display. Glue the pictures under the title: *It's Children's Day! Hurray!*

Circle time

Hello song & puppet (CD1 Track 2; see TB p 17 & 21)
Opening routines (see TB p 16)
Lesson aims (see TB p 18)

Introduce Children's Day.

- Explain that there is a special day each year to celebrate children. Ask children if they want to celebrate Children's Day in English.
- Ask children what they love to do. As they answer, use the puppet to introduce the new words (*talk, run, play, hug my friends*). Children repeat words.
- Ferris Wheel mat on floor or board with flashcards face down (on different colored pods). Use puppet to turn over and name. Children repeat the words.

Game: *Guess and say!*

- Turn the flashcards face down and mix them up.
- Use the puppet to point to one of the flashcards and children guess what it is. Turn the flashcard over and see if they're correct. Repeat several times.

Game: *Mimi says …!*

- Teach children the actions for each word (see below).
- Use the puppet to give instructions, e.g. *Mimi says … talk!* Repeat with all the actions and words.

Table time

Student's Book p 96

Listen and point.

- Hold up your book. Play the audio and point to the pictures in turn.

CD3 Track 52

It's Children's Day. Look! I love to … talk … play … run … and hug my friends!

- Play the audio again. Children listen, point to the pictures in their books, and say the words.

Listen and sing *It's Children's Day*.

- Play the song. Children listen and point to the pictures as they hear the words in the song.
- Play the song again. Children listen and join in singing the song and doing the actions.

CD3 Track 53

It's Children's Day
Hurray, hurray (Wave your arms)
I love to talk (Open and close your fingers)
I love to play (Jump in place)
It's Children's Day
Hurray, hurray (Wave your arms)

It's Children's Day
Hurray, hurray
I love to run
I love to play
It's Children's Day
Hurray, hurray

It's Children's Day
Hurray, hurray
I love to hug
My friends and play
It's Children's Day
Hurray, hurray

Color the frames of the things you love to do.

- Children color the frames of pictures that show what they love to do.

Draw a picture of you doing something you love.

- Children draw a picture of something else they love to do, e.g. read a storybook, watch a movie, ride a bike, etc. Children show each other their pictures.

Say.

- Ask *Do you like Children's Day?*
- Say *Happy Children's Day!* and encourage children to say this to each other and to you.

Activity Book p 96

Find and circle the children doing something different.

- Draw attention to the pictures on the left. Children find and circle the picture in each row that shows a different activity.

Point and say.

- Children point and say what they love to do.

Closing time

Learning review (see TB p 18)
Closing routines (see TB p 16)
Bye bye song and puppet (CD1 Track 3; see TB p 17 & 21)

Project template

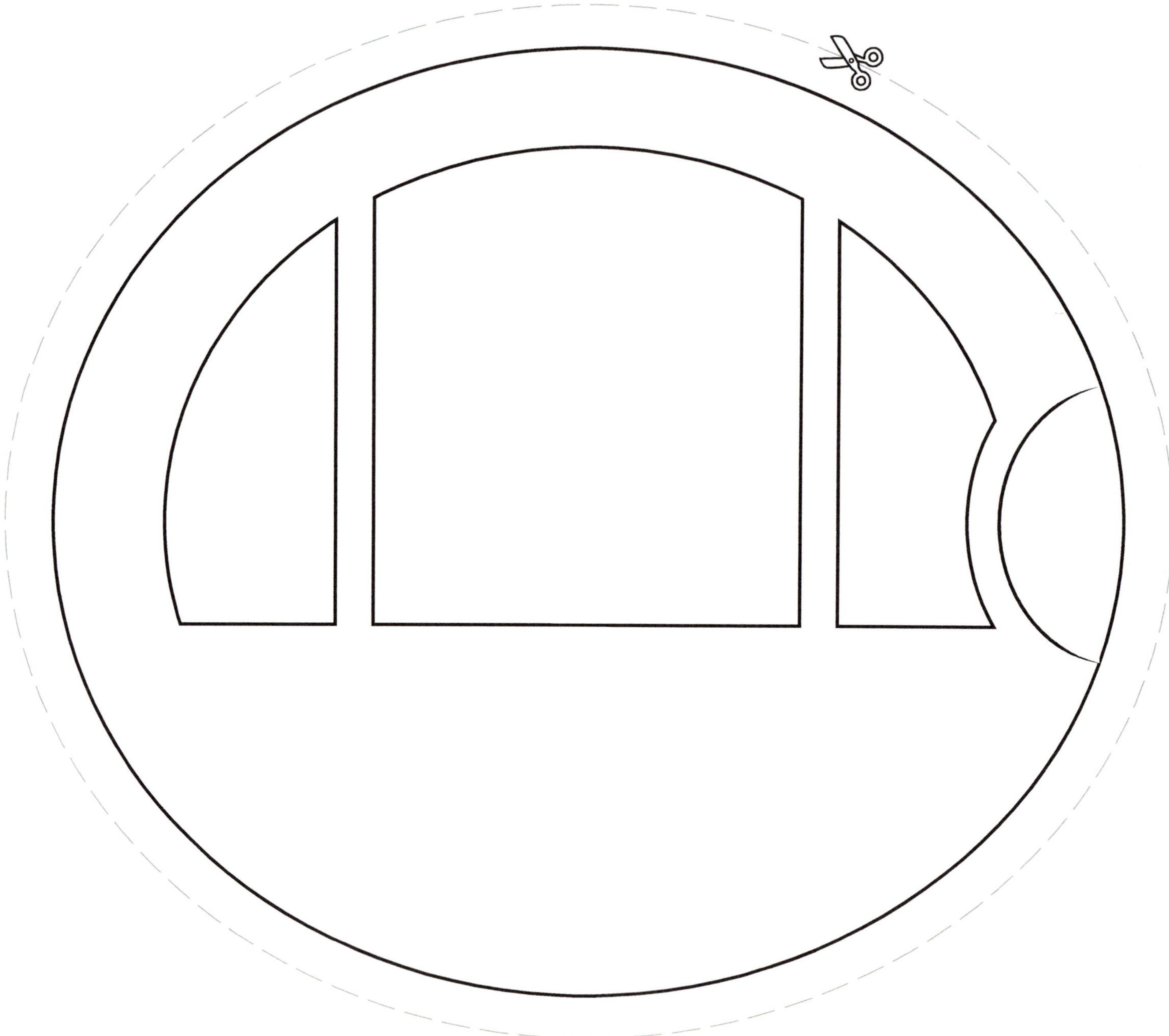

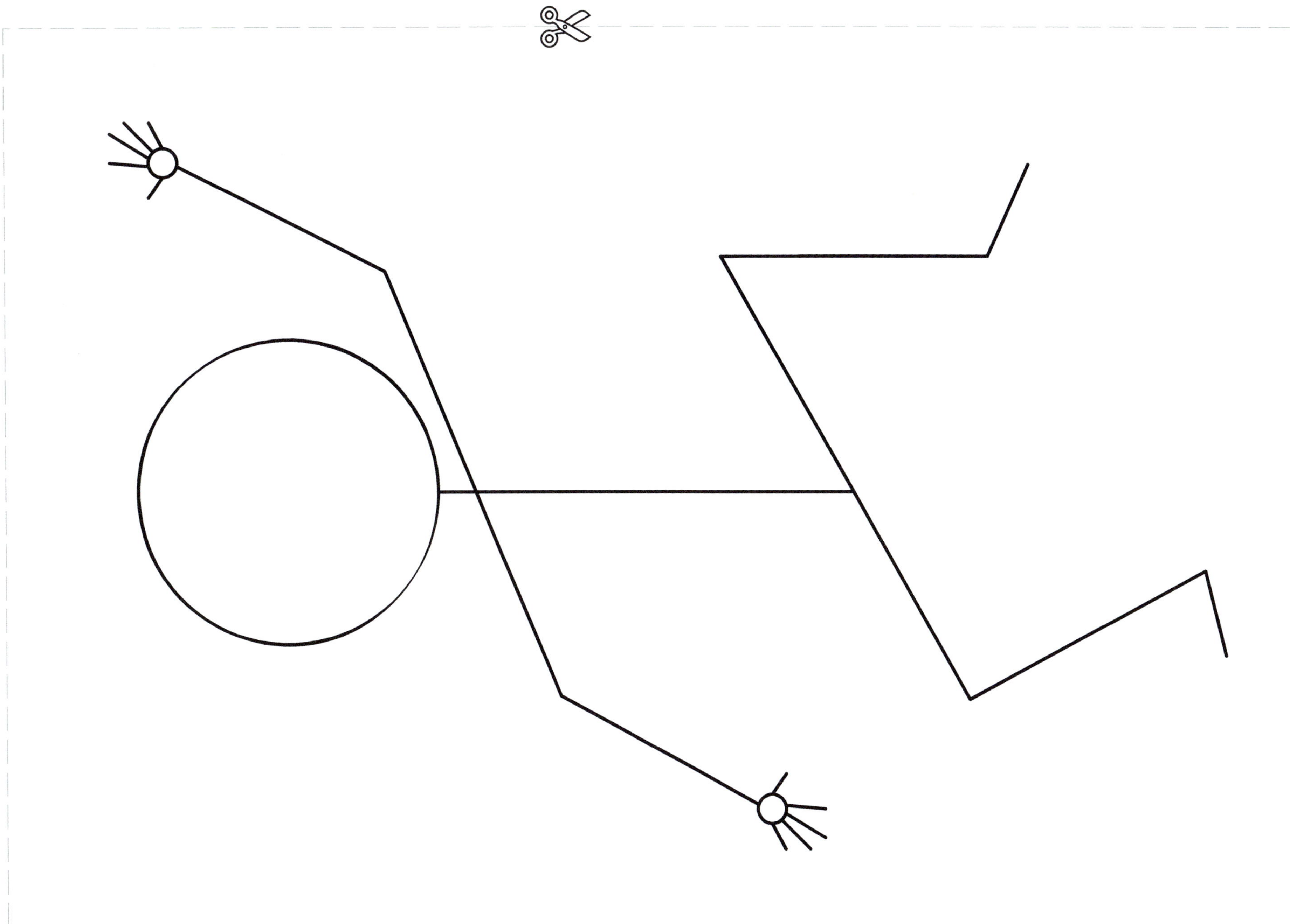

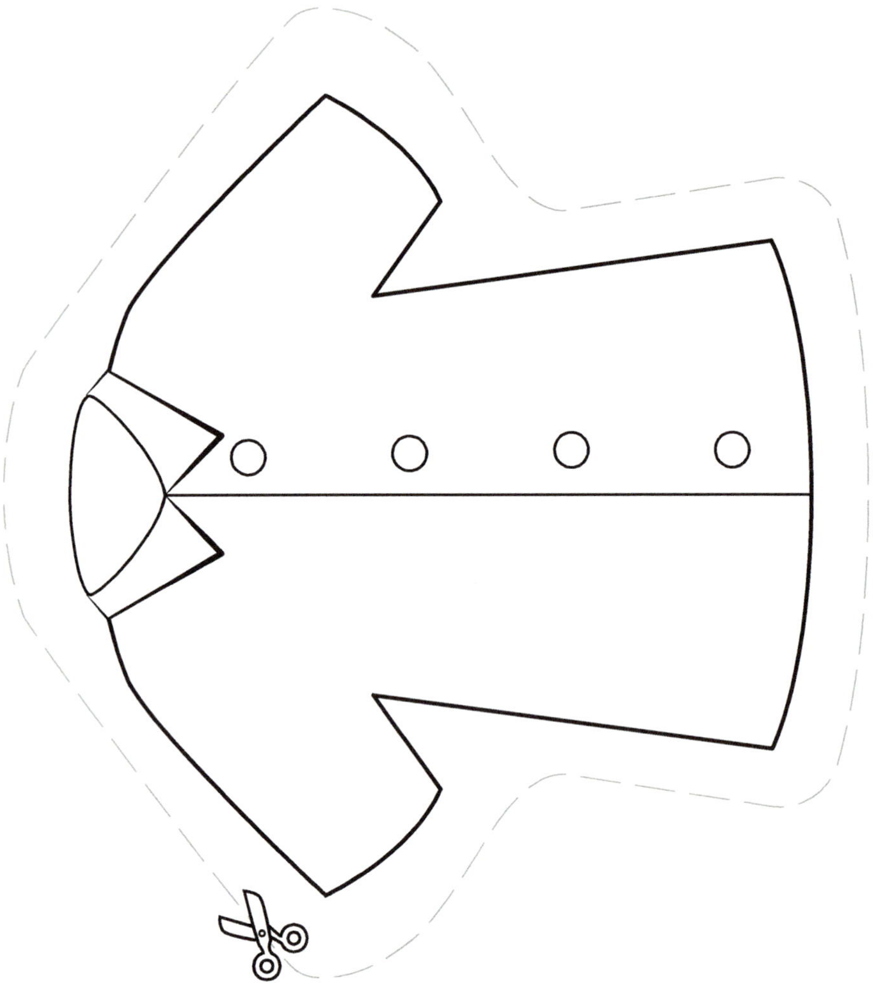

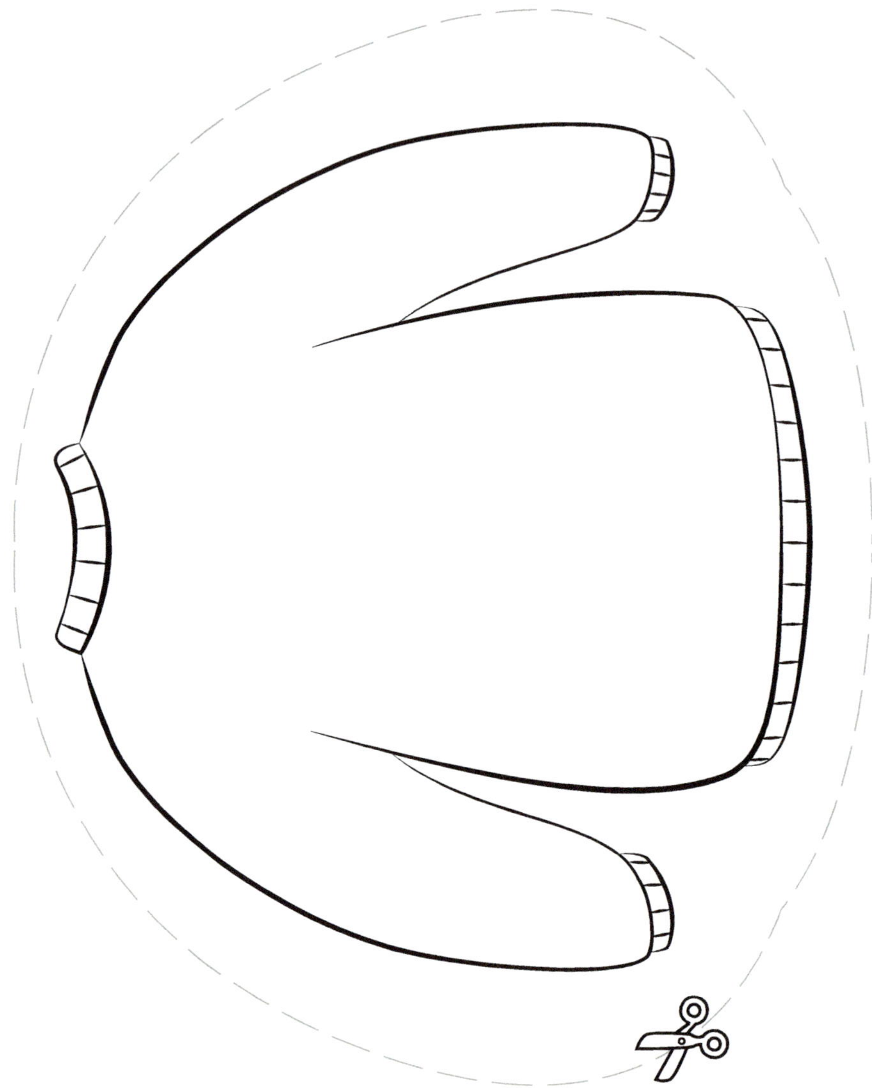

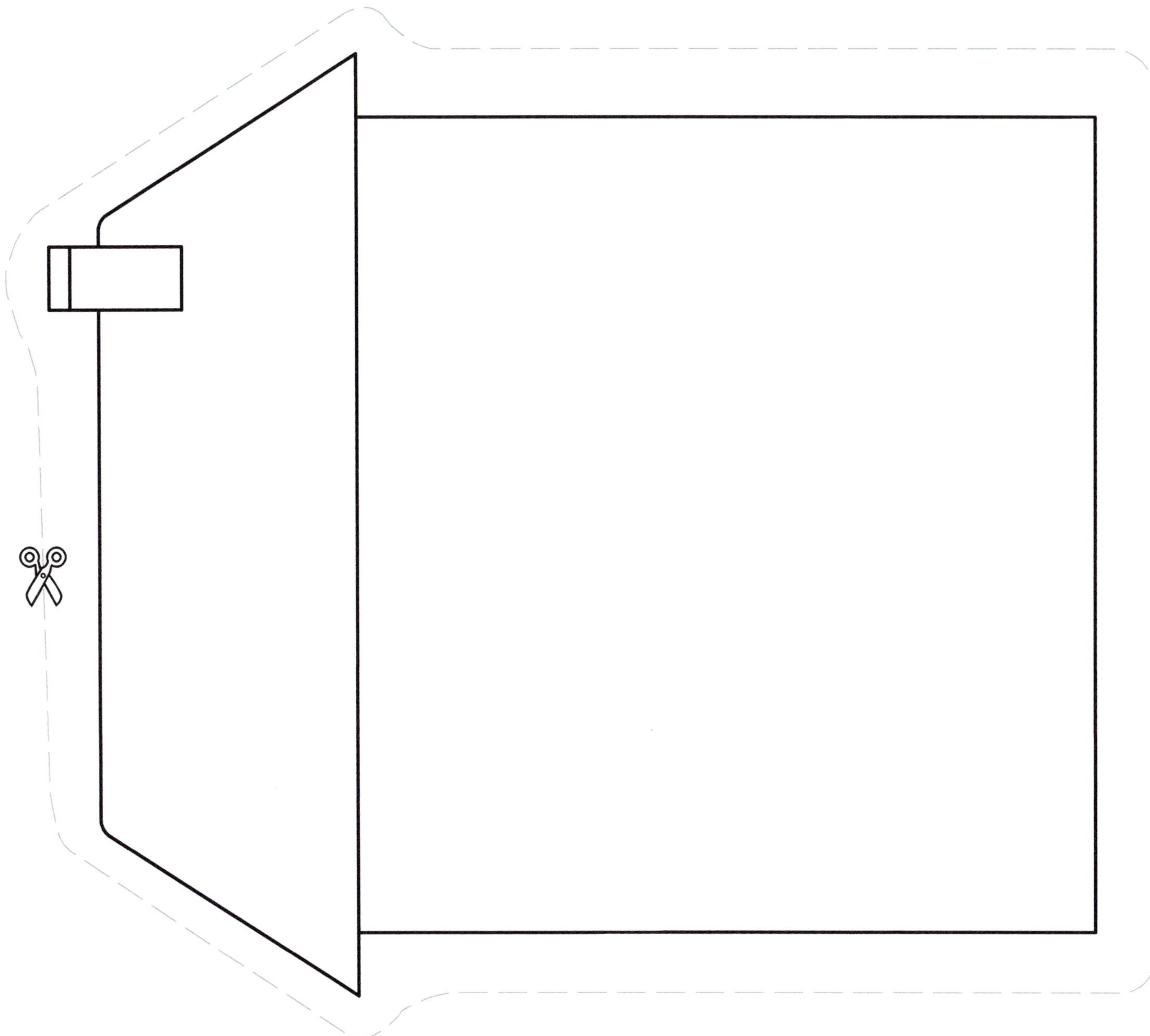

Project template

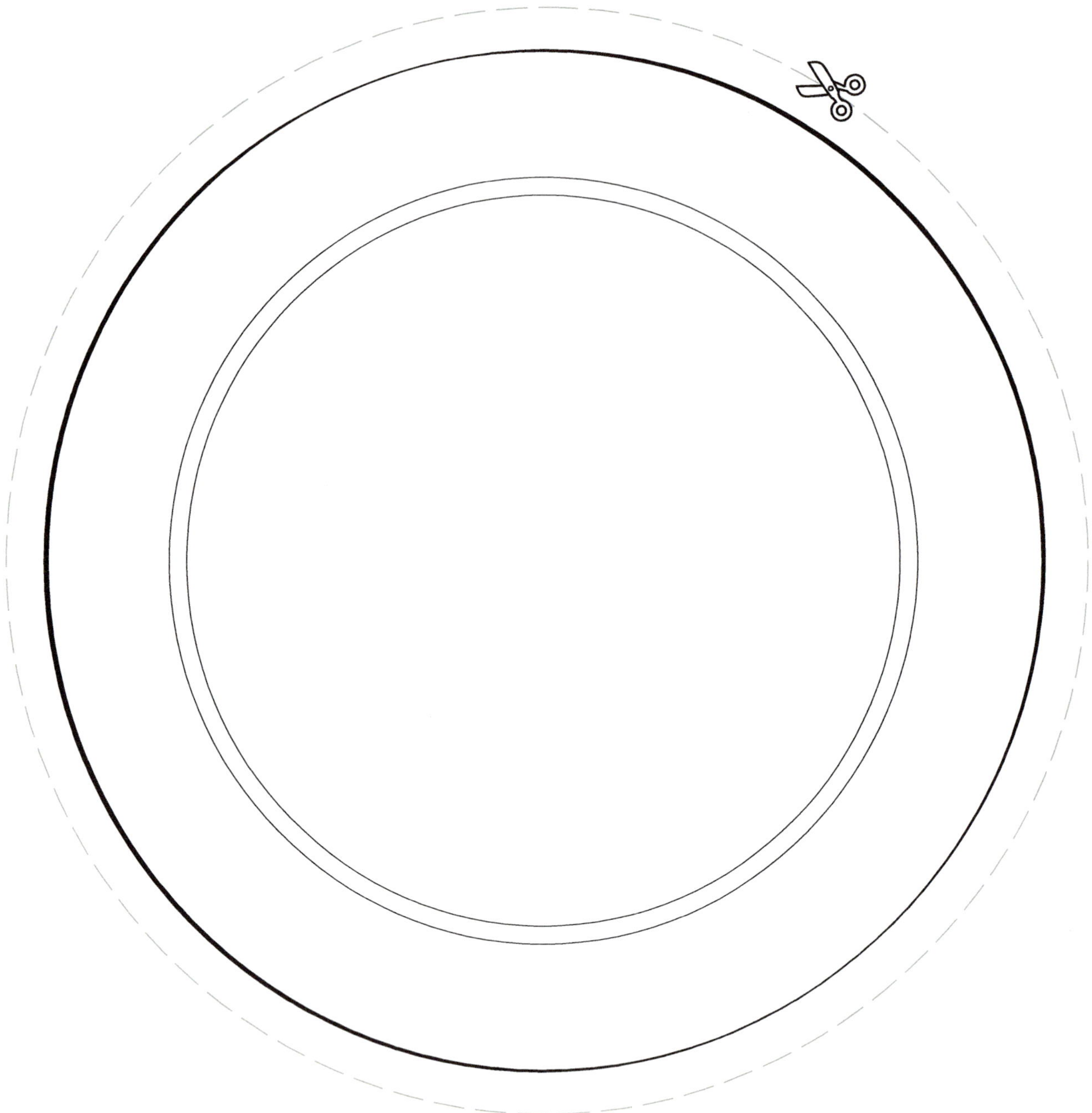

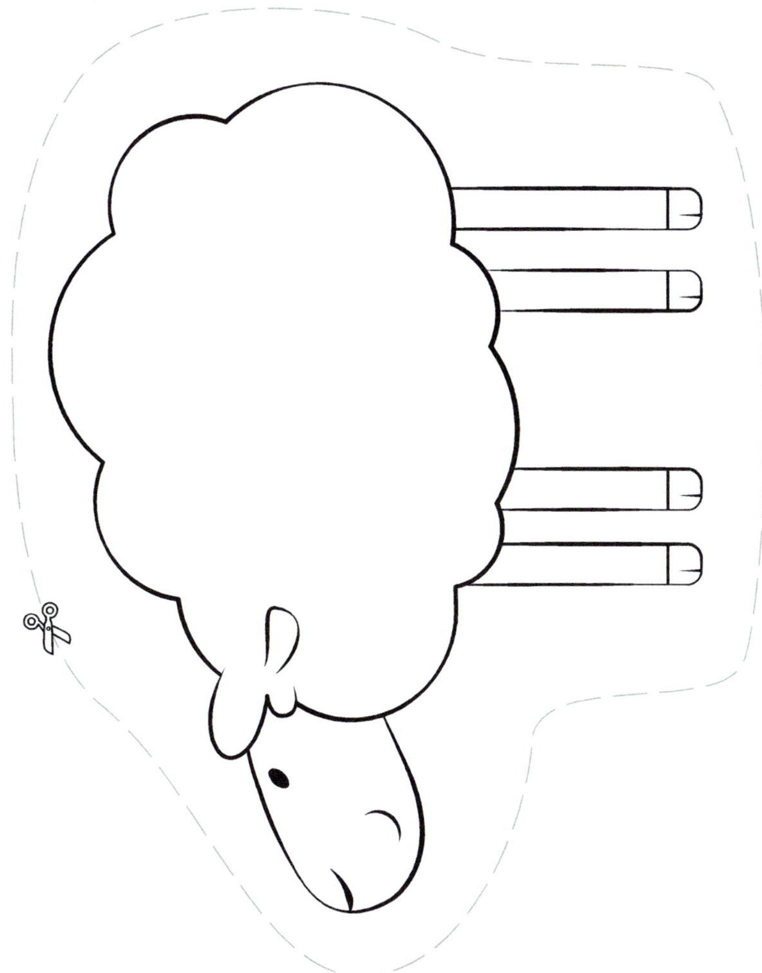

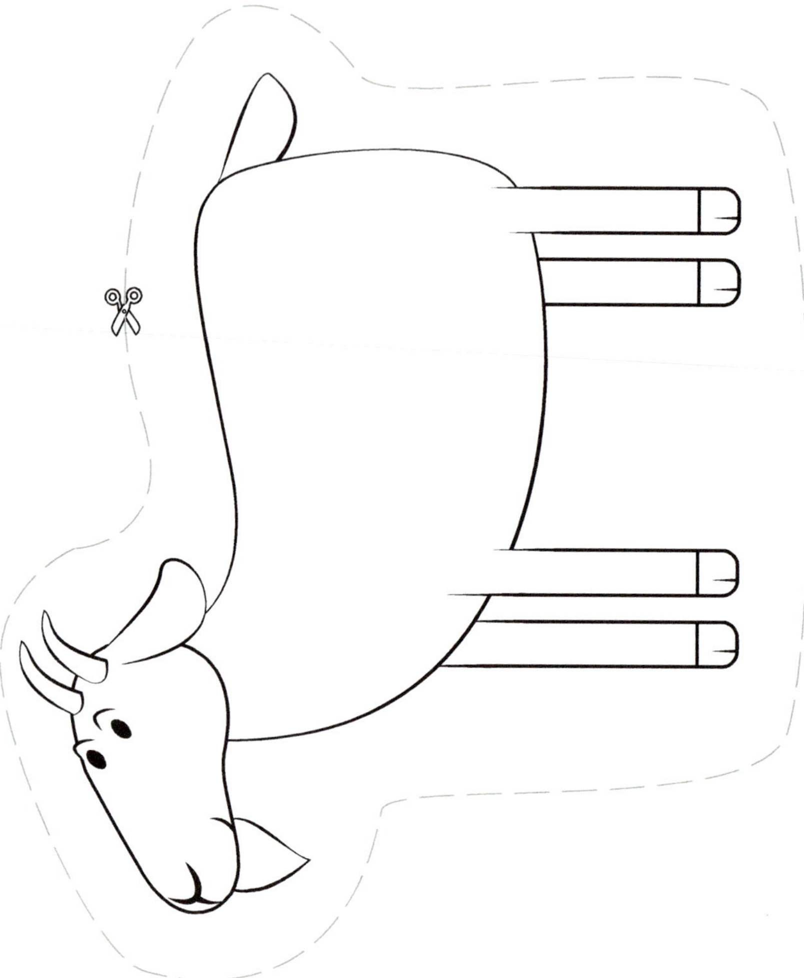

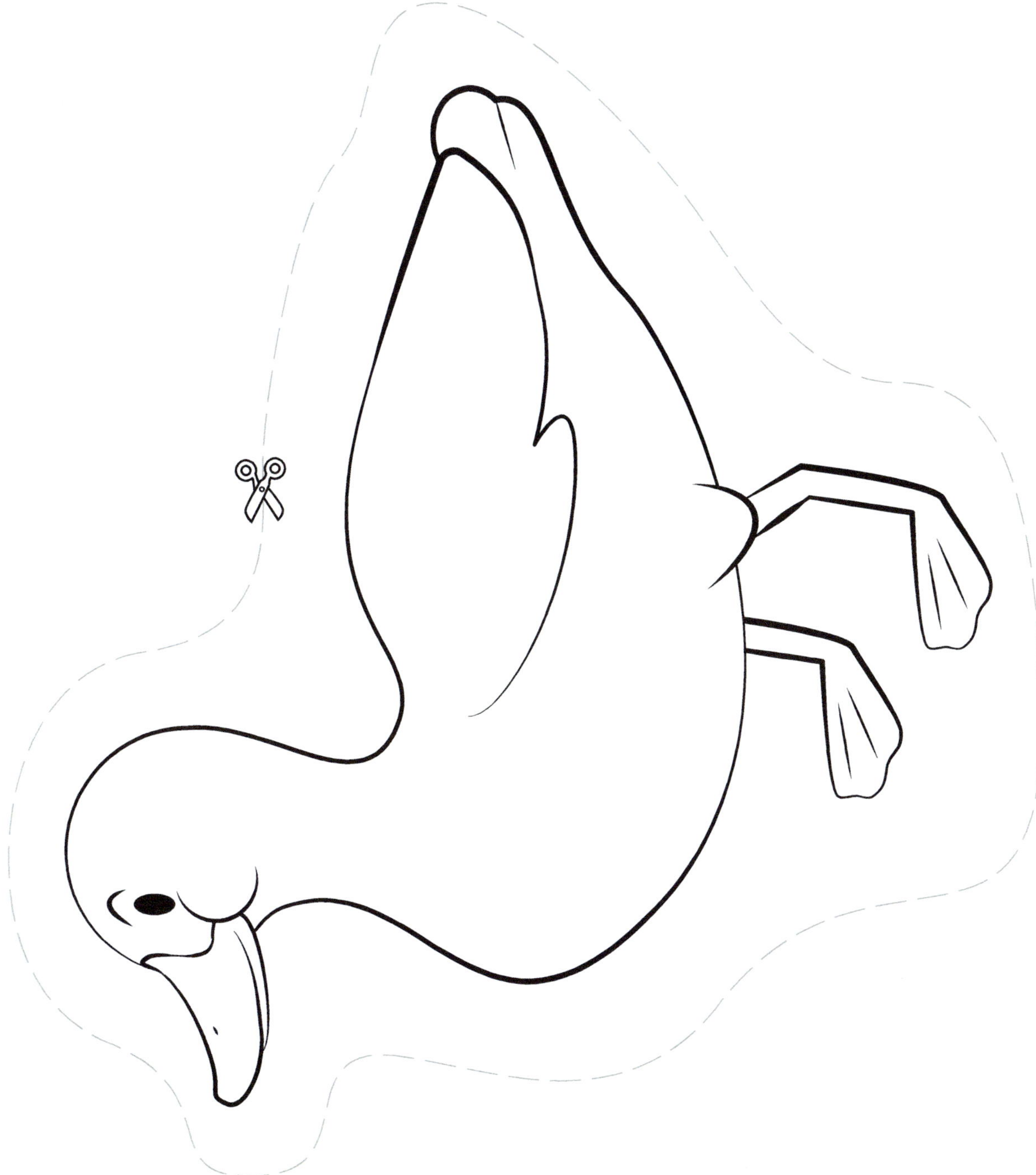

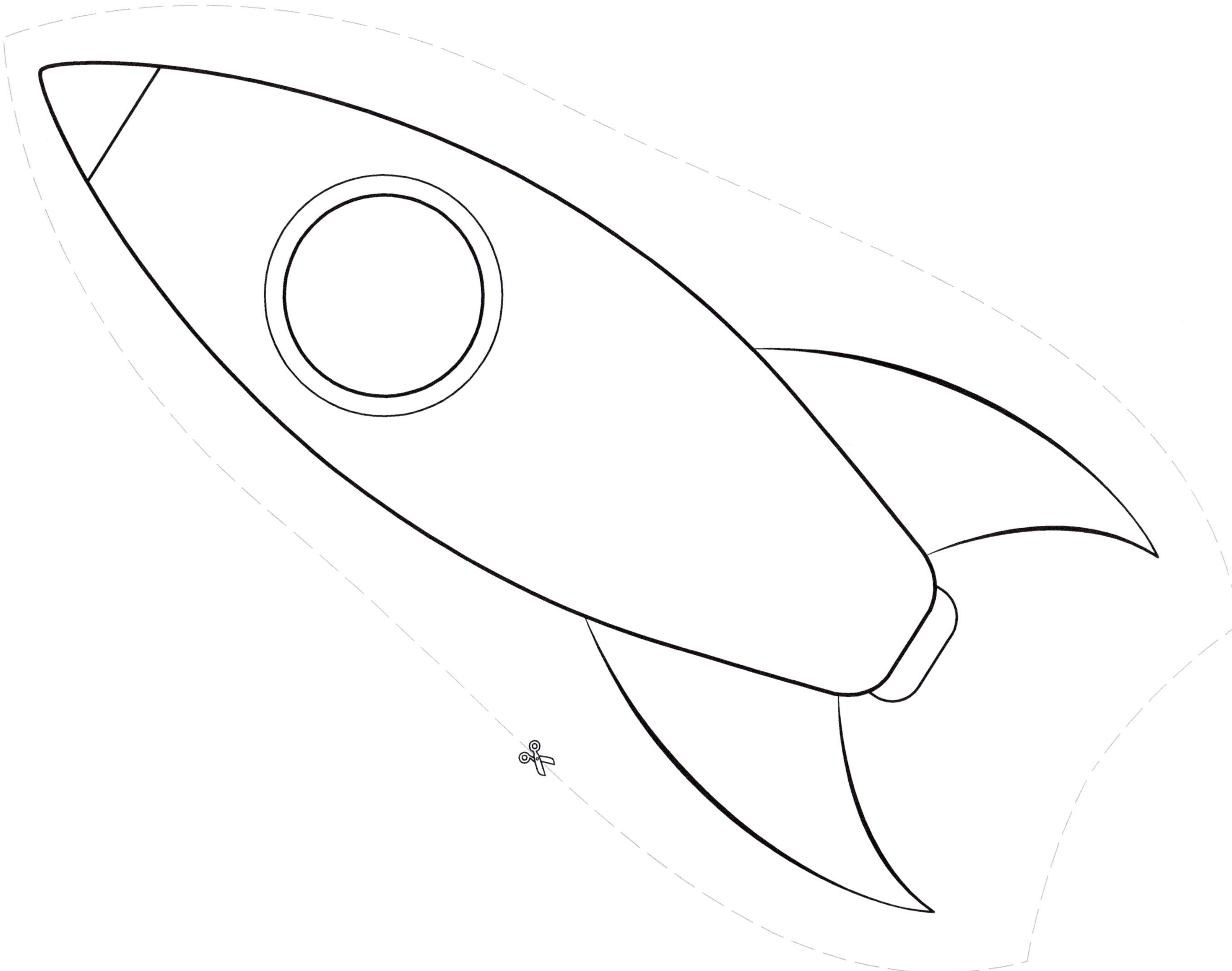